HOW TO STOP UNELECTED JUDGES FROM TRANSFORMING AMERICA

DANIEL E. HOROWITZ

STOLEN SOVEREIGNTY

Published by WND Books, Washington, D.C. WND Books is a registered trademark of WorldNetDaily.com, Inc. ("WND")

Cover designed by Vi Yen Nguyen

WND Books are available at special discounts for bulk purchases. WND Books also publishes books in electronic formats. For more information call (541) 474-1776, email orders@wndbooks.com or visit www.wndbooks.com.

Hardcover ISBN: 978-1-944229-29-0
eBook ISBN: 978-1-944229-30-6

Library of Congress Cataloging-in-Publication Data
Names: Horowitz, Daniel E., author.
Title: Stolen sovereignty : how to stop unelected judges from transforming America / Daniel E. Horowitz.
Description: Washington, D.C. : WND Books, 2016. | Includes bibliographical references and index.
Identifiers: LCCN 2016010876 (print) | LCCN 2016011197 (ebook) | ISBN 9781944229290 (hardcover) | ISBN 9781944229306 (ebook)
Subjects: LCSH: Political questions and judicial power--United States. | United States--Politics and government--2009-
Classification: LCC KF5130 .H67 2016 (print) | LCC KF5130 (ebook) | DDC 347.73/12--dc23
LC record available at http://lccn.loc.gov/2016010876

Printed in the United States of America
16 17 18 19 20 21 LBM 9 8 7 6 5 4 3 2 1

CONTENTS

FOREWORD

Unelected judges are not God.

As I noted in *Men in Black* and *The Liberty Amendments*, of all the possible challenges to the constitutional system our founders lost sleep over, a judicial oligarchy wasn't one of them. Sure, they feared each branch of government would attempt to usurp the power of the people, but they never believed they would be replacing King George with a tyranny of unelected judges in black robes. Yet, that is exactly what has happened over the past half century.

Over the past decade since I wrote *Men in Black*, the court system has reached rock bottom. Not only have they declared themselves the national potentate with the final say over all political questions of our generation, they have redefined marriage, the very foundation of all civilization, from the bench. And as I warned in *Men and Black*, and as this author has elaborated upon at great lengths, the courts have now forayed into the final frontier of judicial tyranny, deciding issues pertaining to immigration and national sovereignty.

We are now at a breaking point at which if nothing is done to rein in the judicial branch of government, we will no longer have representative democracy. We will be denuded of any ability to even restore our Republic through the elected branches of state and federal government because the courts are about to become more powerful than the very monarch against which our forefathers fought with their lives, fortunes, and sacred honor.

My good friend Daniel Horowitz, whom I have the privilege to work with on a daily basis, has picked up the banner as part of the next generation of conservative leaders and has pinpointed the most systemic problem with the judicial oligarchy of all—social transformation without representation. I rarely pen forewords to other books, but I feel the need to promote *Stolen Sovereignty* because this book provides a blueprint for dealing with the most current and existential threats to our Republic that I have decried for years in my books and on my radio program.

With the sad and untimely death of Justice Antonin Scalia, one of the foremost constitutional warriors of our lifetime, the need to reform our judiciary is even more essential. As the courts become more radically hostile to our founding values and the written Constitution, the keys to immigration and religious liberty—perhaps the two most important issues determining the makeup and character of the civil society—hang in the balance of their capricious political views. We the people are left without recourse to affect the outcome or change the courts.

Horowitz has packed it all into this single magnum opus. The proper role of the judiciary, the underpinnings of representative democracy, the foundation of religious liberty, the history of the judicial role in immigration, the history of immigration policy and how we have departed from our founding view on sovereignty—it's all sagaciously researched and beautifully presented in this volume.

Horowitz demonstrates how between judicial tyranny, the secular inquisition, and systemic transformation of our society through immigration—along with the judicial roadblock to reforming these vices—our power of self-governance has been eviscerated. Our sovereignty on an individual, state, and national level has been stolen by the unelected branches of government, collectively disenfranchising the citizenry in the worst way imaginable.

Four of my six books dealt with the immigration issue, and in *Men and Black* I warned how the courts were beginning to make illegal aliens into citizens. This author has done a masterful job presenting the philosophical, historical, and moral case for sovereignty and how our recent immigration policies from both the courts and the administrative state are not only a departure from our values and traditions, they are being implemented without the consent of the people.

This author demonstrates through incontrovertible facts and sound reason how the war on our sovereignty by the judiciary and suicidal immigration policies will create a permanent majority for post-constitutional despotism and spell the end of our republic. This book includes the full legal and policy case against birthright citizenship, counting illegal aliens in the census, refugee resettlement, chain migration, the right of a nation to exclude classes of immigrants, and all of the systemic ways the unelected branches of government have disenfranchised the citizenry through social transformation. The author has isolated and identified the lynchpins to the downfall of our republic and even the essence of our civilization.

Fortunately, all is not lost. As the great Alexis de Tocqueville observed, "[T]he greatness of America lies not in being more enlightened than any other nation, but rather in her ability to repair her faults." The remedies to most of our problems we face in this era of constitutional crisis lie in the Constitution itself.

In *The Liberty Amendments*, I argue that the Framers presciently set forth a process to restore our Republic should the federal government become oppressive by using the convention of the states established in Article V of the Constitution. There is no magic bullet to suddenly kill the century long anti-constitutional socialist utopia that has supplanted our republican form of government overnight. However, we must check all the boxes, take an all-of-the-above approach with unflinching determination to restore the republic through the very founding ideals that made it great in the first place.

In that vein, Horowitz has identified the most imminent threats to our society, security, and system of governance that are all rooted in the erosion of individual and national sovereignty. The author is here to warn us that these ailments are so imminent and terminal that something must be done immediately to put out the raging fire with out of control immigration and the war on religious liberty. Concurrent with a 100-year plan for systemic reforms, we must address these issues immediately.

Unfortunately, as Horowitz proves in vivid detail with impeccable research, if the courts are not stripped of their ill-gotten powers, none of these reforms will be implemented. That is why the author shares with us the most convincing and detailed case for using Congress to reclaim power from the courts. He conclusively proves both the ability and imperative of Congress to strip the courts down to size—from a legal, historical, philosophical, and political perspective. And all of the reforms discussed in this work can be implemented legislatively by the next administration and Congress and do not require constitutional amendments.

Piecemeal changes to the makeup of the courts will not suffice. Anti-constitutionalist judicial opinions have ossified, and American citizens are blocked from overturning these decisions through the democratic process. Only fundamental reforms of the judicial branch, including stripping the judiciary of jurisdiction over foundational issues, can truly remedy the situation.

As the country sits at the crossroads between liberty and tyranny, *Stolen Sovereignty* is one of the most important and timely books for those who seek the path of liberty and self- governance. Agree with all his proposals or not, Horowitz presents a compelling blue print and a rallying cry, chock-full of wisdom, insights, and quotes from our founders and early political leaders regarding the most important systemic political problems of our time.

—MARK LEVIN

INTRODUCTION

On June 26, 2015, the Supreme Court created a constitutional right to gay marriage, forcing states to recognize the status of something that not only is never mentioned in the Constitution but never existed as a legal concept anywhere in the world until fifteen years ago.[1]

At the time, Justice Antonin Scalia pulled the fire alarm and issued a direct and dire warning to the American people: disenfranchisement was coming to the voters by the hands of unelected judges. They no longer have the sovereignty to self-governance and the right to control their own destiny without the new big brother on the block—the unelected courts—making those decisions for them.

In a riveting dissent, which Scalia wrote separately to "call attention to this Court's threat to American democracy," the senior justice issued a rallying cry that all Americans must heed: no social transformation without representation. "To allow the policy question of same-sex marriage to be considered and resolved by a select, patrician, highly unrepresentative panel of nine is to violate a principle even more fundamental than no taxation without representation: no social transformation without representation," he wrote.[2] Alas, the institution that serves as the bedrock, not just for American civilization but all of civilization since the dawn of time, was transmuted by a handful of lower court and Supreme Court justices who never stood for election.

I wrote this book to pick up this banner from the late Justice Scalia and draw attention to just how profoundly the unelected branches of government—the courts and bureaucracy—have transformed our society without any input from the citizenry or recourse to prevent it.

Most importantly, I'd like to build on Scalia's observation of social and societal transformation without representation as it relates to immigration policy. Not only are the courts and the bureaucrats deciding every major societal issue that should be left to the political branches of government, they are now transforming the very membership, size, and orientation of the civil society itself by judicial fiat or lawless executive actions—the most profound and foundational societal transformation of all.

Between a runaway judicial oligarchy and an unaccountable bureaucratic state, our existence as a sovereign nation and our destiny as a civil society entitled to self-determination is under the most imminent, direct and sustained threat since our founding. With the untimely demise of Justice Scalia, the conservative lion on the Supreme Court who issued this very dire warning in the final months of his life, the threat the judiciary poses to our sovereignty has never been greater.

* * *

Amidst the caustic political and social conflicts dividing the country down the middle, we can all agree that the country is more polarized than ever before.

On the one hand Barack Obama won two decisive victories as president. On the other hand, Republicans won both midterm elections with historic landslides down federal and state ballots. They also won substantial victories during the 2015 elections, winning key ballot initiatives on social issues. But even when Obama was re-elected in 2012, it was the most polarizing result in modern electoral history. Obama won just 690 of the 3,144 counties in the country and lost a majority of congressional districts, yet still pulled off a convincing 332-206 Electoral College victory by piling up lopsided margins among minorities in the strategic states. Contrast that to Michael Dukakis who won 819 counties in 1988—more than Obama did in 2012—yet still *lost* the election in a landslide—111-426.[3]

There have always been sharp divisions in this country along ideological and cultural lines, but typically a president who wins an election in a landslide and is re-elected decisively reflects a majority consensus. Yet, as born out by these polarizing numbers and the seething rage across a large section of the country, voters clearly feel disenfranchised as liberals have been able to enact so many transformational policies without popular consent.

As we debate these consequential issues, shouldn't we all agree that these decisions must be made by our elected branches of government? If one side of the political divide believes their views reflect the majority of the public, they should seek to implement those ideas through their elected representatives. That way, each side can strive through the electoral process to win over hearts and minds and move the needle of the political and cultural direction in their preferred path. Hence, Scalia's intuitive principle that all societal transformation should be achieved through the representation of elected officials.

Unfortunately for conservatives, we are confronted with a jarring reality. The left has succeeded in growing the power of the courts and bureaucracy over the rightful predominance of the legislative branch of government, and has irrevocably co-opted those institutions into serving as conduits for their radical and revolutionary ideas—to the point that even if we win back the presidency and elect only constitutional conservatives to Congress, and on a state level to state legislatures, it won't matter.

We are often told that elections have consequences and if we don't like what is happening to our government and society we must do a better job changing hearts and minds, raising money, campaigning, and winning elections. But after winning two smashing victories in the previous mid-term elections, conservatives have painfully learned that elections don't matter—at least not when conservatives win.

Much of this disenfranchisement has been exacerbated by the complete corruption and treachery of the Republican Party at a leadership level. Those narratives are well documented by many conservative authors, and indeed are the relentless focus of my daily and weekly columns at *Conservative Review*. But for the purpose of this book, I'd like to focus on an even more uncomfortable reality confronting American conservatives. The unelected branches hold the keys to our future, and most of what we do through the electoral sphere is bound to fail if we don't build immediate momentum to rein in the courts and the bureaucracy on the most critical, consequential, and foundational issues of our time.

Conservatives could succeed in electing a constitutionalist in the mold of Jeff Sessions, Ted Cruz, or Mike Lee to every House and Senate seat, and it will do very little in staving off the inexorable march towards a post-constitutional Sodom and Gomorrah. In fact, with the morally, intellectually, and legally dyslexic decisions implemented by lawless courts and bureaucrats concerning the most foundational issues, values, and principles of our nation in recent years, I seek to prove that we are *already* living in a modern-day Gomorrah. The same tepid modus operandi of the past from conservative politicians will not suffice to deliver us from the clutches of this debauchery. We have reached rock bottom. We have lost our sovereignty as individuals, as residents of states—and as we shall explore in the following chapters—as an independent nation.

Pick your favorite conservative issue and your preferred policy solution and understand that the courts will toss out many of those policies. There is a standing army of legal professionals waiting to assail religious liberty, create new rights for criminals, and invalidate immigration enforcement acts at the drop of a hat. Furthermore, the entrenched bureaucrats have grown so strong and have placed much of the left-wing agenda on autopilot, making it arduous for the overworked members of Congress and their staffs to properly exercise oversight and ensure that the executive branch is faithfully executing the laws of the land.

THE LOSS OF OUR SOVEREIGNTY

According to Merriam-Webster's dictionary, the word *sovereignty* refers to "a country's independent authority and the right to govern itself."[4] Yet, that right to self-government, even as it relates to the most important issues pertaining to the sovereign people, has been stolen from those who created the nation.

For example, who ever voted to change the orientation of our country? Who voted to completely remake California? Who voted to grant illegal aliens so many rights they were never entitled to?

Who ever voted to resettle endless scores of Sharia-adherent Muslims in their communities without the recourse to properly vet them for ties to terrorism? Who voted to vitiate our long-standing policies of excluding potential criminals and public charges from our immigration system, paving the road to remaking our society with indigent and often criminal elements from other countries?

When was the last time voters actually had a say in issues pertaining to marriage and abortion?

Who voted to allow transgendered individuals paid-leave for hormone therapy in the military?[5]

Who voted to eradicate any mention of God and religion or tear down religious symbols that have decorated our public buildings since before the ratification of the Constitution?[6]

On issue after issue, we are witnessing a precipitous transformation of our society in every way imaginable—and it all appears to be set irretrievably into motion without the ability to stop it through the political process. This has taken a corrosive toll on society and our political system. It has been widely noted that there is more seething rage, despair, and negativity among the voters towards their government than ever before.

Despite the perception that the country has become more liberal on social issues, a recent poll from the *Washington Post* shows that the public is extremely uncomfortable with where things are headed. When surveyed by the *Post* about whether they are comfortable with the direction of the country on social issues, 64 percent of all voters said they felt *uncomfortable* while only 34 percent felt comfortable with the recent social changes. The polarization aspect is even more striking because 45 percent feel "strongly uncomfortable" while only 14 percent feel "strongly comfortable" with the changes. Sixty-eight percent of Independents and even 43 percent of Democrats say they are uncomfortable with the societal transformation.[7]

Clearly, even a public inundated with social licentiousness in every aspect of media, entertainment, and academia, is still uncomfortable with the growing trend of mass societal transformation without representation. And for good reason.

A polarized and diverse country of this size will always reflect sharp political and societal disagreements. But at least when those decisions are made through the political process, there is always recourse for the losing side to force compromises, concessions, and conditions on those changes or they can live again to fight another day and reverse course through the electoral process and see their vision of society actualized through the new representatives.

As Justice Scalia used to say, "Persuade your fellow citizens it's a good idea and pass a law. That's what democracy is all about. It's not about nine superannuated judges who have been there too long, imposing these demands on society."

None of this can transpire when the consequential societal issues of our time are decided by the unelected branches of government. The lack of a legitimate political process has left much of the public—not just dyed- in-the-wool conservatives—feeling incensed or at least uneasy and disenfranchised by coerced societal transformation and the stealing of their sovereignty.

A REPUBLIC ON THE BRINK

Many legal and constitutional scholars who are students of the original interpretation of our Constitution have come before me to sound the alarm on the growing threat of the courts to our democracy. Jurist extraordinaire Robert Bork and talk radio show host and constitutional lawyer Mark Levin did a superb job chronicling how judicial tyranny is destroying our country.[8] But I feel the sense of urgency to expand upon this issue under the rallying cry of "no societal transformation without representation" for a number of reasons.

While the issue of judicial activism is ubiquitously scorned by the professional conservative political class, many of their lead figures scoff at every idea to actually stop this growing tyranny. They wish not to make any drastic changes or rock the boat, and conjure up all sorts of speculative ancillary negative consequences of proposed efforts to do so. They continue to repeat the failed bromide "elections have consequences, go out and win more elections."

Well, I write this book to dissent separately from many in the D.C. conservative intelligentsia to prove that inaction is not an option. These ain't your grandfather's judicial activists. When judges are throwing peaceful Christian elected clerks into jail for not issuing a gay marriage license but mandating the release of criminal aliens into our communities by applying international law, we've got a problem, Houston. The time for opining, pontificating, punditry, and thumb sucking is over.

Things have never been worse than they are today. We are now living through the nightmare scenario portended by our nation's Founders. The Judicial activism and tyranny of the legal profession was set on autopilot long ago and serves as a ratchet system. Once an activist decision is promulgated, in contravention to the plain meaning of our Constitution and years of prior case law, the originalist view becomes lost forever in most cases. They only ratchet up the deviations from the Constitution with the passage of time and each subsequent decision. The culmination of decades' worth of violence to our constitutional system of governance has now reached a feverish pitch and is downright stealing our sovereignty, especially as it relates to marriage, religious liberty, and immigration.

It is no longer sufficient to sneer, scorn, or warn against the judicial tyranny; it's time to fight back and implement immediate reforms or we will cease to exist as a democratic republic and a sovereign nation. Along with Scalia, Justice Samuel Alito issued his own clarion SOS call isolated on the island of the corrupt legal profession. His sentiments perfectly capture the sense of urgency I feel in writing this book:

> Today's decision shows that decades of attempts to restrain this Court's abuse of its authority have failed. A lesson that some will take from today's decision is that reaching about the proper method of interpreting the Constitution or the virtues of judicial self-restraint and humility cannot compete with the temptation to achieve what is viewed as a noble end by any practicable means. I do not doubt that my colleagues in the majority sincerely see in the Constitution a vision of liberty that happens to coincide with their own. But this sincerity is cause for concern, not comfort. What it evidences is the deep and perhaps irremediable corruption of our legal culture's conception of constitutional interpretation.[9]

Alito's dissent serves as a warning that we are no longer living through times when we can redress the corruption in the courts by educating people on the Constitution and forcing Republicans to nominate "strict constructionists." We have failed at that on a large scale. The time for solving the judicial problem through *traditional* means has passed. The time has clearly arrived to strip the courts of significant power and use the elected branch of government to implement those reforms. It is this call to action I seek to expand upon.

That the day of judicial apocalypse is upon us is not surprising to conservatives in the legal profession, but nonetheless, we must all realize the moment *is* indeed upon us, and act accordingly.

I also feel a sense of urgency to strip the courts of their power over societal issues—over and beyond what others have proposed in the past—because of the Obama presidency. The Obama presidency has exacerbated the disenfranchisement of voters both at the judicial and administrative levels.

Obama has replaced roughly 40 percent of the district and 30 percent of the appellate judges on the federal benches. Based on his impeccable track record of nominating unflinching judicial supremacists and post-constitutional activists, we are now confronted with a judicial time bomb, the likes of which we've never seen before. As a number of cases pertaining to illegal immigration, the death penalty, and an array of social issues are placed in front of these new judges for adjudication in the coming years, I fear we are headed for a degree of Orwellian judicial activism that will make the Earl Warren days look like the founding era of our republic. The time to act is now or never.

Moreover, with the untimely passing of Justice Scalia, the man who most passionately warned about social transformation without representation and the court's unprecedented threat to democracy, we have lost our most effective counterbalance on the Supreme Court.

Finally, the Obama years have resulted in a convergence of judicial activism in the courts with an unprecedented culmination of years' worth of administrative power grabs to create the ultimate anti-democratic nightmare scenario of the legislative branch becoming the weakest part of government, especially as it relates to the question of immigration and sovereignty. Obama's unparalleled use of administrative fiat to legislate from the obscure offices of bureaucratic agencies, when coupled with the Orwellian legislating from the high benches of the federal courts, has engendered a new level of disenfranchisement of the voters and their representatives.

While many conservatives are looking forward to the promising prospect of a Republican president in 2017, any hopes of reining in the auto-piloted and ratcheted judiciary and administrative leviathans will be dashed unless immediate systemic reforms are implemented through the people's representatives.

The promise of Republican presidents to nominate only originalist judges is simply insufficient to combat the existing entrenched powers. Even if conservatives successfully scrutinize the few Supreme Court nominees to ensure they are constitutionalists, they rarely have a good track record on all of the lower court appointments. Remember, less than 1 percent of cases appealed to the Supreme Court are granted a hearing, which means the lower courts decide the vast majority of important cases.[10] Moreover, even many of the conservatives within the legal community have become brainwashed into the notion of one-directional *stare decisis*—upholding unconstitutional decisions of past liberal judges as precedent—even if those decisions themselves were reversals of long-standing settled law.

As part of the first order of business for an upcoming Republican administration, a judicial reform package and a plan to permanently restrain the bureaucracy is much more important and vital to our survival as a sovereign and self-determined nation than a policy plan on any single fiscal issue, such as taxes, health care, and Social Security. Moreover, in order to preserve some of the immigration reform ideas we will discuss as part of reclaiming our sovereignty on a national level, we must preempt the courts from stealing our individual sovereignty and right to self-government by striking down those laws and enforcement measures.

To that end, I set out to tell the story of just how unelected bureaucrats have disenfranchised the voters as it relates to the important issues of our time. Most prominently, I seek to lay out a definitive defense of our sovereignty and a full indictment of our current transformation through immigration from a legal, historical, and philosophical perspective. The current transformation of America through imprudent immigration policies are shockingly divorced from our long-held traditions and principles on the issue, as we will chronicle later on in the second half of the book. With the full understanding of the extent and depth of the problem and the imminent inimical harm it is impelling on our prospects of surviving as a democracy and as a sovereign nation-state, we can explore solutions to the problems and how to re-empower the people.

What shall we do as the silent disenfranchised majority? Are we going to sit idly while the courts transform our values and society and outsource our sovereignty to illegal aliens? It's time to break out the 1984 Twisted Sister hit, "We're not gonna take it anymore," and do something about it.

And fortunately, we don't *have* to take it anymore. It's time to use our constitutional powers to strip the courts down to size; to take the ball of activism out of their progressive game. We will refute the arguments of the naysayers by showing how we've long passed the point at which there is any meaningful downside to stripping the courts of jurisdiction. And the most important aspect to this plan is that it does not require a constitutional amendment. It can be accomplished by passing a bill. The same way Republican politicians plan to pass policy reforms, they can—they must—pass judicial reform.

Yes, the courts have spoken. Now it's time for the American people to respond.

1

THE COURTS: NEITHER FORCE NOR WILL

What is a Constitution? It is the form of government, delineated by the mighty hand of the people, in which certain first principles of fundamental law are established. The Constitution is certain and fixed; it contains the permanent will of the people, and is the supreme law of the land; it is paramount to the power of the Legislature, and can be revoked or altered only by the authority that made it.

—SUPREME COURT JUSTICE WILLIAM PATERSON, 1795

How have we sunk so low?

How has our society so rapidly transformed that our Constitution is now considered "unconstitutional"? How have our founding values related to such vital issues as religious liberty, immigration and the role of the courts been flipped on their head—inside out, upside down?

September 3, 2015, should be a day that will live in infamy for the American people. Yet, its significance is completely lost on most Americans. September 3 was the day a federal judge threw a Kentucky clerk in jail for peacefully abstaining from signing a gay marriage license, even though she was following existing state laws.

On that same day, the Ninth Circuit Court of Appeals ordered ICE (Immigration and Customs Enforcement) to suspend the deportation of a twice-deported criminal illegal alien who almost killed an American in a drunk driving incident. Why did she order this undocumented felon released? What was the rationale of Judge Jacqueline Nguyen, an Obama appointee, who issued the order? She applied international law by asserting that because the defendant was a self-described transgendered man he would likely be tortured were he deported to Mexico. The judge then proceeded to chastise the immigration officials for not using the proper "pronoun" when referring to the defendant![1]

Thus, our court system threw a county clerk in jail for being a Christian and released a dangerous illegal alien from ICE custody on the same day. Through these two incidents we see the most profound manifestation of social transformation against the will of the people. The sovereignty and security of the nation was violated, the Constitution was supplanted for international law, and the peaceful adherence to state law and religious liberty—deeply rooted in our nation's history and tradition—was criminalized. At the same time, transgenderism was codified into law and policy, and homosexual marriage was prioritized over religious liberty. All at the hands of the unelected branch of government.

If modern-day America were relocated to the Middle East it would probably be called "Absurdistan." The core of what ails America is that unelected judges, bureaucrats, and political elites are transforming our sovereignty, society, and system of governance without the consent of the governed.

Consider the following legal and political absurdities:

- Courts strike down state marriage laws even though marriage is not discussed in the Constitution and states have plenary power to define it, yet they won't strike down state gun laws that violate the plain language of the Second Amendment.[2] At the same time, some of these same courts have ruled that illegal aliens have Second Amendment rights.[3]

- Christian business owners are coerced into using their private property for activity that violates their consciences, yet Muslims, as employees, can force other business owners to accommodate their religious needs, even when they impede the fundamentals of the job.[4]

- There is near unanimity of opinion among both left and right-leaning politicos, and most likely a growing number of legal "scholars" and judges that there is an affirmative right to immigrate and that sharia-adherent Muslims in Pakistan or Saudi Arabia have a First Amendment religious right to enter our country. Yet, American citizens can't peaceably run their own businesses according to their consciences without government mandates to cover abortion services. Private employers don't have a religious conscience right against coercion to cover abortion services for their own employees, but the government has a fundamental liberty interest in entitling those employees to taxpayer-funded birth control.

- The legal community would have you believe the federal government has the right to regulate inactivity and force citizens to purchase health insurance, yet they don't have the power to prevent illegal aliens from asserting jurisdiction and obtaining citizenship for their children against the consent of the people.

- While our federal government regulates every aspect of the lives of American citizens, they refuse to scrutinize the radical views of foreign nationals when doing background checks on potential immigrants from volatile parts of the world.[5]

- Record waves of illegal and legal immigrants are fundamentally transforming our society, bankrupting our social programs, and endangering our security, *yet the American people were never given a say in the matter*. Worse, the political and legal fields are advancing arguments that will commit us to double down on these failures—all while forgetting the purpose of our government, Constitution, and social compact: protecting American citizens. At present, the future of our immigration policy is in the hands of the United Nations, private refugee contractors, state department bureaucrats, and the immigrants themselves, not the American people through their elected officials.

- States that uphold our sovereignty and federal immigration laws are sued in court and judges prevent them from following congressional statutes. Yet, states that violate our sovereignty and thwart federal immigration law are given a pass. Worse, they are awarded greater representation in Congress through their inflated numbers from their illegal alien population.
- A government that was once committed to shielding its citizens from any undesirable immigration—from public charge to security and cultural threats—is now committed to bringing in anyone and everyone unless they are proven terrorists up front. DHS even instituted a waiver allowing in those with "limited" ties to terrorists—all under the presumption and practice that our nation no longer has sovereignty.[6]
- The Constitutional Convention, out of which was born our supreme law of the land, started and ended with a formal prayer. Yet, we are told we can't pray in public in schools or government gatherings. Our founding presidents proclaimed days of prayer "to promote the knowledge and practice of true religion and virtue" and to "devote the time to the sacred duties of religion in public and in private; that they call to mind our numerous offenses against the Most High God, confess them before Him with the sincerest penitence."[7] Yet, courts are prohibiting the display of religious symbols that have been around since our founding, even though nobody is coerced into serving any particular religion.

The common denominator between all these juxtapositions is that the concepts of fundamental rights, constitutional protections, and the role of government have been distorted so grotesquely beyond anything our Founders envisioned. What is transpiring in our country at present reaches beyond the bounds of the most exaggerated absurdities one could have conjured up just a generation ago.

Is it not fair to ask who voted for this radical departure from our legal system, values, and traditions? When did we ever vote for any of this social transformation? When did we vote to abridge our rights and elevate the rights of foreign nationals?

Of course, these are all rhetorical questions. The people have never had a say in such fundamental transformation of the most important aspects of our society and law. And, as this book will demonstrate, if the courts are not stripped of their ill-gotten power to impel societal transformation, we will lose our ability to restore America even if we elect conservatives to the political branches of government. Worse, we will lose our national sovereignty and be stripped of our ability to reclaim our country from deleterious immigration policies.

THE INCREMENTAL WARPING OF THE JUDICIARY

On July 4, 1776, the Continental Congress adopted the 1,338-word Declaration of Independence, in which they declared, "[W]e hold these truths to be self-evident, that all men are created equal, that they are endowed by their Creator with certain unalienable Rights, that among these are Life, Liberty and the pursuit of Happiness."[8] This earthshattering document reconstructed the relationship of the citizen to its governing authority and established the foundation for the form of government the colonists would create following the Revolutionary War.

Eleven years later, after miraculously shaking off the yoke of the mighty British Empire, the aspirations expressed in the Declaration became a reality in the crafting of the new Constitution for the nascent American republic. As Benjamin Franklin left the Constitutional Convention at Independence Hall, he was reportedly asked by a lady,

"Well doctor, what have we got, a republic or a monarchy?" He famously replied, "A republic, if you can keep it."[9]

Fast-forward 230 years and we are on the cusp of not only losing our republican form of government, but our sovereignty as a nation-state with defined borders and a defined citizenry empowered by the self-determination to govern its own affairs. No, we have not been occupied by a hostile invasion, although we are languishing from endless waves of illegal immigration. We have been occupied by the bloodless revolution of unelected judges and bureaucrats, permanently remaking society and the character of America itself—without the input of the people through their elected representatives.

At the heart of any republican form of government is the principle that all societal and political questions must be addressed by the *political* branches of government—those directly accountable to the people. With the exception of fundamental rights expressed in the Declaration and later enshrined into our Constitution—the right to life, liberty, and pursuit of happiness—which must be protected even against the majority rule in a legislative body, the people's representatives, most prominently in state legislatures, were supposed to have the final say in all societal questions. To do otherwise would violate the other principle of the Declaration: popular sovereignty—government by the consent of the governed.

Although the Framers designed three "equal" and separate branches of government in order to establish checks and balances against usurpation of power and protect individual liberty, the legislative branch of government was envisioned as the dominant branch because all of its members are elected.[10] In the words of James Madison, "In republican government, the legislative authority necessarily predominates."[11]

Conversely, the judicial branch of government was always intended to be the least powerful, especially as it relates to fundamental political issues. "The judiciary, from the nature of its functions, will always be the least dangerous to the political rights of the Constitution; because it will be least in a capacity to annoy or injure them," wrote Alexander Hamilton.[12]

Hamilton, who had a more expansive view of the judiciary than some of the other Founders, contrasted the judiciary from the other two branches thus:

> The Executive not only dispenses the honors, but holds the sword of the community. The legislature not only commands the purse, but prescribes the rules by which the duties and rights of every citizen are to be regulated. The judiciary, on the contrary, has no influence over either the sword or the purse; no direction either of the strength or of the wealth of the society; and can take no active resolution whatever. It may truly be said to have neither FORCE nor WILL, but merely judgment; and must ultimately depend upon the aid of the executive arm even for the efficacy of its judgments.

In explaining why "the judiciary is beyond comparison the weakest of the three departments of power," Hamilton declared that "though individual oppression may now and then proceed from the courts of justice, the general liberty of the people can never be endangered from that quarter."[13]

In other words, courts were never vested with the power to decide broadly consequential societal and political questions not explicitly addressed in the Constitution, such as gay marriage, abortion, and immigration policy. They were primarily created for the purpose of interpreting and plying the meaning of statutes, mediating disputes between individuals and between states, deciding complex separation of powers disputes between the legislature and executive, and several esoteric jurisdictions for which the Constitution granted the Supreme Court original jurisdiction.[14]

Montesquieu, whose writings had a profound influence on the Founders, observed that "of the three powers above mentioned, *the judiciary is, in some measure, next to nothing*."[15] It is likely for this reason that Article III of the Constitution sparked the least controversy and the shortest debate of all the proposed facets of government when our Founders met in Philadelphia at the Constitutional Convention. As Max

Farrand, one of the foremost authorities on the history of the founding, observed, "[T]o one who is especially interested in the judiciary, there is surprisingly little on the subject to be found in the records of the convention."[16]

The only role the courts had in striking down laws passed by Congress, even in the view of those Founders who believed in such a power, was when those laws blatantly violated the plain meaning of the Constitution *at the time it was written*. In that sense, as Hamilton concluded, "the power of the *people* is superior to both [the legislature and judiciary]; and that where the will of the legislature, declared in its statutes, stands in opposition to that of the people, declared in the *Constitution*, the judges ought to be governed by the latter rather than the former."[17] The popular will of the legislature expressed through the mandate given to it by voters was supposed to be out of reach from the courts except for when the majoritarian rule in the political branches of government infringed on the life, liberty, and property rights of the citizenry, as plainly and incontrovertibly defined in the Constitution.

It is for this reason that the courts were not subject to the checks and balances of the political branches except for impeachment. As Mark Levin has observed in *Men in Black*, "Judges are appointed for life *because* they're not politicians. And because they're not politicians, they're not directly accountable to the people and are not subject to elections."[18] Additionally, this is why there was no direct remedy to overrule a court's decision. They were to have "neither force nor will" with regard to political issues. Consequently, there was no reason to overrule them because they never had jurisdiction over governing the nation; they had the power to offer *opinions* in individual "cases and controversies."

There's a reason why the Constitution uses the words "cases and controversies" to describe the scope of the court's power of adjudication.[19]

Senator Oliver Ellsworth, the primary drafter of Article III and the man often referred to as "the father of the national judiciary," promised the people of his state that the federal judiciary was "not to intermeddle with your internal policy."[20] One could only imagine what Ellsworth, the first chairman of the House Judiciary Committee and the third chief justice of the Supreme Court, would say about the modern courts preventing states from protecting their people and their sovereignty from violent criminal aliens. Redefining marriage is a form of "meddling" that would have been beyond his comprehension.

As Justice Joseph Story, one of the most authoritative early commentators on the Constitution, wrote of the original plan to create the judiciary, "There was nothing in the plan, which directly empowered the national courts to construe the laws according to the *spirit* of the constitution."[21] Preeminent historian and expert on the Constitutional Convention Max Farrand noted that "not a word" in the proceedings of the convention indicate that the federal courts had the power "to declare laws null and void."[22] Farrand also noted that the power to strike down laws was very clearly articulated and desired by those promoting the "Council of Revision," a form of government in which a committee of respected political leaders and legal scholars would have the power to nullify laws passed by Congress. But that system was soundly rejected.

The original vision of the judiciary is vividly on display not just in theory—before the ratification of the Constitution—but in practice during the early years of the Supreme Court. When President John Adams asked John Jay to accept the nomination as the next chief justice of the court, Jay demurred. He noted that he left the court in 1795 because the court was so weak in its ability to shape the national government.[23]

Despite the tumultuous first century of our nation's history, this aspect of our government, more or less, worked as planned. Aside from a few exceptions, the courts deferred to the political branches of government for most key political and societal questions, relegating their authority to calling the balls and strikes on interpreting the laws.[24]

The first major strike against the Framers' conception of the judiciary was orchestrated early on in 1803 by Chief Justice John Marshall in *Marbury v. Madison*.[25] By establishing the power of judicial review, Marshall opened the door for the view of the court as the final arbiter of every important ideological debate in this country, although Marshall himself never envisioned the Court as the *final* arbiter, but merely as an arbiter of constitutional disputes.

Our Founders were appalled by this power grab. Writing to his friend William Jarvis in 1820, Jefferson chastised his view that courts are "the ultimate arbiters of all constitutional questions." He admonished Jarvis that this was "a very dangerous doctrine indeed, and one which would place us under the despotism of an oligarchy." He prophetically warned that such power is "more dangerous as they are in office for life, and not responsible, as the other functionaries are, to the elective control." "The Constitution has erected no such single tribunal, knowing that to whatever hands confided, with the corruptions of time and party, its members would become despots," wrote an aging but passionate Jefferson.[26]

However, even Marshall never intended for the court to decide societal and political issues or to rewrite the Bill of Rights, enumerated powers, and federalism from the bench. Marshall merely said that "in *some cases*, then, the Constitution must be looked into by the judges" in order to resolve specific cases.[27] The issue over which Marshall exercised judicial review in *Marbury* was what we would consider nowadays an "inside baseball" dispute between two government agencies and an "in-the-weeds" analysis of standing before the court. It wasn't the future society or sovereignty of a nation at risk. Ironically, he was overturning a law that, in his estimation, unconstitutionally *expanded* the original jurisdiction of the Supreme Court.[28]

Further, it was clear even from the early supporters of judicial review that the Supreme Court only had the authority to strike down laws passed by the people's representatives when they flagrantly violated the Constitution. Hamilton envisioned the role of the courts in the realm of judicial review as enforcing "certain specified exceptions to the legislative authority." Those specified exceptions referred to laws that were "contrary to the manifest tenor of the Constitution," such as punitive and retroactive criminal laws.[29] Justice James Iredell, one of the early vocal proponents of judicial review, conceded that "the Court will never resort to that authority but in a clear and urgent case."[30]

The act that Justice Marshall overturned was a section of the Judiciary Act of 1789. That congressional statute expanded the scope of the court's original jurisdiction explicitly spelled out in the Constitution, and therefore, clearly met this criterion laid out by Hamilton. Overturning laws on social questions regarding concepts that never existed until this generation certainly doesn't fit this criterion.

Somehow the power of judicial review expressed in *Marbury* has been transmogrified into complete authority over the future of sovereignty, marriage, culture, and the power to regulate every industry in our economy.

Starting in the FDR-era, accelerating during the Warren court of the '60s, and now crystallizing during the modern era of Obama, the courts—aided by the left-wing takeover of the legal profession—have gradually yet relentlessly turned the governing arrangement on its head by completely reinterpreting the most foundational aspects of our Constitution. Judges who were supposed to be immune to politics have enshrined their political and social preferences into the Constitution itself. What is in the Constitution, they refuse to recognize as a fundamental right and defend from the encroachment of the other branches of government. Yet, what is not in the Constitution they have installed as new and evolving fundamental rights.

Charles Evans Hughes, who served as chief justice during the bulk of FDR's tenure, was the embodiment of the early pioneers of judicial activism. As a leading progressive during the early part of the twentieth century, Hughes famously said during a speech in 1907, "We are under a Constitution, but the Constitution is what the judges say it is."[31] Years later, Justice William Brennan, a key judicial supremacist on the Warren court, boasted to his law clerks that "with five votes you can do anything around here."[32]

By applying precedent after each discovery of new rights in the Constitution—rights that never existed at the time of its crafting—the Courts have now become the predominant branch of government, with

"Will and Force" on almost every issue that matters in our lives. Basic rights of religious liberty and property rights of American citizens have been disregarded, while new rights—such as the right to an abortion, gay marriage, privacy, "dignity," guaranteed outcomes, and the right to immigrate—have been retroactively backfilled into the Bill of Rights through the preposterous, open-ended expansion of the equal protection and due process clauses of the Fourteenth Amendment.

However, even some of the early pioneers of judicial activism still had limits to their hubris in violating the Constitution and playing the role of God in society. Even after thirty years on the court, Associate Justice William Douglas, a liberal activist appointed by FDR in 1939, encouraged his colleagues in a 1970 case "to adhere to the mandate of the Constitution, and not give it merely that meaning which appeals to the personal tastes of those who from time to time sit here."[33]

Yet in recent years, the courts have taken the "legislative powers" they plundered from the elected branches to a new level. Whether it is mandating access to health care, education, gun rights, or release from detention for illegal aliens, or indicating that all children born to illegal aliens are entitled to citizenship, the courts are in the process of remaking society itself—without any recourse for the citizenry to fight back—even through their elected representatives.

Judge Richard Posner, a Reagan appointee to the Seventh Circuit Court of Appeals, recently suggested the Constitution as written is completely dead. He even brazenly admitted that judges no longer need to sincerely swear allegiance to the Constitution but to law *created* by the Supreme Court. "It's funny to talk about the oath judges take to uphold the Constitution since the Supreme Court has transformed the Constitution in its decisions. The oath is not really to the original constitution, or to the constitution as amended. It is to some body of law created by the Supreme Court. You can forget about the oath. That is not of significance."[34]

In many respects, we have reached the final frontier of judicial tyranny. After conferring super rights on a panoply of "protected classes" of

Americans—at the expense of the fundamental inalienable rights of *all* citizens—the courts are now copying and pasting their contrived rights and potentially applying them to all 7.3 billion people in the world.

As Justice Alito noted in his dissent on the marriage case, the inexorable and degenerative trajectory of judicial tyranny has become "irremediable."[35] The early judicial activists had established the perfect system to void out our Constitution while simultaneously, yet ironically, enshrining their anti-constitutional priorities as the law of the land into that very same Constitution.

The paradoxical view of the judicial tyrants goes something like this:

> Our Constitution and founding documents cannot possibly be the inviolable and eternal law of the land because of the original sin of slavery. No system that could have blessed such an abomination may be respected to define and guard the boundaries of liberty and fundamental rights. The same way the Constitution got it wrong on slavery and rights for native blacks, they erred on every other social value as it relates to liberty and the role of government. As such, the Constitution as it was originally founded is irrelevant to our times.

To continue this train of thought and take it to its logical conclusion, one would expect the judicial supremacist doctrine to continue as follows: "and therefore, we must amend the Constitution or work as a nation to adopt a new system of government, a new standard for defining the contours of liberty."

However, being the savvy and clever politicians they were, the pioneers of judicial activism understood that the Constitution is beloved by the people, and, outside of seminars to captive audiences of the elite ruling class, trash-talking our founding is not very popular. Moreover, why pursue the nearly impossible process of amending the Constitution when they could unilaterally change it and disenfranchise the people with the gradual, yet steady reinterpretation of the Constitution disguised under an incomprehensible system of legal fog?

This is where the paradox of the judicial supremacists comes into play. Instead of adopting a new Constitution, they gradually ratcheted up the reinterpretation of the Fourteenth Amendment based on their thesis of a flawed founding. They contend that the Fourteenth Amendment, which rectified the original sin of slavery, also rectifies every grievance they perceive until the end of time. Gay marriage, transgender rights, abolishing the death penalty, abolishing school prayer, affirmative action, illegal aliens' rights, you name it, it's in the Fourteenth Amendment under the due process and equal protection clauses. Even further, these phantom *positive* rights are retroactively reincorporated into the original Bill of Rights at the time of the founding and are binding against all state and federal legislation to the contrary.

Accordingly, in one brilliant stroke of legal hocus-pocus, our original Constitution has been ruled unconstitutional for something completely different and often antithetical to the original draft. Yet, at the same time it's all retroactively written into the Constitution via the Fourteenth Amendment. No constitutional amendment or input from the people has been necessary to carry out this gradual coup.

Thurgood Marshall, the partner in crime on the high court with Earl Warren and William Brennan during the '70s and '80s era, when judicial activism was taken to a new level, embodies this paradoxical approach of "the Constitution is unconstitutional." Speaking at a bicentennial celebration of our Constitution on May 6, 1987, Marshall trashed our Founders and Constitution instead of celebrating them.

He began his discussion with a frontal assault on the Founders:

> I cannot accept this invitation, for I do not believe that the meaning of the Constitution was forever "fixed" at the Philadelphia Convention. Nor do I find the wisdom, foresight, and sense of justice exhibited by the Framers particularly profound. To the contrary, the government they devised was defective from the start, requiring several amendments, a civil war, and momentous social transformation to attain the system of constitutional government, and its respect for the individual freedoms and human rights, we hold as fundamental today.

He then proceeded to declare the Constitution dead. This, *after* spending twenty years on the Supreme Court sworn to uphold the very document he detested:

> While the Union survived the civil war, the Constitution did not. In its place arose a new, more promising basis for justice and equality, the Fourteenth Amendment, ensuring protection of the life, liberty, and property of all persons against deprivations without due process, and guaranteeing equal protection of the laws.[36]

Let's indulge this thought process for a moment. Marshall was suggesting that the Constitution was completely rewritten as a result of the Fourteenth Amendment. So perhaps the judicial activists are correct in their philosophy and indeed are in possession of a legitimate fixed constitutional anchor and unbending system of governance, albeit not the one established in 1789, but the one they perceived to have been adopted in 1868.

Perhaps we should then follow the "Constitution of the Fourteenth Amendment," at least as the judicial activists interpret it? But this presents a conundrum for the judicial tyrants. After all, how could they conceive of rights to sodomy, mandating gay marriage on the states, and granting an array of rights to illegal aliens? These concepts were either unknown or as rabidly opposed by the very framers of the Fourteenth Amendment as they were by the Framers of the original Bill of Rights.

That is why Thurgood Marshall proceeded to note that the Fourteenth Amendment was insufficient as written because "almost another century would pass before blacks were granted true equality." He therefore echoed the national anthem of the judicial tyrant movement in singing the praises of a "living and breathing document." That the Fourteenth Amendment forever entrusted the legal profession to rectify every other perceived injustice until the end of times—all backfilled into that amendment and reincorporated into the rest of the original Constitution.

The one challenge confronting those who seek to disenfranchise the voters and their elected representatives through the Fourteenth

Amendment is section 5 of that amendment, which explicitly grants *Congress* the power to define its contours. "The Congress shall have power to enforce, by appropriate legislation, the provisions of this article," reads the end of the Fourteenth Amendment.[37] An identical provision is also in the Thirteenth and Fifteenth amendments. So how could the courts claim absolute power over the Fourteenth Amendment and use it to bastardize the rest of the Constitution?

Enter Justice William Brennan and his "ratchet theory." In *Katzenbach v. Morgan*, Brennan wrote an opinion upholding the power of Congress through section 5 of the Fourteenth Amendment to *expand* upon the scope of rights expressed in that amendment (even if it infringes on state powers under the Tenth Amendment), over and *beyond* what the courts had discovered at the time. But like a ratchet, Congress can only move forward in creating new rights, not backward, when defining the contours of the Fourteenth Amendment clauses, such as equal protection, due process, and privileges and immunities. Congress could not, in the politically convenient view of Brennan, "exercise discretion in the other direction . . . to restrict, abrogate, or dilute these [Fourteenth Amendment] guarantees."[38] And of course, in his estimation, the "guarantees" of the Fourteenth Amendment are fully defined by—you guessed it—the courts.

Cutting away the convoluted legal contortions, what Brennan was in fact telling Congress is, "Sure, you can *accelerate* the social justice religion in accordance with our views all you want, but you can never pass laws in contravention to the prevailing views of the legal profession, even when the Constitution explicitly grants you that authority." In other words, if Congress wants to mandate transgendered bathrooms on the states under the equal protection clause, it is their right to do so, but if they want to (properly) define the citizenship clause of the Fourteenth Amendment as excluding those here in contravention to our laws from birthright citizenship for their children, well, Brennan already told us what he thought of that in 1982.[39]

While the Brennan ratchet theory has seldom been used in practice in its original application, as the case law on section 5 of the Fourteenth Amendment is scant, the rationale behind his ratchet theory is what drives their phantom legal theory. It is the embodiment of the entire legal profession, and indeed the bureaucratic branch of government, in their pursuit of disenfranchising the people with the coerced acceptance of their worldview.

You will often hear from liberals a sanctimonious reverence for *stare decisis*, the accepted precedent of previous court rulings. But as we will study later on, their respect is only one directional. They have no problem overturning the original meaning and intent of the Constitution as well as one hundred years of case law in pursuit of the malleable social justice utopia. But once that breach in the Constitution is delivered in the form of even a 5-4 opinion in a single court case, that decision becomes immutable, settled law and cannot be overturned. At that point, the new court-manufactured right can and will only be augmented until we reach a point when we have come full circle and flipped the Constitution on its head. Hence, the ratchet.

Margaret Thatcher often decried the "ratchet effect" of British politics in which liberal policies were only expanded during Labor rule but never reversed during the rule of moderate Tories.[40] The same can be said of our political system between the truculent and effective Democrats and the feckless Republicans. But that is politics. There is still some recourse through the electoral process to remedy that. The same cannot be said of the ratchet wielded by the unelected judges.

Even John Marshall in *Marbury*, while instituting judicial review and subjecting the legislature to the final constitutional decisions of the Court, noted that the scope of judicial review was limited to anchoring the laws of Congress to "unchangeable" constitutional law.[41]

Certainly Marshall would have agreed with Associate Justice John Marshall Harlan II, known as the "great dissenter" on the Warren court in the '60s, when he expressed his exasperation with societal transformation without representation:

> The Constitution is not a panacea for every blot upon the public welfare nor should this court, ordained as a judicial body, be thought of as a general haven of reform movements.[42]

Harlan was merely echoing the sentiments of our Founders, who unambiguously instructed us on constitutional construction and interpretation. Toward the end of his life, Jefferson advised his colleagues to hark "back to the time when the Constitution was adopted, recollect the spirit manifested in the debates, and instead of trying what meaning may be squeezed out of the text, or invented against it, conform to the probable one in which it was passed."[43]

There is no greater tyranny than the retroactive creation of an ever-elastic set of laws that is anchored to nothing more than the political judgment of unelected judges at the time they woke up that day. Taken to its logical conclusion, this means there is nothing the courts cannot do in the realm of politics, even against the will of the elected political branches of federal and state governments, so long as the legal profession deems and cultural elites decree it.

Rather than the Constitution serving as a "living and breathing document," an ideal the judicial tyrants so passionately extol, the Constitution is nothing but a dead artifact if its words no longer have any meaning. This is why Justice William Paterson, a founder, an original member of the Senate Judiciary Committee, and early member of the Supreme Court asserted that by definition a constitution must be "certain and fixed" and contain "the permanent will of the people" until it is altered by the very same authority.[44]

Madison warned that once our nation would deviate from the original meaning of the Constitution, "there can be no security for a consistent and stable [government], more than for a faithful exercise of its powers."[45] This degree of despotism and disenfranchisement is not only the most severe deviation from the founding role of the judiciary imaginable; it is *antithetical* to the republican form of government our Founders established.

PROTECTING OUR "NEAR-PERFECT" FOUNDING DOCUMENTS

In reality, the true story of fundamental rights and the role of the courts in our system of government is the exact opposite of the views expressed by Thurgood Marshall and championed by the contemporary legal profession. While only God's laws are perfect, the founding of our country was as close to perfection as practicably possible and far superior to the founding of any other nation. That near perfection was expressed through the Declaration of Independence in 1776, thirteen years before the adoption of the Constitution.

I refer to the Declaration as a near-perfect document because it reflects the self-evident truths of the laws of nature and of nature's God, which are indeed perfect. The self-evident truth that all men are created equal means nobody has fewer rights, but nobody has super-protected *privileges* either. As such, the people are entitled to popular sovereignty, the ideal that abjures any form of government not created by the consent of the people. Yet, government through consent must be created in order to protect the equal fundamental rights, which are the right to life, liberty, and the *pursuit* of happiness, not *guaranteed* happiness or guaranteed outcomes. The Declaration was limited to only a few fundamental rights—negative rights—because only those listed in the Declaration and later extrapolated upon in the Constitution were God-given. By definition, everything else is man-made and can only be dealt with through the political process, not enshrined as fundamental rights—out of reach from the republican system of elected representatives.

Our Constitution was ratified over a decade later built upon these self-evident truths under God. However, there was one glaring flaw—the native black population was completely excluded from the very essence of the principles espoused in the Declaration. So does this mean our entire founding and Constitution were fatally flawed?

Of course not.

Slavery was neither invented nor enhanced by the founding of the republic; in fact, it was set on the inevitable path to the ash heap of history by the founding itself. Slavery was a reality in the colonies for over a hundred years, and that was not going to change under British rulers who stood to benefit from the economy generated from slavery. Once they shook off the yoke of the British, the Founders were confronted with a choice: they could continue the failed system of the Articles of Confederation, which allowed the sovereign southern states to continue slavery and would have enshrined slavery as the law of those lands forever, or they could form a federal union with those states and strive toward a time when slavery would be abolished across the board. Forming a federal union with a ban on slavery in the Southern states was not an option because those states would not have joined that union. Not only would slavery have remained in those states indefinitely, but none of us would enjoy the freedoms we have today had they blocked the founding over the issue of slavery.

Immediately upon the founding of the country, slavery became one of the most contentious issues. It led to a bloody civil war, which, as hoped by many original Founders, ended slavery and charted a course toward full equal rights via the Thirteenth, Fourteenth, and Fifteenth amendments, although it unfortunately took a long time for society to fully adopt the laws in practice.

Thus, as Edward Erler, a Claremont Institute constitutional scholar, explains, "[T]he Civil War was fought to extend to principle of consent to all the governed, and with the adoption of the Thirteenth and Fourteenth Amendments, the Constitution for the first time came into formal harmony with the principles of the Declaration of Independence." Consequently, "the idea that the thirty-ninth Congress was engaged in completing the founding was expressed so frequently during debates that one can hardly doubt that it was the ruling paradigm."[46]

What Erler proves from endless quotes of the Founders and the members of the "Fourteenth Amendment Congress" is that, in fact, the Fourteenth Amendment permanently anchored the Constitution in the inviolate principles of the past—the Declaration of Independence—and not some phantom, unknown, and infinitely adaptable political doctrine of future generations.

Thus, there is no room—under the guise of expanding civil rights—

to add additional super rights, such as abortion, gay marriage, abolishing of the death penalty, or affirmative action, to the self-evident truths of inalienable rights. And there certainly is no room to suggest that the Fourteenth Amendment intended to grant rights and citizenship to foreign nationals who infiltrate the society against the consent of the people. As we will explore later, the notion of super rights for favored classes and citizen rights for illegal aliens breaches the very underpinnings of the Fourteenth Amendment, which was built upon the principles of true equality and popular sovereignty rooted in governance by consent.

While there always have been and always will be disagreements over esoteric constitutional principles, such as disputes over separation of powers, there can never be any changes to the boundaries of fundamental rights.

President Calvin Coolidge noted in his July 4, 1926, speech commemorating the 150th anniversary of the Declaration, that although the Founders knew that times and technology would change and progress, the ideals expressed in this document were to be interminable. In his own words:

> If all men are created equal, that is final. If they are endowed with inalienable rights, that is final. If governments derive their just powers from the consent of the governed, that is final. No advance, no progress can be made beyond these propositions. If anyone wishes to deny their truth or their soundness, the only direction in which he can proceed historically is not forward, but backward toward the time when there was no equality, no rights of the individual, no rule of the people. Those who wish to proceed in that direction can not lay claim to progress. They are reactionary. Their ideas are not more modern, but more ancient, than those of the Revolutionary fathers.[47]

What Coolidge was noting is that, unlike the shallow-minded bleeding-heartedness of the Left, the spectrum of liberty is not an infinite straight line; it's a bell curve. You have to get it just right and freeze it at the peak. That peak was established by the Declaration of

Independence, ratified by the Constitution despite the gaping hole of slavery, and repaired by the Fourteenth Amendment in 1868. Any attempt to "expand rights and liberty" runs off the cliff of Liberty Mountain toward the backside of Tyranny Slope.

Granting super rights to protected classes *necessarily* leads to the infringement of basic rights of every other citizen. As John Quincy Adams once said, "[T]his is a land, not of privileges, but of equal rights. Privileges are granted by European sovereigns to particular classes of individuals, for purposes of general policy; but the general impression here is that privileges granted to one denomination of people, can very seldom be discriminated from erosions of the rights of others."[48]

For example, with the creation of a fundamental right to gay marriage—a concept that never existed until fifteen years ago—individuals are now suffering from the loss of their religious liberty, private property rights, and livelihood—our most foundational and unchangeable rights.

By granting illegal aliens rights to be released into the country, serviced with education and health care and citizenship for their children—all at taxpayer expense—the courts are infringing on the liberty and property rights of the American citizen not to mention the very essence of the social contract and consent-based popular sovereignty—the foundation and preamble of our founding.

Not only do court-created super rights violate the principle of popular sovereignty; they undercut the other principle of the Declaration—that all men are created equal. Court-mandated affirmative action and the requirement of equal outcomes in the private economy and society in general necessarily abrogate the equal opportunity that provides the underpinnings of a just and moral government.

Hence, when it comes to asserting rights beyond our founding rights, more is less. Any other popular or unpopular political or societal change willed by a group of people is designed to be executed through the elected branches of government and not retroactively enshrined into our Constitution, lest we slip into the nightmare scenario we are confronted with today—stolen sovereignty and the road to irremediable despotism.

As we embark on the mission to restore our republic to the values it was founded upon, let us not feel intimidated by the pseudo intellectualism and righteous indignation of those who defend judicial tyranny in the media, academia, and the supercilious legal profession. Let us not forget our history and founding, for, as President Reagan warned, "If we forget what we did, we won't know who we are."[49] Let us rally around the words of one of the early Supreme Court justices, Joseph Story, who respected the Constitution as it was written and understood the proper role of the judiciary relative to the sovereignty of the people:

> "Let us never forget, that our constitutions of government are solemn instruments, addressed to the common sense of the people and designed to fix, and perpetuate their rights and their liberties. They are not to be frittered away to please the demagogues of the day. They are not to be violated to gratify the ambition of political leaders. They are to speak in the same voice now, and for ever. They are of no man's private interpretation. They are ordained by the will of the people; and can be changed only by the sovereign command of the people."[50]

2

COURTS AND OBAMACARE: LIMITLESS FEDERAL POWER

I'm not particularly interested in the 18th Century, nor am I particularly interested in the text of the Constitution. I don't believe that any document drafted in the 18th century can guide our behavior today.

I think we can forget about the 18th century, much of the text. We ask with respect to contemporary constitutional issues, ask what is a sensible response.

—JUDGE RICHARD POSNER, GOP-APPOINTED JUDGE,
SEVENTH CIRCUIT COURT OF APPEALS

It's understandable why, despite the growing malfeasance of the court system on constitutional issues, even conservatives would be reluctant to either ignore the court's opinions or pass legislation stripping their power. Nobody wants chaos and instability and a lack of uniformity in law. Plus, it was always thought that as much as the courts illegally created *new* rights for protected classes, we would need them for the instances in which the other branches of government—both federal and state—abused *their* power. After all, the political branches of government regularly infringe on the authentic inalienable rights of the citizenry, which are supposed to be walled off even from majoritarian legislative rule.

However, the recent court decisions and the growing judicial time bomb make it clear that this time has long passed. The courts are irreparably corrupt, unflinchingly political, and devoid of any coherent jurisprudence. The majority of the courts like to have it both ways. They invent new rights that are not written in the Constitution and allow the other branches of government to blatantly violate the most sacred property and liberty rights expressed in the preamble of the Declaration and the Constitution.

Based on a number of recent cases, it is clear that conservatives cannot even count on benefiting from the anti-constitutional jurisprudence of the courts when the policy or political outcome benefits them. That is because the courts have no consistent *legal* jurisprudence other than siding with the preferred left-wing *political* outcome and backfilling it with incomprehensible and appallingly hypocritical legal analysis. When it suits their preferred outcome, they will side with the states over the federal government and vice versa, even when the legal rationale is internally conflicting. In one decision they will side with ballot initiatives over elected officials; in the next decision they will rule against the popular will. No matter what, the outcome is never in doubt. The Democrat political position will be victorious in the courts. The legal claptrap merely served as the stuffing.

What is striking in each high-profile case we will explore—Obamacare, marriage, religious liberty, and immigration—is that *all* of the Democrat-appointed judges, from the district and appellate courts all the way to the Supreme Court, rule on the side of the legal/constitutional question that helps Democrats politically. Meanwhile, Republican-appointed judges are often split. This imbalance on the courts has completely disenfranchised conservatives. Now that the courts are 100 percent political and decide all-important societal questions, conservatives can't even rely on Republican judges to counter the

Democrat ones. This has created a growing permanent majority on the benches of those who will always distort their legal arguments in order to side with the Left on major societal questions for political reasons.

CONTORTING THE CONSTITUTION FOR POLITICAL REASONS

One of the striking features of the paradoxical legal philosophy of the judicial tyrants is that they are willing to bless the legislative power grab over the people when it comes to regulating the economy. Yet, they are all too alacritous to render Congress impotent in deciding the will of the people as it relates to the political and societal debates of our time.

On the one hand, they magically broaden and amplify the enumerated powers of the Commerce, Necessary and Proper, and General Welfare "clauses" of the Constitution—all but voiding out the power of the people and states expressed in the Ninth and Tenth Amendments. On the other hand, they say the Fourteenth Amendment prevents Congress or state legislatures from working out their internal social and political conflicts because the newly discovered fundamental rights (which were blithely ignored when examining economic regulations) would be violated.

Then again, this legal enigma is only perplexing to those expecting a rational and impartial legal opinion from the courts. The sad reality is that the new, outcome-based model of jurisprudence is actually very consistent and coherent—that is to say, whatever benefits the left-wing political agenda is legal and constitutional; whatever hinders it is unconstitutional.

As Judge Posner brazenly proclaimed, "The time to look at precedent, statutory text, legislative history, that's *after you have some sense of what is the best decision for today.* Then you ask whether it is blocked by something that happened in the past."[1] Never mind that "what is sensible" is a matter of public policy reserved for the *elected* branches of government, whereas the Constitution, precedent, and statutory text are precisely and exclusively the legal purview of judges who do not face the electorate.

The juxtaposition of the recent Obamacare and marriage cases offers a superlative glimpse into a full array of these politically motivated paradoxes in judicial tyranny.

If there was ever a prime opportunity for the courts to invalidate a law passed by the political branch of government to protect a fundamental liberty, it was the two opportunities the court had to invalidate Obamacare. In 2012, twenty-six states filed joint or separate lawsuits against Obamacare along with the National Federation of Independent Business.[2]

The central question before the courts in *National Federation of Independent Business v. Sebelius* (and a couple of parallel cases in the court system) was whether the federal government had the power to coerce an individual to purchase a private product—health insurance. Unlike car insurance at a state level, which mandates insurance for the activity of driving a vehicle on the road, Obamacare was placing a new federal regulation on a person's mere existence. Does the federal government now have the power to not only regulate anything and everything but to now even regulate inactivity?

It's important to note that the legal question was completely divorced from the political or policy question. From a conservative policy perspective, the individual mandate was not even the central or most onerous part of Obamacare, such as the price-hiking coverage mandates, Medicaid expansion, and endless rules and regulations on doctors and hospitals—all of which contributed to the precipitous rise in costs for health care and health insurance.[3] The legal question was not whether this was a prudent policy; it was whether the federal government has the power of coercion on inactivity.

A judge could be a bleeding-heart liberal who believes in single-payer health care as a matter of policy, but were he to adhere to any semblance of constitutional jurisprudence, he must rule this law way out of bounds of the scope of Article I enumerated powers. Yet, they knew that because the coverage mandates and subsidies were inextricably tied to the unconstitutional individual mandate, and would have countermanded the entire policy they supported, they had to remake the Constitution in order to save the program.

Our detractors will accuse us of a double standard—desiring the courts to stay out of the issues we want unchanged but overturn the laws we dislike. "They like judicial activism when it benefits them," is a common refrain from the other side of the legal community.[4] But this is really simple; it's not about activism or restraint. It's about whether we believe in the Constitution as it was written.

If liberals desire to revert back to pre-Marshall days, when the court lacked the power of judicial review, let's shake on it and go back in time to absolute majoritarian rule. On net, it would certainly be superior to the existing judicial oligarchy that promotes the liberal political agenda without any recourse to stop it. But now that we've given the courts that power to strike down federal statutes in addition to interpreting their application, they must use the original Constitution, not the Democratic Party platform, as their blueprint for judicial review. By ruling the individual mandate of Obamacare constitutional, the courts are now saying that the federal government has the power to regulate *all* activity and *all* inactivity. This is a prima facie contortion of the entire founding of our Republic and the whole concept of enumerated powers.

Regulating inactivity and coercing people to actively engage in commerce would most certainly fit the description of an "act contrary to the manifest tenor of the Constitution," of which Alexander Hamilton believed the court had an obligation to nullify.[5]

Honest people can disagree over gray areas and the contours of the enumerated powers, but once you believe that there *are* no contours or boundaries, the powers of the federal government are not limited and enumerated; they are boundless and infinite. What was so earth-shattering about the Obamacare ruling, and what should alarm every American, is that there is now nothing beyond the reach of the federal government because the courts have empowered them to regulate even inactivity. Congress can pass a law mandating three hours of exercise on a treadmill per week, punishable with a $1,000 fine for those who disobey the order. They can force us to eat a plate of broccoli every day. Remember, these are not necessarily dumb laws; they would actually go a long way in combating obesity in this country. But they are lawless "laws" nonetheless; they are patently and incontrovertibly unconstitutional. And if the courts are going to exercise judicial review, they must interpret the Constitution that was adopted by the states in 1789.

Yet, every single Democrat-appointed judge ruled that the Constitution permitted the federal government to compel someone to enter into commerce and purchase a private product. And in what has become a pattern even in the most egregious cases, several Republican-appointed judges ruled the same way.

When the case finally reached the Supreme Court, Chief Justice Roberts was faced with a dilemma. On the one hand, there was no way someone who had staked out his career as a conservative could interpret the commerce clause as including the power to regulate inactivity. On the other hand, as witnessed by his change of heart and his later absurd opinions upholding Obamacare, he was clearly intent on preserving Obamacare at all costs. He therefore proceeded to rewrite the legislation from the bench and upheld the individual mandate as a function of Congress's power to levy taxes.[6]

But Roberts's opinion is absurd on its face because if the federal government lacks the authority to coerce someone to eat broccoli, how does levying a $1,000 "tax" on that inactivity make it better? Again, what can be said of our Constitution as a doctrine of only enumerated powers if the government can circumvent those constraints by calling it a tax?

Moreover, not only did Roberts and the other leftists completely rewrite the Constitution; they set a precedent by rewriting a congressional statute from the bench. Congress never wrote the individual mandate law as a tax to collect revenue for specific government services; they wrote it as a *regulation* enforced through a *penalty* to coerce something for which Roberts admitted they lacked the power to regulate.

In reality, the commerce clause was not only never intended to empower the federal government to regulate inactivity; it was never conceived as a proactive green light to regulate any activity simply because it moves across state lines. In 1829, Madison wrote that the commerce clause had already been abused by that time, noting that it was "intended as a negative and preventive provision against injustice among the States themselves, rather than as a power to be used for the positive purposes of the General Government."[7] This reflects his observation at the time of the founding that the commerce clause was "an addition which few oppose and from which no apprehensions are entertained."[8]

As Justice Thomas noted in a 1995 case regarding the ban of handguns within one thousand feet of schools, "at the time the original Constitution was ratified, 'commerce' consisted of selling, buying, and bartering, as well as transporting for these purposes."[9] The purpose of regulating "commerce among the several states" was to break down trade barriers between the states, not to prohibit products and services or create mandates on the people.

At the time, Thomas warned that "[A]t an appropriate juncture, I think we must modify our commerce clause jurisprudence."[10] Sadly, instead of recalibrating their jurisprudence to match the original intent of the document they swore to uphold, just a generation later many of those same justices stepped on the gas pedal of post-constitutional jurisprudence and redefined the commerce clause as empowering the federal government to compel one to engage in commerce.

The modern-day judicial assault on the commerce clause is just as bad as the adulteration of the necessary and proper clause, or elastic clause.[11] The necessary and proper clause was also never designed to add entire *new* spheres of power to the federal government. It was merely concocted to grant Congress the flexibility to exercise the *existing* enumerated powers without violating existing rights of the people or powers of the state. For example, Congress has the power to tax and has the power to raise an army and a navy. Applying the elastic clause as it relates to our national security needs in the modern era would vest Congress with the authority to use their *existing* taxing authority to further protect the people by funding an air force.

Necessary and *proper* are words descriptive of a *means* to achieve the ends of "securing the blessings of liberty" as prescribed in the Declaration of Independence.[12] This clause was certainly never intended to create a *new* power as an *end* to itself—one that would run counter to the ideals of individual rights, and certainly not to the point of penalizing inaction for simply existing without purchasing a private product. This clause was a call for the people's representatives to use prudence and common sense in using existing tools, at least when not in conflict with existing constraints on their power, to achieve the desideratum expressed in the preambles of the Constitution and Declaration.

For example, it's not outlandish to presume that some of the policy objectives laid out in this book—abolishing birthright citizenship for illegals, excluding illegal immigrants from the census, and stripping the courts of jurisdiction over societal issues—are quintessential applications of this clause. For without those reforms, we will no longer have liberty, property rights, and sovereignty as a nation, nor will we have recourse through our elected representative to ever restore our Republic. Don't hold your breath waiting for any federal judge to uphold potential congressional legislation dealing with those issues on account of the necessary and proper clause.

Amazingly, despite the incontrovertibly limited scope of the commerce and necessary and proper clauses, all but one Democrat-appointed judge ruled that one can be compelled to engage in commerce.[13] On the other hand, several GOP-appointed judges sided against the Constitution. Some of these justices were appointed by President Bush—after the much-vaunted push by the conservative legal community to pick originalist judges.[14] The courts have failed to properly use judicial review in the few instances where they held the legitimate power to do so. Thus, the days when conservatives could benefit from the power of the judiciary in order to promote liberty have long past.

COURTS REWRITE STATUTES FROM THE BENCH

In many respects the Supreme Court's decision in *King v. Burwell* upholding the federal subsidies to states with federal health insurance exchanges was even more egregious and nakedly political than the first Obamacare case concerning the individual mandate. With this decision, Chief Justice Roberts has paved the way for endless executive usurpations of congressional statutes and the prospect of the courts literally rewriting laws from the bench in order to preserve liberal policies.

In *King v. Burwell*, the question before the court was even less political in nature than the individual mandate case.[15] Plaintiffs sued the Obama administration for granting tax credits to those who purchased health insurance under Obamacare in the thirty-four states where the state failed to set up a health care exchange. Under the unambiguous language of the law, tax credits were only to be doled out to those purchasing insurance in exchanges "established by the State."[16] This lawsuit didn't even involve any judicial review of the constitutionality of the law, nor did it deal with the prudence of the broader health care scheme. At its core, interpreting the plain meaning and application of congressional statutes is *exactly* what the courts were established to do.

Even a champion of Obamacare must concede that the plain language of the law limited the tax credits to those states that established a *state*-based exchange. The clear intent of the law was to serve as an incentive for states to follow the law and establish exchanges. Given that thirty-four states failed to set up their own exchanges, this should have been a no-brainer decision even for Democrat-activist judges. The consequences of invalidating those subsidies should have played no role in their strict responsibility to interpret the statutes as written and clearly intended. This is exactly why federal judges don't stand for election.

Yet, not only did every single Democrat-appointed judge throughout the *King v. Burwell* (and parallel court cases) litigation vote to rewrite the law, but so did a number of Republican-appointed judges.[17] And at the Supreme Court, both Chief Justice Roberts and Associate Justice Kennedy joined all of the liberals in striking the word *state* from the statute and rewriting it to include those who purchased insurance under federal exchanges.

"In this instance, the context and structure of the Act compel us to depart from what would otherwise be the most natural reading of the pertinent statutory phrase," wrote Chief Justice Roberts.[18] He concluded with the following dangerous precedent on the power of the courts: "A fair reading of legislation demands a fair understanding of the legislative plan. Congress passed the Affordable Care Act to improve health insurance markets, not to destroy them. If at all possible, we must interpret the Act in a way that is consistent with the former, and avoids the latter."[19]

What Roberts was essentially saying is that anytime the policy of a bill goes off the rails and is in need of a political fix, the courts have the power and desire to help fix the law in the event of litigation against executive overreach in defying the plain meaning of the law.

It's important to remember that this decision had nothing to do with Obamacare, although it had the potential to strike down Obama's subsidies and cause a chain reaction in dismantling the rest of the high-profile program. The broader implication of this decision is that the court can now serve as a super-legislature, albeit an unelected one, with the power to consider the *political* implications of interpreting laws as written, and if it deems those implications to be contrary to their desired political outcome, they can rewrite the law from the bench.

Scalia, in his dissent, ominously warned of the fallout from this decision:

> Just ponder the significance of the Court's decision to take matters into its own hands. The Court's revision of the law authorizes the Internal Revenue Service to spend tens of billions of dollars every year in tax credits on federal Exchanges. It affects the price of insurance for millions of Americans. It diminishes the participation of the States in the implementation of the Act. It vastly expands the reach of the Act's individual mandate, whose scope depends in part on the availability of credits. What a parody today's decision makes of Hamilton's assurances to the people of New York: The legislature not only commands the purse but prescribes the rules by which the duties and rights of every citizen are to be regulated. The judiciary,

> on the contrary, has no influence over . . . the purse; no direction . . . of the wealth of society, and can take no active resolution whatever. It may truly be said to have neither FORCE nor WILL but merely judgment.[20]

The *King v. Burwell* decision should serve as the final straw for anyone holding out hope that we can still benefit from an activist Supreme Court when justices strike down laws and executive decisions conservatives deem harmful and unconstitutional. From the fact that every Democrat-appointed judge was willing to rewrite the law, it is plain as day that the courts have become results-oriented, basing their decisions on their preferred political outcome rather than deciding the narrow legal questions presented to them on their own logical and constitutional merits. And since even a number of Republican judges joined in such a rancid usurpation of power, we must conclude that conservatives can never count on Republican presidents to appoint only originalists to the bench with a success rate that will even the score against the Democrats' impeccable record of appointing judicial tyrants.

A "COMPELLING GOVERNMENTAL INTEREST" . . . *REALLY?*

Aside from the lawsuits challenging the constitutionality of the individual mandate and the federal subsidies to states that failed to set up an insurance exchange, a number of private religious institutions filed lawsuits against the requirement in the law that these organizations provide contraception and abortifacient coverage in their health care compensation packages.

After losing their case to directly force religious employers to cover abortifacients in their health insurance compensation plans, the Obama administration concocted a new scheme. Any objecting organization must send a cumbersome form to the Department of Health and Human Services (HHS) stating the grounds for the religious objections. If they are approved for the exemption, HHS then requires the insurance provider of that organization or a third party to provide the contraception coverage separately.

Hence, they are still forcing religious institutions to be complicit in violating their religious consciousness with their own private property and businesses. This is the most flagrant violation of the First Amendment's right to religious freedom and federal law, which protects the exercise of religious freedom except in case of a "compelling governmental interest."[21] We have now reached silly season in our moral-legal ethos that providing taxpayer funds to subsidize everyone's birth control is a compelling government interest—enough to infringe on the religious and property rights of private entities.

Yet, appallingly only one circuit court out of over half a dozen cases throughout the appellate level sided with the religious institutions.[22] Once again, every Democratic appointee sided with the Obama administration against the Constitution; a number of Republican appointees did as well.[23]

* * *

With the ruling on Obamacare, the economic component of the legal ratchet of social justice is complete. The screw is as tight as can be, with nowhere for liberty to go. The federal government can either tax or regulate both activity and inactivity. What this means in the long run is that as the courts create new fundamental rights and brazenly decide all societal issues in favor of the most liberal causes, we will never benefit from their looseness with "liberty" on the other hand to protect the most fundamental liberties of bodily integrity and private property rights when the other branches of the federal or state governments infringe on them. It should be abundantly clear that any effort to reform the courts by regulating and limiting their power will always serve as a net positive for the Constitution and representative government.

3

THE COURTS REMAKE CIVILIZATION AND THREATEN RELIGIOUS LIBERTY

Conscience is the most sacred of all property; other property depending in part on positive law, the exercise of that, being a natural and inalienable right.

—JAMES MADISON

In chapter 2, we explored how the courts believe government has the power to regulate or tax all activity and *inactivity*. But that all-powerful leviathan suddenly becomes impotent to reserve its prerogative to define marriage as it has been defined since time immemorial for purposes of federal law (as it relates to the federal government) and state law (as it relates to state government). The juxtaposition of the court's marriage and Obamacare rulings demonstrates its purely naked politics.

Concurrently, as the courts give the other branches of the federal and state governments a green light to infringe on civil liberties and private property rights with Obamacare mandates, their gay marriage decision is now telegraphing the message to those same entities that they can infringe on the most foundational right of religious liberty, as it must yield to the newly created *super right* of the broader homosexual agenda.

Unfortunately, this paradox is no enigma. The Founders foresaw the possibility that a government powerful enough to infringe on property rights would also promote societal transformation and violate religious liberty. As John Witherspoon, a signer of the Declaration, presciently warned, "There is not a single instance in history, in which civil liberty was lost, and religious liberty preserved entire. If therefore we yield up our temporal property, we at the same time deliver the conscience into bondage."[1]

Witherspoon's nightmare has come true. With the ability to tax and regulate almost every act—and in the case of Obamacare, even inaction—government, not God, has become the source of those rights. It was only a matter of time before this hundred-year march toward government control of private property and commerce (*pursuit of happiness*) would inevitably lead to the curtailment of religious *liberty*.

To understand why the courts' "legal" decisions ratifying the homosexual political and social agenda are actually rooted in the *erosion* of rights and a war on religious liberty, we must first understand the central question before the courts in the marriage cases and again hark back to the foundation of fundamental rights we explored in chapter 1.

The question at hand in the marriage case was not whether homosexuality is a sin or a virtue or anything in between. It was not a question concerning the prudence of redefining marriage. Those are societal and political questions that should be left to the people, yet those were the very questions that were stripped from them. The legal question was whether there is a federal constitutional right for same-sex partners to obtain a marriage license, thereby preventing the people or legislators of sovereign states from defining marriage.

This marriage case was not a question of religiosity or a debate over culture. That is a societal conflict that will be settled outside of court. Even the strongest supporter of homosexuality or the idea of a same-sex marriage cannot deny that there is no mention of *any* form of marriage in the Constitution. States have unconditional authority over marriage. So how could a court rule that the people through ballot initiatives and state legislatures are precluded from defining marriage as it has always been since the existence of both the original Constitution and the ratification of the Fourteenth Amendment?

The answer, of course, is that this was nothing but pure politics, backfilling the legal analysis with their "living and breathing" ratchet theory of the Constitution in order to achieve the desired political outcome. They had to concoct a new super right that was lost on us for the first 225 years of our republic. But in creating that super right, as is always the case on the bell curve of liberties, they *necessarily* had to abridge the natural inalienable right to religious liberty.

In the infamous same-sex marriage case of 2015, Justice Anthony Kennedy didn't just redefine marriage from the bench. He remade our Constitution and our entire system of governance. After asserting that the framers of the Fourteenth Amendment couldn't possibly know "the extent of freedom and all its dimensions," Kennedy invoked twenty-three words that will forever endanger our sovereignty unless the courts are stripped down to size: "and so they entrusted to future generations a charter protecting the right of all persons to enjoy liberty as *we* learn its meaning."[2]

The "we" is, of course, referring to the courts. Now, picture any left-wing social policy, from amnesty for illegal aliens to transgender bathrooms, and you can easily see how any future court can use those twenty-three words to "discover" infinite "rights" and backfill them into the Fourteenth Amendment.

Let's unpack the legal fiction behind the gay marriage case.

In order to assert a new fundamental right, plaintiffs claimed that state marriage laws violated their "substantive" due process under the Fourteenth Amendment. Now, if you notice, the word *substantive* might not be in *your* version of the Constitution, but it is evidently written in invisible ink in the version used by the judicial tyrants. As anyone with even a rudimentary understanding of the Constitution knows, the term due process mentioned in the Fifth and Fourteenth Amendments refers to a *process* and *procedure* that is required before denying someone his or her *inalienable* rights—life, liberty, and property—via imprisonment, fines, or death.

In one of the clever tricks of the legal tyranny community over the past century, they created a legal fiction known as *substantive* due process and differentiated it from *procedural* due process—the only real due process mentioned in the Constitution. That way they could concoct new fundamental rights and insert them into the Constitution, even though constitutional due process merely referred to a process in safeguarding inalienable and finite rights. The Founders never meant to create a new, undefined, and ever-evolving basket of rights as ends in themselves.

Substantive due process has become the porta-potty of post-constitutional jurisprudence for those too cowardly to pursue their societal transformation through the democratic process. It is a legal fiction meant as a means to an end—that is, societal transformation via "judicial legislation."[3]

In the mind of Alexander Hamilton, the parlance of "due process" was unambiguous. While defining the term in 1787, he declared that the "words '*due process*' have a *precise technical import*, and are *only* applicable to the *process and proceedings* of the courts of justice."[4] It was never designed to create a single new right beyond protecting the fixed rights that are self-evident under natural law with a fair process in court. It was a directive, for example, that before someone is hanged for murder or treason, to make sure you got the right guy and he is indeed guilty of the crime.

Like every legal fiction designed to supplant the Constitution, substantive due process started out in baby steps. After all, everyone agrees there are gray areas in terms of what denotes a violation of liberty. For example, one would say that a hypothetical state or federal law requiring that all citizens walk the streets without clothes would be defined as a violation of liberty.

Therefore, even as late as this generation, the courts still claimed to abide by a very narrowly defined and strict definition of a substantive due process violation. In 1997, there was a case before the Supreme Court, *Washington v. Glucksberg*, regarding physician-assisted suicide that mirrored the arguments proponents of homosexual marriage have employed. The Court ruled in favor of the state 9–0 in declining to assert a fundamental right to physician-assisted suicide.[5] Three of the justices—Kennedy, Breyer, and Ginsburg—completely contradicted themselves with the ruling on marriage in *Obergefell*.

The respondents in *Glucksberg*, led by Washington physician Harold Glucksberg, asserted a "liberty interest" and fundamental right to assist terminally ill patients in committing suicide. They contended that the state law banning assisted suicide violated their "substantive" due process under the Fourteenth Amendment.

On paper, the respondents in *Glucksberg* had a much better case than those who sought to invalidate state marriage laws. They were asserting the right of self-sovereignty and were simply asking the state to not interfere with their act. On the other hand, in the *Obergefell* case, they were asking for a state benefit and affirmative recognition, the opposite of the relief the respondents sought in the assisted-suicide case.

Yet, in *Glucksberg*, the court shredded the idea that there is a fundamental right under the Fourteenth Amendment to assisted suicide. The litmus test the court used, based on decades of past precedent, in determining whether the due process clause of the Fourteenth Amendment protects a specific act is whether the asserted right is "deeply rooted in this Nation's history and tradition," and "implicit in the concept of ordered liberty," such that "neither liberty nor justice would exist if they were sacrificed."[6]

Chief Justice Rehnquist, writing the unanimous opinion (although the four liberals disagreed slightly with the reasoning in a concurring opinion), noted that bans on suicide were a part of Anglo-American common law for seven hundred years and that "by the time the Fourteenth Amendment was ratified, it was a crime in most States to assist a suicide."[7] So, rather than the asserted right having deep roots in history and tradition, Rehnquist observed that the state laws *banning* assisted suicide were rooted in history and tradition. This was similar to Scalia's point in his dissent in *Obergefell* when he observed that every state defined marriage as between one man and one woman at the time the Fourteenth Amendment was ratified.[8]

Now, ask yourself this question: how can anyone assert such a claim for a concept that was not even conceived until this generation, thereby bypassing the political process to create that right? Say what you want about homosexuality in general, but even the most ardent activist cannot assert that a same-sex marriage is "deeply rooted in this Nation's history and tradition," and "implicit in the concept of ordered liberty," such that "neither liberty nor justice would exist if they were sacrificed."

Yet, by creating such a super right, what the court has said is that homosexuals are now a protected class entitled to the same extra privileges the courts have gradually granted chosen demographics. By circumventing the political process to create a new fundamental right and protected class, the court has codified into law the antireligious bigotry we've witnessed over the past few years.

DENYING RELIGIOUS LIBERTY

The inalienable liberty and property rights of religious Americans are now necessarily forced to yield before the man-made super rights on steroids when the two are in conflict. We have descended to such tragic depths of anti-constitutional dyslexia that the few rights that are the epitome of "deeply rooted in this Nation's history and tradition"—namely, religious liberty and property rights—are now being infringed by a "right" that, whatever you think of the policy and values behind it, is antithetical to an ideal deeply rooted in history and tradition. Ironically, the concept of gay marriage violates natural law as established by nature's God—the very source of our rights in the first place.

Clarence Thomas eloquently observed how the granting of such a super right would necessarily come into conflict with religious liberty—the most foundational right. "It appears all but inevitable that the two will come into conflict, particularly as individuals and churches are confronted with demands to participate in and endorse civil marriages between same-sex couples."[9]

Thomas also saw right through the majority opinion and revealed that the assault on religious liberty was not some unintended consequence of their opinion; it was *part and parcel* of it:

> The majority appears unmoved by that inevitability. It makes only a weak gesture toward religious liberty in a single paragraph. And even that gesture indicates a misunderstanding of religious liberty in our Nation's tradition. Religious liberty is about more than just the protection for "religious organizations and persons . . . as they seek to teach the principles that are so fulfilling and so central to their lives and faiths." Religious liberty is about freedom of action in matters of religion generally, and the scope of that liberty is directly correlated to the civil restraints placed upon religious practice.[10]

Justice Scalia commenced his masterful dissent in *Obergefell* observing how the courts have taken this political question away from the people, even though the process was actually working quite well:

> Until the courts put a stop to it, public debate over same-sex marriage displayed American democracy at its best. Individuals on both sides of the issue passionately, but respectfully, attempted to persuade their fellow citizens to accept their views. Americans considered the arguments and put the question to a vote. . . . Win or lose, advocates for both sides continued pressing their cases, secure in the knowledge that an electoral loss can be negated by a later electoral win. That is exactly how our system of government is supposed to work.[11]

Throughout the past decade, thirty-two states have enacted laws—via ballot referendums—reaffirming the traditional definition of marriage while other states were gradually redefining it.[12] The left-wing political movement in this country enjoys control over all of the venues of information dissemination—such as entertainment, media, academia, and nonprofits. This applies doubly as it relates to the issue of homosexual marriage. If this was such a winning issue, as they boldly asserted, why couldn't they just let the political process unfold, and in all likelihood, within one election cycle they could have overturned the marriage laws through ballot initiatives? It's not as though conservatives were asserting that gay marriage is affirmatively unconstitutional, so they could have done this at a state level with simple majorities. No constitutional amendment was required. Yet, *we* are the ones who are forced to pursue constitutional amendments to merely restore the Constitution to its original meaning?

The true motivation of enshrining this into the Constitution was to strip the political branches of their power to craft statutes and conditions protecting religious liberty. If conservatives continue to legitimize this lawlessness by asserting that our only recourse to abiding by the Constitution is to pursue constitutional amendments, we will lose our country before that nearly impossible process gets off the ground. We will also lose our right to religious liberty.

Kim Davis, who was clerk of Rowan County, Kentucky, for twenty-seven years, was sent to jail for refusing to issue marriage licenses to gay couples following the 5–4 marriage decision in *Obergefell*.[13] The media brainwashed the public into thinking that this woman was ignoring the "law of the land." But who has the law on their side?

Kim Davis worked in the clerk's office for almost three decades, predating even the human concept of a homosexual marriage. In 2004, 75 percent of the state's voters agreed to preemptively protect against the assault on marriage by defining it as a union between a man and a woman. One can be the most pro-homosexual "rights" activist in the world, but to uphold our legal framework, he'd have to concede that the federal Constitution is silent on marriage and that it has always been a state institution. Marriage as it was always understood is the law of the land in the state of Kentucky. Is Davis violating the law of the land? Or were Kennedy and the other four justices, as well as lower court judges, violating the very essence of the Constitution, Bill of Rights, and endless pages of their own precedents on substantive due process rights?

We live in dark times when the court's own public vitiation of the Constitution, Declaration of Independence, and inalienable rights can infringe on religious liberty and have the power to deny due process to religious people in order to serve the ever-evolving nakedly *political* due process.

Anyone who tells you we shouldn't strip the courts of their power over political issues, such as the definition of marriage, clearly is not paying attention to the dramatic, despotic turn the courts have taken—even beyond the previous generation of judicial activism. This is tyrannical, unsustainable, and the antithesis of every solitary tenet of the Constitution and Declaration. We cannot wait any longer to bring the power back to the people through the elected branches of government.

HITTING ROCK BOTTOM: CREATING POSITIVE RIGHTS

There is one other major outcome of this decision that reveals just how negatively consequential this decision is—over and beyond the marriage or religious liberty issues. This court opinion was not about homosexual rights, equality, or marriage. It was about permanently remaking the Constitution in a way that will allow all subsequent justices to create new rights and laws from the bench without any limitations. And yes, that will include expanding rights to illegal aliens.

When our founding documents mentioned "rights," they always referred to protection from a *negative* action, such as a fine, imprisonment, or capital punishment without due process. For example, an American has the right not to be fined for simply existing and not actively purchasing a private product: health insurance. Oh, wait . . . the courts ruled that no such right exists, but I digress. What the *Obergefell* decision accomplished is that it invented the right to a *positive* benefit, a government-sanctioned status and recognition of a marriage certificate.

Clarence Thomas, in his scholarly dissent, trenchantly made this observation:

> The Court's decision today is at odds not only with the Constitution, but with the principles upon which our Nation was built. Since well before 1787, liberty has been understood as freedom from government action, not entitlement to government benefits. The Framers created our Constitution to preserve that understanding of liberty. Yet the majority invokes our Constitution in the name of a "liberty" that the Framers would not have recognized, to the detriment of the liberty they sought to protect. Along the way, it rejects the idea—captured in our Declaration of Independence—that human dignity is innate and suggests instead that it comes from the Government. This distortion of our Constitution not only ignores the text, it inverts the relationship between the individual and the state in our Republic.[14]

Thus, with this decision by the court, not only was the sovereignty of the states violated; the sovereignty of the individual was erased. The individual's innate rights can henceforth only be defined by the unelected courts.

Remember, even Justice John Marshall, the father of judicial review, wrote that the plain words of the Constitution cannot be "extended to objects not . . . contemplated by the framers."[15] How then could Justice Kennedy possibly have the impertinence to crown himself a judicial monarch to redefine the Constitution and the building block of all civilization?

Let's hark back to Madison's warning in 1824 about the consequences of deviating from the original interpretation of the Constitution at the time it was adopted:

> I entirely concur in the propriety of resorting to the sense in which the Constitution was accepted and ratified by the nation. In that sense alone it is the legitimate Constitution. And if that be not the guide in expounding it, there can be no security for a consistent and stable, more than for a faithful exercise of its powers. . . .What a metamorphosis would be produced in the code of law if all its ancient phraseology were to be taken in its modern sense.[16]

What a metamorphosis indeed! As the public jailing of Kim Davis shows, the most inalienable rights of liberty are no longer "shielded from" government action in order to yield to an Anthony Kennedy–made entitlement *to* a government benefit.

Scalia recently commented that although the majority of the court has been liberal and post-constitutional since he sat on the bench in 1984, and has been heading down the slippery slope ever since, "at the bottom of that slope, I can't imagine how you can go any further, is the right to same-sex marriage."[17] We've reached rock bottom.

AN ILLEGITIMATE AND HYPOCRITICAL COURT OPINION

While conservatives never like to advocate chaos by disobeying a court decision, we must ask ourselves at what point are we going to draw the line? Not only was this decision the most profound gyration of the Constitution, natural law, and inalienable rights imaginable, it was nakedly political and devoid of any legitimacy for a number of reasons.

First, under the code of conduct for the judiciary, judges are supposed to recuse themselves when they are clearly indissolubly tied to a particular political outcome with such fervor.[18] Ruth Bader Ginsburg and Elena Kagan demonstrated before the case even reached the court that they were cheering for gay marriage. They officiated at gay marriages and publicly championed the cause.[19] In that respect, the authentic outcome of the *Obergefell* case should have been 4–3 in favor of the states that wanted to preserve their definition of marriage.

But aside from the two reliable post-constitutionalists, Anthony Kennedy has exhibited such a duplicitous political desire to institute gay marriage over the years that it should leave no doubt in anyone's mind that there was not a shred of legal jurisprudence behind his opinion. His emotional rant in *Obergefell* and public break with the Constitution as it was originally written should render the entire decision null and void. Further, his hypocrisy on federalism from previous decisions reveals an undisguised political motivation for specific, and often diametrically opposed outcomes.

When I first read the decision, I was embarrassed for Kennedy and for the country that a Supreme Court justice could write such juvenile rantings masked as a legal opinion. He concocted new fundamental rights to "nobility," "dignity," "the right to define and express their identity," and not to be "stigmatized."[20] If that is the new standard from which God-given rights can be supplanted and swapped for man-made rights, there is no limit to what the courts can devise as a political tool to achieve their ends. How can such an opinion be taken seriously?

It's not a secret that four of the Supreme Court justices and countless lower court judges believe in the paradoxical "anti-constitutional constitutional doctrine" we explained in chapter 1. But with this decision built upon those twenty-three infamous words we highlighted earlier, Anthony Kennedy made it clear there is now a majority on the Supreme Court who believe liberty is man-made and is given over to the courts, not the people, to decide. Those words should haunt every American of all political persuasions because they will create a permanent judicial oligarchy with boundless and unchecked political power unless they are reined in by the people.

Kennedy's raw hypocrisy gets worse. Just two years before the final marriage case, Kennedy authored the 2013 opinion in *United States v. Windsor*, striking down the Defense of Marriage Act (DOMA).[21] Although states issue marriage licenses and have the full power over marriage, the federal government still needed to define marriage for its own purposes in its inevitable interaction with the civil society, such as it relates to immigration policy or monetary benefits for federal employees. Additionally, DOMA protected the states that still defined marriage as a marriage from lawsuits on behalf of those states that redefined the institution. To be clear, DOMA did not interfere or prevent states from choosing to redefine marriage to include homosexual couples, and in fact, a number of states and the District of Columbia adopted gay marriage since DOMA's passage in 1996.

Nonetheless, Kennedy authored the 5–4 opinion striking down parts of DOMA asserting that the federal law infringed on the state power over marriage. You will jump out of your seat when you see what Kennedy said about state authority over marriage just two years before he redefined it from the bench and took the issue away from the states.

"[R]egulation of domestic relations is an area that has long been regarded as a virtually exclusive province of the States," declared Kennedy while citing from previous cases.[22] "[T]he Federal Government, through our history, has deferred to state-law policy decisions with respect to domestic relations," concluded a disingenuous Kennedy.[23]

Once again, when a "lower level" marriage/social issue is before the court, Kennedy uses every argument he can muster to achieve the liberal result, even if that jurisprudence necessarily precludes him from going a step or two or five further. Yet, just two years later, Kennedy overturned the state marriage laws of thirty-two states under a rationale that never existed until this generation.

How can Kennedy say that the *elected* branch of the federal government cannot define marriage for its *own* purposes because *states* have exclusive power and then, just two years later, create a *federal* constitutional right from the *unelected* bench precluding *states* from defining marriage as it has always been defined by those very states he so recently observed exclusively crafted the marriage laws since the nation's founding? How can he say that state laws with regard to marriage are supreme and then force every state to redefine its very essence?

There is no answer other than to say that "choosing a political outcome first, then backfilling the legal rationale later"—even when it is self-contradictory—is overt political lawlessness that violates the Constitution and the popular sovereignty of thirty-two state ballot initiatives and state legislatures. Furthermore, it overturned years' worth of court precedent that Kennedy himself signed onto. Once again, we see that the concept of *stare decisis*—legal precedent—is one-directional. Hence, the socialist ratchet we spoke of in chapter 1.

OUTSOURCING YOUR REPRESENTATION

While discussing hypocritical legal analysis in order to achieve desired political goals, it's important to introduce one more case that reveals the transparent political motivations of Kennedy and the four Democrats on the court.

Just a few days after rewriting the Constitution and countermanding the preamble of the Declaration, Kennedy signed onto a majority opinion in a seemingly unrelated case, *Arizona State Legislature v. Arizona Independent Redistricting*, a decision that reveals even more hypocritical legal analysis designed to net the opposite result when it suits his personal politics.[24] This case involved the Arizona state legislature suing for control over the redistricting process in their state after voters handed over the power of redistricting to an unelected commission. Writing for the majority, Ginsburg ruled that when Article I, Section 4 of the Constitution grants the "Legislature" control over the manner in which federal elections are conducted in the state, it really also means the people of the state through ballot initiatives.[25] This, despite the fact that the Constitution mentions the word *legislature* seventeen times, and in most cases, it's impossible to be describing anything but its plain textual meaning.

As Thomas observed in his dissent, the majority (of which Justice Kennedy was a cosigner) extolls the virtues of ballot initiatives and allowing the people of the state to decide redistricting, even though this is one of the few things preempted by the plain language of the federal Constitution. Yet, these same justices, during the same term, gaily overturned ballot initiatives of thirty-two states dealing with one of the most foundational and contentious societal issues of our time—all for highbrow concepts that are never mentioned anywhere in the Constitution and are indeed an anathema to the Tenth Amendment and to the concept of fundamental rights—based on nature's God.[26]

How ironic that Justice Ginsburg sanctimoniously extolled the right to ballot initiative enshrined in Arizona's Constitution, which as she noted, passed "by a margin of more than three to one." Do you know what other Constitutional amendment passed by a margin of three to one? The Kentucky constitutional marriage amendment—the same law county clerk Kim Davis was upholding when she was ordered jailed on account of violating the "law" promulgated by these very same five justices!

The only semblance of consistency here is the desire of the courts to violate the Constitution and disenfranchise the people. In the Arizona redistricting case, they were able to kill two birds with one judicial stone—outsource the people's representation to an unelected commission while overturning the plain meaning of the elections clause of the Constitution.

JUST WHAT *IS* MARRIAGE?

To strike down the state marriage laws, the court declared that marriage is no longer a special union between one man and one woman. As such, they had an obligation to explain to the country what a marriage *is*. This is where they were appallingly silent. This case is different from all other areas where the courts strike down state or federal statutes. Normally, when the courts strike down a law they deem unlawful, the law reverts back to what it was before the passage of the "flawed" statute. In this case, nothing predated "traditional" marriage.

This leads to the question none of the proponents of redefining marriage from the bench could answer. If marriage is no longer limited to one man and one woman, why should it not include polyamory, polygamy, and incestuous relationships? Again, were marriage to be redefined through the *political* process, these are the particular conditions that can be worked out. But if courts are going to find an inalienable right to a homosexual marriage, and state recognition thereof, why do those rights not extend to the aforementioned, nontraditional relationships, so long as they are consenting adults?

This was the question posed by Justice Alito to Mary Bonauto, the lawyer arguing the case on behalf of the same-sex couple. She had no legitimate answer.[27]

Checkmate.

In fact, there are three reasons why the aforementioned relationships should have a *stronger* case in their quest for marriage recognition than homosexual couples, if we are to consider Anthony Kennedy's opinion the law of the land.

First, from a natural-law perspective, polygamist, polyamorist, and incestuous marriages can result in procreation. And in the case of polygamy, it is certainly more rooted in history than homosexual marriages. While marriage encompasses a lot more than simply having children, procreation has been the hallmark of the institution since its inception because civilization could not perpetuate itself without it. That is the defining characteristic differentiating a marriage from any other friendship or relationship.

Moreover, so much of Kennedy's ruling is rooted in his fabrication of new constitutional rights; namely, the right to "dignity," "nobility," protection against stigmas, and the right to "define and express their identity." If Kennedy believes it is his responsibility and prerogative to bestow those new post-constitutional rights on, perhaps, the most powerful and trendy class of people in the country, how much more so for a group that is still scorned, stigmatized, and denied their dignity to express their identity? Homosexual marriage is in vogue and glorified by Hollywood, whereas these other relationships are still heavily stigmatized. Don't they need an even greater degree of protection?

Where is *their* right to love?

Third, what about the children of these relationships? Shouldn't we be concerned with removing the stigma from their children just like Kennedy was so concerned in regards to the stigma against adopted children of homosexual relationships?[28] And unlike children of homosexual relationships, which by definition are only adopted, polygamist or incestuous relationships can produce biological children. Don't these biological children deserve at least as much protection against stigma as the adopted children of homosexuals?

Again, we are not making political and societal arguments here. Courts should be concerned with legal arguments, and it is simply indefensible to deny multiple partners—threesomes or tensomes—the dignity of a marriage license. Imagine how well rounded the children would be—having the luxury of multiple caretakers.

Picture a middle-aged man who tragically loses his wife to cancer in her forties and views his daughter—who is a spitting image of his late wife—as his next soul mate to console him over the heartbreaking loss? Doesn't this scenario epitomize "the highest ideals of love, fidelity, devotion, sacrifice, and family" Kennedy referenced at the conclusion of his illogical and tempestuous screed?[29]

Yet, amazingly, Kennedy blatantly limited his decision to two individuals in the most brazen act of legislating from the bench of all time—restructuring the foundation of civilization:

> The nature of marriage is that, through its enduring bond, *two persons* together can find other freedoms, such as expression, intimacy, and spirituality. This is true for all persons, whatever their sexual orientation. . . . There is dignity in the bond between *two men or two women* who seek to marry and in their autonomy to make such profound choices. . . . A second principle in this Court's jurisprudence is that the right to marry is fundamental because it supports a *two-person union* unlike any other in its importance to the committed individuals.[30]

As Chief Justice Roberts noted in his dissent, Kennedy's insertion of the adjective "two" into his edict redefining marriage as between any two individuals of the same or opposite sex makes it clear that personal social preference now trumps legal consistency.[31]

Moreover, if the Court can decide what is now a marriage, doesn't that mean they get to decide what is no longer a marriage and when a marriage ends? That is a question Chancellor Jeffrey Atherton, a Tennessee judge, rightfully posed last September. He declined to rule on a divorce case, noting, "[W]ith the U.S. Supreme Court having defined what must be recognized as a marriage, it would appear that Tennessee's judiciary must now await the decision of the U.S. Supreme Court as to what is not a marriage, or better stated, when a marriage is no longer a marriage." Atherton added, "[T]he conclusion reached by this Court is that Tennesseans have been deemed by the U.S. Supreme Court to be incompetent to define and address such keystone/central institutions such as marriage, and, thereby, at minimum, contested divorces."[32]

JUDICIARY BY OPINION POLL

Let's cut through the political correctness for a moment. There is only one justification for redefining marriage for eternity—out of the reach of the people—to include homosexual marriages, yet tacitly exclude polygamist marriages: public opinion polls. Anyone who believes that legal decisions should be governed by subjective opinion polls should simply run for Congress, not serve on the court.

Carving out a new super right for homosexual couples alone, rather than all consenting adults, permanently endows them with a protected-class status that will trump religious liberty in ways even the past generation of social justice judicial activists never envisioned.

Yet, this is exactly the rationale used by Judge Posner, one of the circuit court judges who struck down a state marriage law, in justifying his change of heart on the constitutionality of state marriage laws. Explaining his evolution on the question since 1992, Posner admits that public opinion was the driving force behind the change and was even "*required* to make the judicial creation of such a right acceptable." This highly respected jurist appointed by Reagan then went on to fully repudiate the Constitution as written—like the worst of the Democrat-appointed judicial tyrants:

> Federal constitutional law is the most amorphous body of American law because most of the Constitution is very old, cryptic, or vague. The notion that the twenty-first century can be ruled by documents authored in the eighteenth and mid-nineteenth centuries is nonsense.[33]

We have come full circle with judicial tyranny. Even the most respected GOP-appointees now believe the Constitution is dead. Yet, they have the unbridled temerity to suggest that instead of judges stepping aside from constitutional questions altogether, it is their job to act like legislators and craft sensible public policy that reflects their myopic view of public opinion. They never stop to question why, if they are vested with the power to concoct law *and* change the Constitution—a power greater than that of the legislature—they are not subject to elections just like the legislators.

Posner also expressed the same paradoxical view that we referred to back in chapter 1, of using the Constitution to render the Constitution unconstitutional. "The time to look at precedent, statutory text, legislative history, that's after you have some sense of what is the best decision for today." This explains why Posner relied so heavily on the same convoluted bastardization of the Fourteenth Amendment to sustain his policy preference, even though at the same time he believes the writings from the 1800s are "very old, cryptic, or vague."[34] In the view of the judicial tyrants, because the Fourteenth Amendment is vague, they can backfill it with an ever-evolving set of ethics championed by the extreme left.

How portentous and haunting was the warning of Judge Farrar in 1867 when after observing that the Fourteenth Amendment made no fundamental change to the Constitution, he urged the people to "watch narrowly every amendment which may be proposed, and see that there lurks not, under some plausible covering, any latent mischief which may sap and undermine the foundation of some efficient support to the constitutional fabric which it cost our fathers so much to raise, and their children so much to defend."[35]

In reality, there is nothing vague or cryptic about the Fourteenth Amendment, nor is there any enigma about the scope, boundary, or source of fundamental rights. The Fourteenth Amendment was designed to ensure that freed slaves and their offspring were granted the same inalienable rights as all other citizens. During the debate over the Fourteenth Amendment, Rep. John F. Farnsworth (R-IL) noted that everything in what would become section 1 of the Fourteenth Amendment was taken straight from the Fifth Amendment and inspired by the Declaration. He observed that the only new language, "the equal protection of the laws," was not new at all to the original Constitution but indeed the "very foundation of a Republican government." How can a subject "have and enjoy equal rights of 'life, liberty, and the pursuit of happiness' without 'equal protection of the laws'?" asked Farnsworth.[36]

Unlike Posner, who believes that original intent is the *last* thing to be examined and only if it comports with the modern political agenda, James Wilson, among the greatest of all Founders and a member of the original Supreme Court, was very clear about how to apply the Constitution. "The *first* and governing maxim in the interpretation of a statute is to discover the meaning of those who made it," he said.[37]

In 1833, Justice Joseph Story posed the following rhetorical question in his treatise on the Constitution: "What is to become of constitutions of government, if they are to rest, not upon the plain import of their words, but upon conjectural enlargements and restrictions, to suit the temporary passions and interests of the day?"[38]

Almost two centuries later we have seen exactly what becomes of such a government.

AN ASSYLUM ON EARTH FOR RELIGIOUS LIBERTY

As we've demonstrated throughout this chapter, the marriage case is riddled with layer upon layer of lawlessness, absurdity, and naked political ambition. There is perhaps no other case this century that will prove more harmful—both as a direct threat to religious liberty and an indirect threat of expanding the court's power to every issue known to man.

One would expect such a radical decision to be supported by a fringe group of judges. Yet, every single Democrat-appointed judge who heard a case dealing with marriage decided to redefine the institution from the bench. On the other hand, as was the case with the Obamacare decision, at least half a dozen GOP-appointed judges voted to toss out state marriage laws.[39]

Anyone who tells you electing more Republicans to appoint "originalist" judges to the bench is a panacea to this terminal illness of the legal profession is not paying attention. Judge David Bunning, the district judge for eastern Kentucky who threw Kim Davis in jail and mocked the natural law expressed in the Declaration of Independence, was appointed by George W. Bush and recommended by GOP Senate leader Mitch McConnell.[40] This is the same Mitch McConnell who said that gay marriage is the law of the land and that Americans must rely on the courts to protect religious liberty.[41]

But instead of protecting religious liberty, the one legitimate function of the courts, the marriage decision is now encouraging liberal states to violate the private property rights and religious conscience of individuals who wish to abstain from servicing gay weddings with their property or livelihood. With the Kline family bakery in Oregon being fined $137,000 for not baking a cake for a same-sex ceremony and the Gifford family in New York being fined for not lending out their private farm for a lesbian service, super rights—concocted by unelected judges—now supersede the most inalienable rights of conscience and private property.[42]

James Madison referred to religious conscience as the most sacred of property rights. It is the very impetus for the founding of this country by the Pilgrims, who came here to escape religious coercion at the hands of the Church of England. Now we are seeing homosexuality being elevated to the status of a national religion. There is no class of persons in this country that have reacted more viscerally and fascistically to those who dissent from their dogma.

With states now taking their cue from the Supreme Court, it's time for conservatives in Congress and the next Republican president to pass civil rights–style legislation protecting religious liberty. While the federal government has no right to concoct new rights for protected classes and impose it upon the states—as the Supreme Court did with gay marriage—the elected branch of the federal government has a sacred responsibility to protect the people against states that blatantly infringe on the most fundamental rights. Congress must pass federal legislation barring any state or federal branch of government from punishing individuals who refuse to service with their private property acts that violate their consciousness.

Obviously, the courts will attempt to invalidate any law protecting inalienable rights and assert that it violates the super rights they concocted for special classes. After all, in their Orwellian world, the Constitution is unconstitutional. This is why, as we will explain in detail in chapter 9, it is so important that any religious liberty legislation be drafted in a way that explicitly strips the courts of the power to strike down laws pertaining to religious freedom.

PRESERVING THE REVOLUTIONARY LEGACY

At some point, we will have to reassert the power of the legislature over the judiciary, and that time is now. There is no choice. For some perspective on just how breathtakingly far we have fallen into the abyss of tyranny and post-constitutional Gomorrah, consider the warning from Judge Robert Bork in 1996, following the first major activist court decision on behalf of homosexual super rights:

> Even in the depths of the Warren Court era some of us thought that the Court's performance, though profoundly illegitimate, could be brought within the range of the minimally acceptable by logical persuasion or the appointment of more responsible judges, or both. We now know that was an illusion. A Court majority is impervious to arguments about its proper behavior. It seems safe to say that, as our institutional arrangements now stand, the Court can never be made a legitimate element of a basically democratic polity.[43]

Bork uttered those words twenty years ago, when we stood at the foot of the mountain of judicial tyranny redefining marriage and sexuality from the bench. This was long before the Obamacare decisions and numerous egregious immigration decisions and other radical anti-constitutional jurisprudence foisted upon us even by Republican-appointed judges. And yet it was clear as day to him that the courts were irredeemably broken and that the notion of Republican presidents turning the tide significantly by appointing originalist judges was illusory and an exercise in pink unicorns.

If the next president fails to act on this issue immediately—both by promoting legislation protecting liberty and private property and by stripping the courts of the power to adjudicate societal questions—the trajectory of religious tyranny will easily lead to the criminalization of the practice of major religions. Islam, which, ironically, has been treated as a favored class, will likely get a special exemption. And if, as a people vesting power in the federal government, we cannot protect religious liberty, there is no purpose to our federal union, and indeed, no purpose to America itself.

As the British redcoats were preparing to invade the colonies following the signing of the Declaration of Independence, Sam Adams summed up the coming fight as follows: "Our contest is not only whether we ourselves shall be free, but whether there shall be left to mankind an asylum on earth for civil and religious liberty."[44]

After 240 years of serving as that asylum for religious liberty, have we regressed as a people so deeply that we will obsequiously accept the judicial tyranny of a few flawed individuals in robes who overturn the preamble of the very document that spawned our independence and affirmed the very rights they seek to expand? If the spirit of liberty runs through your veins, you must shout from the rooftops, "Hell no!" and start rejecting the illegitimate coup d'état of the unelected oligarchy.

4

VIOLATING SOVEREIGNTY: THE ULTIMATE DISENFRANCHISING OF A NATION-STATE

The jurisdiction of the nation within its own territory is necessarily exclusive and absolute. It is susceptible of no limitation not imposed by itself. Any restriction upon it deriving validity from an external source would imply a diminution of its sovereignty to the extent of the restriction and an investment of that sovereignty to the same extent in that power which could impose such restriction. All exceptions, therefore, to the full and complete power of a nation within its own territories must be traced up to the consent of the nation itself. They can flow from no other legitimate source.

—CHIEF JUSTICE MARSHALL, 1812

Courts have long stolen the sovereignty of the individual and the state to govern its affairs within their constitutional realms. The next and final frontier of judicial tyranny is to steal the sovereignty of the nation-state itself—to change the orientation and membership of the society without the input of the existing members.

Justice Scalia recently commented that "he can't imagine how you can go any further" down the "slippery slope" of judicial tyranny than creating "the right to same-sex marriage."[1]

Sadly, there is one final step on the inexorable road to judicial autocracy—creating an affirmative right for foreign nationals to immigrate here and steal citizenship for their children. This eventuality, which is already at our doorstep, will harm our society and economy, and abjure our sovereignty—all without the people's consent.

The same judges who repudiate the Constitution as written and call upon judges to do "what is sensible," if left to their own devices, will discover these new rights for illegal aliens. They will discover an affirmative right to immigrate and render everything our Founders and early courts said about sovereignty obsolete and inapplicable in the modern era. Yes, we are headed to a time when courts will issue judicial amnesty, even if the political branches are committed to enforcing the laws.

The courts are an existential threat to our future as a civilization and a nation-state. If conservatives don't immediately address the growing judicial crisis, the entire preamble of the Constitution—what is left of it—will apply to all 7.2 billion people in the world. That is why I have chosen to dedicate the longest section of this book to judicial tyranny as it relates to immigration and sovereignty.

* * *

Nothing undermines the self-determination of a society and the sovereignty of a nation-state more than illegal immigration or the refusal of the political class to keep out those who will harm or transform the existing society. Yet, in an increasingly disquieting trend, the courts have undermined the self-determination of American citizens by stripping them of the ability to secure their own future and society against those who illegally infiltrate America. The courts have ratcheted up their wholesale invention of constitutional rights for illegal immigrants, undermining the ability of voters to use their elected representatives to prevent illegal immigration.

However, it wasn't always this way. There was a time when the courts ruled that Congress has full "plenary" power over the issue of immigration—both to exclude and deport immigrants for whatever reason it choses. They believed it was settled law, rooted in the foundation of a sovereign nation, that only the elected representatives of the people can make decisions about the future membership of their society, leaving the courts with no jurisdiction to get involved so long as those laws don't abridge the inalienable rights of citizens.

To understand the importance of congressional plenary power over immigration and how the courts deemed it settled law, we must first explore the myth of constitutionally mandated birthright citizenship for illegal aliens—the most profound assault on the sovereignty of any nation. By proving conclusively that there is no concept of birthright citizenship for illegal aliens rooted in American law, or indeed any nation-state, it will shed light on the view of the courts for over one hundred years upholding the full power of Congress to regulate immigration and naturalization, as well as deportations and exclusions. We can then appreciate the breathtaking departure from that tradition perpetrated by contemporary courts.

THE MYTH OF BIRTHRIGHT CITIZENSHIP

The American people are being told by the political class that there is nothing they can do to prevent future waves of illegal immigrants from coming here, unilaterally declaring political and legal jurisdiction, and securing citizenship and welfare benefits for their children. We are told there is no recourse through our elected representatives to prevent illegal immigrants from gaining a legal foothold in this country, all because of a footnote from an opinion of one of the most radical post-constitutional justices of this century, William Brennan Jr.

If you are scratching your head, wondering how our own Constitution can be used as a suicide pact against us by foreign countries, join the club. This irrational sentiment expressed by a number of conservative and liberal pundits alike undermines the very fabric of the social contract, popular sovereignty, and the republican form of government established by the preamble of the Declaration of Independence and the Constitution.

Several dozen illegal aliens from Mexico and Central America are now suing three Texas counties for denying their children birth certificates unless they produce valid identification.[2] In addition to bastardizing the citizenship clause of the Fourteenth Amendment, they are of course invoking the "equal protection" clause. The government of Mexico has filed an amicus brief in this lawsuit against Texas.[3]

There is a very simple yet vital question that must be asked at this juncture in our journey as an enduring nation-state: do we as a society have the inviolable right to control our sovereignty and reserve that prerogative, through our elected representatives, to prevent people from asserting immigration and citizenship rights against our will? Or do foreign nationals and foreign governments have the right to assert jurisdiction in our country and obtain citizenship and fundamental rights of the society—without any recourse to stop it? The answer is very simple to anyone who has a firm grasp on our founding values.

It is incontrovertibly clear from a wealth of statements by our Founders before the ratification of the Fourteenth Amendment and from a hundred years of case law after its ratification that Congress has plenary power over immigration, specifically to deny entry or deport those here illegally, and even to deny due process in doing so.

First, we must discuss the erroneous notion of unconditional birthright citizenship even for all legal immigrants and then we can prove—even from the writings of its supporters—that this system of citizenship cannot be conferred upon children of illegal immigrants and was never meant as such. Even the proponents of birthright citizenship for legal children back in the 1800s would have been appalled by the application of this principle to children of those who violate our sovereignty.

The prevailing interpretation of the citizenship clause of the Fourteenth Amendment—now used to grant automatic citizenship to children of both parents who are illegal aliens—is erroneous and preposterous. Section 1 of the Fourteenth Amendment states, "All persons born or naturalized in the United States, and subject to the jurisdiction thereof, are citizens of the United States and of the State wherein they reside."[4] Everyone agrees with the basic concept of birthright citizenship as plainly stated in the first part of this clause—that generally speaking those born in America are to be automatic citizens. But in addition to the requirement that a child be born on American soil, the plain reading of the citizenship clause adds another requirement: "*and* subject to the jurisdiction thereof." As we all know, there are no superfluous clauses in this tightly drafted document we call the US Constitution.[5] Clearly, the Framers were drawing some limitation beyond simply being born on American soil.

Fortunately, we need not speculate about their intent. The purpose of this amendment was to overturn the *Dred Scott* case and ensure guaranteed citizenship to all former black slaves born in America.[6] At the same time they wanted to limit citizenship to those subject to our jurisdiction, which excludes those who are not legal permanent residents of this country, such as sojourners and visitors, and certainly illegal aliens.

The 1866 Civil Rights Act, which was the forerunner to the Fourteenth Amendment, reads, "All persons born in the United States, and not subject to any foreign power, excluding Indians not taxed, are hereby declared to be citizens of the United States."[7] Anyone who is here illegally or on a temporary visa is still subject to the jurisdiction of his or her own country of origin and was never meant to be included in the Fourteenth Amendment's citizenship clause. As Rep. James F. Wilson of Iowa, then chairman of the House Judiciary Committee and a drafter of the Fourteenth Amendment, explained, the 1866 act was meant to grant citizenship to all those born in the United States, "except that of children born on our soil to temporary sojourners or representatives of foreign Governments."[8]

But even legal immigrants who are still citizens of foreign countries are excluded from the term "subject to the jurisdiction of." As Sen. Lyman Trumbull of Illinois, the chairman of the Senate Judiciary Committee, said during the debate over the Fourteenth Amendment, "subject to the jurisdiction" of the United States meant subject to its "complete" jurisdiction, "not owing allegiance to anybody else."[9] Of course anyone present inside American territory is subject to our *partial* jurisdiction in the sense that they have to obey our laws and are subject to criminal prosecution for disobeying our laws. But when congressional drafters added the second phrase of jurisdiction to the citizenship clause, they were clearly limiting citizenship to those who, in the words of one of the key drafters, were subject to the "complete" jurisdiction as Americans.

Sen. Jacob Howard of Michigan, the principle author of the citizenship clause of the Fourteenth Amendment, explicitly said that candidates for citizenship must be born here *and* not owe allegiance to any another authority. Echoing Trumbull, he said "a full and complete jurisdiction" means "the same jurisdiction in extent and quality as applies to every citizen of the United States now." He made it clear that allegiance "will not, of course, include persons born in the United States who are foreigners, aliens, who belong to the families of ambassadors or foreign ministers accredited to the Government of the United States."[10] If we can be sure that even children of Indian tribes were excluded from automatic citizenship, certainly temporary visitors from foreign countries were meant to be excluded as well. After all, members of Indian tribes and their parents were actually born on American soil and they were somewhat subject to America's protection.

Everyone agrees that children born to Indian tribe members or foreign diplomats were excluded from automatic citizenship under the Fourteenth Amendment. Two subsequent court cases made that clear. It's also clear from the fact that Congress had to explicitly grant citizenship to Indian tribes in 1924 via statute that they were obviously excluded from automatic constitutionally mandated birthright citizenship.[11]

In the 1872 *Slaughterhouse* cases, dealing with a variety of Fourteenth Amendment questions regarding the rights of butchers, including those of former slaves, the court interpreted the definition of numerous clauses for the first time since it was ratified.[12] In defining the citizenship clause, Justice Samuel Miller noted, "[T]hat its main purpose was to establish the citizenship of the negro can admit of no doubt."[13] He went on to say, "the phrase, 'subject to its jurisdiction' was intended to exclude from its operation children of ministers, consuls, and citizens or subjects of foreign States born within the United States."[14]

In *Elk v. Wilkins* (1884), the court enshrined the dicta of *Slaughterhouse* into law by ruling that a man born on an Indian reservation who voluntarily left the Indian society and lived with the rest of the American population is not an automatic citizen under the citizenship clause.[15] Writing for the majority, Justice Gray asserted that the phrase "subject to the jurisdiction" is "not merely subject in some respect or degree to the jurisdiction of the United States, but completely subject to their political jurisdiction and owing them direct and immediate allegiance."[16]

Justice Gray's opinion was guided, in part, by an 1873 legal opinion from Attorney General George Henry Williams, a senator at the time the Fourteenth Amendment was ratified, stating that the Fourteenth Amendment did not mean to include all aliens:

> The word *jurisdiction* must be understood to mean absolute and complete jurisdiction, such as the United States had over its citizens before the adoption of this amendment . . . Aliens, among whom are persons born here and naturalized abroad, dwelling or being in this country, are subject to the jurisdiction of the United States only to a limited extent.[17]

The notion that the framers of the Fourteenth Amendment desired to include illegal aliens in birthright citizenship is contrary to the explicit language and context of the amendment. It's as absurd as the notion that the due process and equal protection clauses of that same amendment were designed to mandate the recognition of homosexual marriage. It ties into the broader agenda of the Left to assert that the Fourteenth Amendment was designed to remake our Constitution and society rather than fix the one grave flaw—slavery and the mistreatment of native blacks since the colonial days.

Imagine the reaction of Chairman Wilson were he to witness

the modern hijacking of his work. Wilson spoke emphatically of the 1866 Civil Rights Act, from which the language of the Fourteenth Amendment was copied almost verbatim, that it was "establishing no new right, declaring no new principle. . . . It is not the object of this bill to establish new rights, but to protect and enforce those which belong to every citizen."[18]

Could any of Wilson's colleagues possibly have conjured up a right to a gay marriage certificate or birthright citizenship for those who violate our sovereignty? Would Wilson have ever envisioned a new right undermining "those [rights] that belong to every citizen?"

WONG AND THE COMMON-LAW DISCUSSION

Opponents of US sovereignty hang their hats on the 1898 *Wong Kim Ark* decision in which Justice Gray interprets the Fourteenth Amendment as granting birthright citizenship under the interpretation followed by English common law. In that case, he opined that an American-born son of Chinese immigrants was automatically a citizen, and in broader dicta (nonbinding rhetoric), appears to adopt the rationale of *jus soli*, citizenship by birth on the soil.[19] Bizarrely, Gray overturned his own decision in *Elk*, but seamlessly obfuscated the fact that he had authored that opinion.

Let's put aside everything we believe as conservatives for a moment and take the activist ruling of *Wong* as impregnable constitutional law. As such, the Fourteenth Amendment would compel Congress and the executive agencies to grant citizenship to all children of legal immigrants. Although we all agree as a matter of policy that it is a good idea to grant children born to legal permanent residents citizenship, by accepting the 1898 court decision as settled law, thereby enshrining birthright citizenship into our Constitution, we'd have to swallow a number of ridiculous notions.

We'd be ignoring the intent of the drafters of this amendment, who clearly had no intention to mandate birthright citizenship for all immigrants. While originalists like to focus on text, in this case the text fits in exactly with the intent of the drafters, as demonstrated by the transcript of the congressional debates. In this case, we'd be overturning the most logical meaning of the text of the citizenship clause, rendering the second phrase all but superfluous. Even under common law, children born to foreign diplomats were not automatic citizens. By interpreting the phrase "subject to the jurisdiction thereof" as merely limiting those individuals and nobody else, there would be no further addition made by the second phrase of the clause. That exclusion was already baked into the cake.

What is most appalling about this activist decision is that Justice Gray was bizarrely adopting English common law's view of citizenship, which was antithetical to what our Founders believed. As Chief Justice Fuller noted in his dissent in *Wong*, the revolutionary-era feudal system of English common law was rooted in the fact that men are subjects of the state by virtue of being born on the soil.[20] This is antithetical to the consent-based notion of citizenship expressed by our Founders.

As Professor Edward Erler observed, citing Thomas Jefferson in *Notes on the State of Virginia,* "not all the principles of the English constitution (and common law) were adopted by America, but only its 'freest principles,' i.e., those compatible with natural right and natural reason."[21] How ironic that Jefferson used this phrase when discussing his concerns about unbridled immigration from countries with fewer freedoms from which immigrants "will bring with them the principles of the governments they leave."[22] Jefferson would roll over in his grave knowing that one hundred years later a federal judge would use the feudal system of English common law to establish a policy that would eventually bring in endless numbers of immigrants who "will bring with them the principles of the governments they leave!"

In reality, unqualified birthright citizenship is antithetical to the consent-based view of citizenship our Founders established, which made acceptance to the society and expatriating from the society a consensual act, not one compelled or barred by birth on the soil.

The Left believes, as with most constitutional issues, that the Fourteenth Amendment overturned the fundamentals of the original

Constitution. In this case, they believe that rather than simply granting automatic citizenship to freed blacks who were living here for hundreds of years, the Fourteenth Amendment remade citizenship as one attached to the soil, in the mold of common law. The problem with that, as Erler noted, is that at the very time they adopted the Fourteenth Amendment, Congress repudiated English common law's view of citizenship just as the Founders had done long before the era of the Fourteenth Amendment.[23]

In 1868, along with the Fourteenth Amendment, Congress passed the Expatriation Act, which codified a long-held belief of our Founders that every citizen has the inalienable right to expatriate. During the floor debate, in the very same year they passed the citizenship clause, members of Congress directly linked the right to expatriate to repudiating the concept of birthright citizenship inherent in the feudal system. Rep. George Woodward (D-PA) proclaimed, "It is high time that feudalism were driven from our shores and eliminated from our law, and now is the time to declare it."[24]

Another problem with adopting Justice Gray's broader application of English common law, instead of the consent-based allegiance passed down by the parents of the child, is that all children born to American citizens abroad after passage of the Fourteenth Amendment would not automatically be citizens, as noted by then Chief Justice Fuller in his dissent.[25]

Fuller further noted that by mandating automatic citizenship for all children of immigrants—no matter the circumstances—the Fourteenth Amendment would have the power "to cut off the legislative power from dealing with the subject."[26] Article I Section 8 of the Constitution grants Congress plenary power over naturalizations.[27] Fuller observed "the right of a nation to expel or deport foreigners who have not been naturalized or taken any steps toward becoming citizens of a country is as absolute and unqualified as the right to prohibit and prevent their entrance into the country."[28]

Reading the Fourteenth Amendment as establishing automatic and unqualified birthright citizenship for all aliens under all circumstances would completely vitiate that core-enumerated power. Unless there would be no other way to read the plain language of the Fourteenth Amendment than as a mandate based on territorial jurisdiction instead of political jurisdiction (before 1898 nobody read it this way), it is simply imprudent to interpret it in the most stringent manner. Doing so would have the effect of almost completely voiding an enumerated power of the people's representatives concerning the most vital aspect of a society.

Finally, it's important to remember that the Fourteenth Amendment itself, under section 5, grants Congress the power to enforce the provisions of the amendment.[29] To interpret the Fourteenth Amendment so as to void an entire enumerated power is absurd in light of Congress's power to interpret the amendment itself. Certainly, in any case of ambiguity, we must "err" on the side of caution and not strip the consent of citizenship from the society and its representatives. Congress unambiguously has the authority to interpret the scope of its jurisdiction over immigration and can pass laws clarifying in which instances the children of immigrants are entitled to citizenship.

BIRTHRIGHT CITIZENSHIP TO ILLEGALS COUNTERMANDS SOVEREIGNTY

Freeze-frame at this point.

It is already hard to swallow the notion of automatic birthright citizenship for all *legal* immigrants as a constitutional *mandate*, irrespective of their allegiance to or citizenship of another nation. Yet, the pseudo-conservative pundits in the political class want to extrapolate this terrible decision to children of illegal immigrants. As if it wasn't enough to accept the activist 1898 court case from the segregationist justices, proponents of anchor citizenship for illegal immigrants rely on a footnote in Justice William Brennan's 1982 *Plyler v. Doe* opinion—a decision that absurdly forced taxpayers to fund K–12 education for illegal immigrants.

In that footnote, which is nothing more than dicta (nonbinding comments not relevant to the case), Brennan quotes "one early commentator" noting that "given the historical emphasis on geographic territoriality, bounded only, if at all, by principles of sovereignty and allegiance, no plausible distinction with respect to Fourteenth Amendment 'jurisdiction' can be drawn between resident aliens whose entry into the United States was lawful, and resident aliens whose entry was unlawful."[30]

There you have it; American citizens—through their elected representatives—have no recourse to prevent future illegal immigrants from obtaining citizenship against their will all—because of the nonbinding footnote of one of the most radical justices of the twentieth century, from a case reversing precedent and relying on the English feudal system that was twice repudiated. This is what passes for constitutional scholarship among our political elites.

Even if one accepts the concept of birthright citizenship based solely on geographic jurisdiction, there is a huge difference between the legal permanent resident who was the subject of the 1898 court case and the illegal immigrants of today. The justices in *Wong* awarded the child citizenship because his Chinese immigrant parents were "domiciled" in America (legally, before the ban on Chinese immigration). As Professor John Eastman has noted, "domicile" is a legal term of art; it means "a person's legal home," according to *Black's Law Dictionary*, and is often used synonymously with "citizenship."[31] Undoubtedly, those here in contravention to our laws, unlike Wong Kim Ark's parents, cannot unilaterally declare domicile in our country. And as we will see, Justice Gray and other judges of the time always used that term exclusively for those who were legitimately residing in this country on a permanent basis and who were admitted with the legal consent of the people.

This all leads to a much more fundamental and vital discussion about sovereignty. There is simply no way our Constitution can prohibit our elected representatives from preventing illegal immigrants from driving their pregnant wives to the border, and assuming the border patrol fails to catch the speeding vehicle in time—poof!—that baby is a citizen.

The notion that illegal immigrants can unilaterally declare citizenship for their kids against the will of the people and the laws duly passed by the people's representatives, and that those representatives would lack any recourse to stop it even prospectively, violates the very essence of consent-based citizenship. The concept of consent-based citizenship serves as the bedrock of popular sovereignty, territorial sovereignty, and republicanism—all built upon the social contract. The preamble of the Declaration of Independence was rooted in the principle that to protect natural rights, people are entitled to popular sovereignty—to form a government that derives its powers "from the consent of the governed."

Professor Erler has been a leading voice observing how birthright citizenship for illegal immigrants, and indeed the entire premise of illegal aliens' securing of rights and benefits, violates the social contract in the most foundational way. In an essay on birthright citizenship, Professor Eastman cites Erler regarding the relationship between citizenship and the social contract: "[T]he social contract requires reciprocal consent. Not only must the individual consent to be governed, but he must also be accepted by the community as a whole. If all persons born within the geographical limits of the United States are to be counted citizens—even those whose parents are in the United States illegally—then this would be tantamount to the conferral of citizenship without the consent of 'the whole people.'"[32]

Simply put, stealing our sovereignty and robbing our birthright to grant citizenship to those who force their way into our country represents the most grievous violation of the very philosophy behind our system of governance.

THE CASE FOR CONGRESSIONAL AUTHORITY OVER IMMIGRATION

Although there was never a direct court case pertaining to birthright citizenship for illegal aliens, by exploring the hundred years of settled law covering Congress's plenary power over immigration, we can prove conclusively that the courts would never have granted that right to illegal aliens. As an added benefit we will also see that our history is replete with examples of Congress and the executive branch using its power to categorically exclude or deport noncitizens for any reason—a vital power that is now being challenged by the political elites in both parties.

It's often said that illegal immigration is a relatively recent phenomenon, but given the fact that Congress started regulating immigration in 1875 and 1882 by barring immigrants from China, as well as an array of categories of people they deemed undesirable (public charge, criminals, those with mental or physical illness, etc.), there were plenty of cases where people were deemed inadmissible and deported in the late nineteenth century.[33] By studying the laws of the time and the relevant court cases, one is struck by one overarching theme: Congress has full authority to restrict or deport any alien and even deny them due process rights, much less rights and benefits of US citizens—and certainly, presumably, citizenship itself. This often extended to people who previously resided in the country legally, not to mention those who were never granted lawful residence, and in fact, were present in the country illegally.

In *Chae Chan Ping v. United States* (1889), commonly referred to as "the Chinese Exclusion Case," the court ruled unanimously that immigration officials had the right to deny entry to a Chinese immigrant who was reentering the country after a brief return to China.[34] This individual came to the United States in 1875, before the 1882 law restricting immigration from China, and lived in San Francisco legally for twelve years. In 1887, he took a trip back to China, armed with an official certificate allowing him reentry as a legal immigrant. Nonetheless, he was denied reentry upon his return on September 7, 1888, because Congress had passed a new law repealing the exemption for those reentering the country who were already residing in the United States before enactment of the 1882 law.

In a long-winded decision that focused mainly on the power of a new statute to countermand an earlier treaty with China, the court upheld the decision of the immigration officials acting in accordance with the immigration restrictions passed by Congress. It can truly be said that Chan Ping got screwed in the worst possible way, and we can certainly second-guess the prudence and motivations behind the laws and policies established at that time. But that does not change the fact that Congress, as empowered by the citizenry, has full legal authority to defend the country's sovereignty and restrict entry to any noncitizen for any purpose. And despite the harsh nature of these retroactive laws of exclusion, even for existing legal resident immigrants, the executive branch faithfully executed these laws. Here is what Justice Field wrote on behalf of the unanimous opinion:

> That the government of the United States, through the action of the legislative department, can exclude aliens from its territory is a proposition which we do not think open to controversy. Jurisdiction over its own territory to that extent is an incident of every independent nation. It is a part of its independence. If it could not exclude aliens it would be to that extent subject to the control of another power.[35]

The decision continues with a powerful expression of popular sovereignty manifested through the right to keep out anyone or any class of people the elected branch of government chooses to exclude.[36] Justice Field closed by drawing upon the diplomatic correspondence from six secretaries of state about the importance of regulating immigration and reserving the prerogative to preserve the sovereignty and our republican form of government.[37] These quotes predated the time when Congress formally placed restrictions on immigration nationwide, but reveals how important it always was to reserve the right to exclude various immigrants when the need arose.

There can be no ambiguity left after reading this decision that this court would never have conferred citizenship—the highest benefit of all—upon children born to those who sneak into our country in clear violation of our laws.

COURT DENIES DUE PROCESS TO APPEAL DENIAL OF ENTRY

In 1892, Justice Gray, the same author of the *Wong* birthright citizenship case, took the court's deference to Congress and immigration officials a step further. In *Nishimura Ekiu v. United States*, the court affirmed the right of immigration officials to deny a Japanese woman entry into the country *and* deny her (procedural) due process in proving she had a right to land. She claimed her husband was residing legally in San Francisco, but she did not know the address and was deemed inadmissible as a public charge.[38] This decision was reinforced three years later by Justice Marshall Harlan in *Lem Moon Sing v. United States* when the Court denied procedural due process rights to a Chinese reentrant who was known to have lived in the country for years as a businessman but was turned away at the port because Congress had already invalidated the landing certificates of all Chinese immigrants.[39]

Here are the relevant quotes from Justice Gray, with my emphasis added:

> *It is an accepted maxim of international law that every sovereign nation has the power, as inherent in sovereignty, and essential to self-preservation, to forbid the entrance of foreigners within its dominions*, or to admit them only in such cases and upon such conditions as it may see fit to prescribe. . . .

As to such persons, the decisions of executive or administrative officers, acting within powers expressly conferred by congress, are due process of law.[40]

Putting aside the importance of this decision in affirming the plenary power of Congress to bar entry and in denying the court's jurisdiction to even overrule such a decision, there are two other important outcomes of *Nishimura Ekiu*: (1) It established that those who are not legally domiciled in the country do not have constitutional rights of due process as it relates to their desire to remain in the country; congressional laws are due process in immigration. And (2) it established that temporary housing of the alien on American soil for logistical reasons until he or she is deported does not grant that person constitutional rights as a legally domiciled immigrant. In the words of the court, it "left her in the same position, so far as regarded her right to land in the

United States, as if she never had been removed from the steamship."[41]

There is no doubt that had this woman given birth to a child during the time she was onshore, that child would never have been granted citizenship by Justice Gray—the very author of the birthright case—because, in his own words, she was not legally domiciled, even though she was granted permission to temporarily come ashore. How much more so this would apply to those who snuck into our country in full violation of our laws without ever seeking permission.

Those seeking to apply Gray's birthright ruling in *Wong Kim Ark* to illegal aliens are willfully overlooking the twelve instances in which he referred to "domiciled" immigrants in that case. They also conveniently ignore his opinion six years earlier in which he clearly held that an alien *not* legally domiciled in this country is as if he is standing *outside our soil* as it relates to due process rights, much less the right to assert jurisdiction on behalf of his child.

CONGRESSIONAL POWER TO DEPORT

In *Fong Yue Ting v. United States* (1893), Justice Gray went a step further.[42] On May 5, 1892, Congress passed a law ordering that all Chinese laborers found without a certificate after a year of residency be subject to deportation.[43] Again, for purposes of comparing to modern concepts, these people would be the equivalent of legal permanent residents, not illegal aliens.

Yet, Justice Gray reiterated his decision in *Nishimura Ekiu* and lauded Justice Field's decision in *Chae Chan Ping* sustaining the right of Congress to regulate immigration for the purpose of upholding the integrity of national sovereignty.[44] He took it a step further and declared, "the right of a nation to expel or deport foreigners who have not been naturalized, or taken any steps towards becoming citizens of the country, rests upon the same grounds, and is as absolute and unqualified as the right to prohibit and prevent their entrance into the country."[45]

As unfair as it sounds to *ex post facto* invalidate one's legal status, Gray noted that "having taken no steps towards becoming citizens, and incapable of becoming such under the naturalization laws, and therefore remain subject to the power of Congress to expel them or to order them to be removed and deported from the country whenever, in its judgment, their removal is necessary or expedient for the public interest."[46]

These three cases form a concrete foundation for upholding the plenary power of Congress to secure our sovereignty and deny entry of all immigrants even without due process beyond the opportunity to present their case to an executive official. They also clearly express the principle that anyone not legally domiciled in the United States is not entitled to any rights whatsoever and it is as if they are *not physically present on our shores.*

APPLYING SOVEREIGNTY TO RADICAL ISLAMIC IMMIGRANTS

As for expelling legal immigrants who were accepted into the country with the consent of the people and who have not committed a crime, while as a matter of policy most would find the idea uncomfortable, it is important to not dismiss the *legal* precedent vouching for the prerogative to do so.

At present, among the many peaceful Muslim immigrants we have in this country, there are clearly many who have retained allegiance to the ideology of their home countries. Almost on a daily basis, Muslim immigrants (and citizens) are arrested for plotting terror attacks, collaborating with terrorists, or attempting to join ISIS and al-Qaeda. There are a number of Islamic leaders in this country who engage in subversive activity that might not meet the threshold of treason, which would allow us to denaturalize a citizen, but would meet the threshold to deport an immigrant.

It's important we remember that, as it relates to radical Islamists who have not yet obtained citizenship, they can be deported. Even the dissenting justices in *Fong* only opposed a categorical deportation of an entire race simply based on prejudice against who they were, after we had consensually and specifically brought them in by force of a treaty. They also felt that the requirement to register to remain in the country and be searched without due process, in some ways, was worse than simply deporting them as a national expression of sovereignty. Finally, the dissenting justices were clear that their limitation on the power to expel legal immigrants was during a time of peace and with regard to immigrants from peaceful nations.[47] Nobody can assert that same principle to the subversive Muslim immigrants from countries hostile to our values during a time of war.

In the case of our contemporary problem with radical and subversive Islamic immigrants, it would be appropriate to apply the maxim of Emer de Vattel, the noted Swiss expert on international law:

> Every nation has the right to refuse to admit a foreigner into the country, when he cannot enter without putting the nation in evident danger, or doing it a manifest injury. . . . Thus, also, it has a right to send them elsewhere, if it has just cause to fear that they will corrupt the manners of the citizens; that they will create religious disturbances, or occasion any other disorder, contrary to the public safety. In a word, it has a right, and is even obliged, in this respect, to follow the rules which prudence dictates.[48]

AN ENDURING PRECEDENT

These cases remained precedent for almost a full century.

In *United States v. Ju Toy* (1905), the Court took *Nishimura Ekiu* and *Fong* a step further and ruled that there are no procedural due process rights to a trial by jury to those denied reentry even if the immigrant alleges that he had already become a citizen before departing.[49] Justice Holmes, writing for the majority, asserted that the determination of whether to believe the claim "may be entrusted to an executive officer, and that *his decision is due process of law*," so long as it comports with the statutes passed by Congress and so long as the individual remained outside the United States.[50]

Moreover, the Court, once again, reasserted the principle that physical presence within the boundaries of the country—without lawful admission—does not grant the petitioner due process rights. "The petitioner, although physically within our boundaries, is to be regarded as if he had been stopped at the limit of our jurisdiction, and kept there while his right to enter was under debate," wrote Holmes.[51] There can be no doubt that those who are undeniably in the country illegally are not deemed as present in the country for due process rights, much less securing citizenship for a child born during that time. The child would be considered born right by the boundary, according to settled law.

In *Low Wah Suey v. Backus* (1912), the Court refused to review the deportation order against a Chinese immigrant accused of prostitution, even though she was married to a US citizen and was a mother to an American-born child.[52] In 1907 and 1910, Congress passed laws ordering the deportation of any alien who engaged in prostitution.[53] In a unanimous opinion, the court noted that although given her status this was "a hard application of the rule of the statute," the "situation was one of her own making" and the Court had no business second-guessing Congress or rewriting the statute.[54]

During the post–World War II era of communism, the courts continued to uphold the power of Congress and the executive branch to deport aliens without judicial review with the same intrepidness of the 1890s era courts. In *Shaughnessy v. United States ex rel. Mezei* (1953), the Court upheld a decision from the Truman administration to deny a Romanian immigrant who had been living here for twenty-five years, reentry into the country after visiting his dying mother in Europe. And because no other country would accept him, Shaughnessy was detained on Ellis Island for twenty-one months. The denial of entry *and* detainment were ruled lawful and not in violation of due process rights, pursuant to the Chinese exclusion cases and a wealth of case law in the intervening years.[55]

And drawing upon *Nishimura Ekiu* and a number of later decisions, the Court made it clear that his temporary dwelling on Ellis Island did not bestow him with constitutional rights, even though he had previously lived here legally for twenty-five years!

> But such temporary harborage, an act of legislative grace, bestows no additional rights. Congress meticulously specified that such shelter ashore "shall not be considered a landing," nor relieve the vessel of the duty to transport back the alien if ultimately excluded. And this Court has long considered such temporary arrangements as not affecting an alien's status; he is treated as if stopped at the border.[56]

Justices Jackson and Frankfurter dissented, but only because they felt a legal permanent resident should not be indefinitely detained without procedural due process.[57] However, as it relates to the right of Congress to deport even a long-standing legal permanent resident, even the dissenters were unequivocal. "Due process does not invest any alien with a right to enter the United States, *nor confer on those admitted the right to remain against the national will*," they wrote.[58]

Even in the few instances where the earlier courts had sided with immigrants over immigration officials, it was either due to the presumption that the petitioner was possibly a US citizens, the immigrant was a long-standing permanent resident who was denied even an administrative hearing to present his case, or it was a matter of statutory interpretation—not a question of constitutionality.[59]

It wasn't until 2001 in *Zadvydas v. Davis* that five post-constitutional justices began mandating the release of criminal aliens from detention when every effort was made to deport them.[60] And even those justices affirmed the validity of *Shaughnessy* and one hundred years of precedent,[61] although, as Justice Scalia observed in his dissent, that case now "stands unexplained and undistinguished" and "obscured in legal fog" by the courts' activism.[62] However, for our purposes *Shaughnessy* is incontestable precedent, as it should be in the eyes of a legal profession that idolizes *stare decisis*. It is the most inviolable of settled law.

As noted, illegal aliens who give birth here against the national will are not even viewed as being within our territorial jurisdiction. It is from this principle that we can prove indisputably that those living here illegally cannot be granted geographical jurisdiction to satisfy even the misinterpreted reading of the Fourteenth Amendment's requirement that the immigrant be "subject to the jurisdiction thereof."

In one of the cases cited in the 1953 decision, *Kaplan v Tod* (1925), the court denied citizenship and relief from deportation to the daughter of a naturalized citizen who emigrated from Russia. On July 20, 1914, the Kaplan family came to Ellis Island to reunite with the father of the family, who had been working in the country for a few years. The thirteen-year-old daughter was deemed inadmissible for being "feeble minded," but because of the outbreak of World War I, her deportation was delayed. She was handed over to the custody of the Hebrew Aid Society, which had her live together with her father until she was ordered deported in 1923.[63]

In the meantime, the father had become a citizen three years earlier, and asserted that because his daughter was under twenty-one at the time of his naturalization and was living in the United States, she should be automatically granted citizenship alongside him, pursuant to longstanding law. But in a unanimous and terse decision, the Court swatted down the petition:

> Naturalization of parents affects minor children only "if dwelling in the United States." The appellant could not lawfully have landed in the United States in view of the express prohibition of the Act of 1910 just referred to, and until she legally landed "could not have dwelt within the United States."[64]

The Court backhandedly rejected the notion that she "dwelt within the United States," even though she physically lived with her father for nine years on American soil, partly with temporary permission from the government. That is because "she was still in theory of law at the boundary line, and had gained no foothold in the United States" and had never "been dwelling in the United States within the meaning of the Act."[65]

Now stop for a moment and compare the language of the naturalization statute for those immigrant children seeking naturalization together with their parents to the wording of the Fourteenth Amendment governing those born here.

The Fourteenth Amendment requires that the child be born here and "subject to the jurisdiction thereof." It is indisputable that even according to those opinions in which jurisdiction means territorial jurisdiction and not political jurisdiction (absurdly rendering the phrase superfluous, as noted earlier), the language of "subject to the jurisdiction" is certainly more restrictive than the purely geographical and literal phrase "dwelling in the United States." After all, everyone concedes that Indian tribes and children born to foreign diplomats were excluded by this phrase, even though they are physically born on our soil.

Yet, the Court ruled in 1925, based on uncontested precedent, that those living here unlawfully don't even satisfy the meaning and intent of "dwelling in the United States"—even in a case where they were granted temporary permission to live here on humanitarian grounds. It is therefore simply preposterous to assert that those who willfully violated our laws and snuck into the country without permission can secure jurisdiction for their children against the consent of the nation. As the Left would say, it's "settled law" that illegal immigrants are considered "at the boundary line, and had gained no foothold in the United States," irrespective of where they reside now.

After having read the rich history of our settled law, including decisions from the very justice who erroneously invented birthright citizenship for all legal immigrants, now consider what the courts have done in our generation. We have gone from a nation having the sovereignty to deport even legal immigrants without judicial review to mandating full constitutional rights for illegal aliens and the release of dangerous illegal aliens into our society against our consent, as we will explore in the next chapter. Stolen sovereignty, indeed.

The bottom line is that a country can never be forced to issue citizenship against its will, for if that were the case, it would cease to be a sovereign country "free from external control," as the term is defined by Webster's dictionary.[66]

THE MOST PROFOUND USURPATION OF OUR SOVEREIGNTY

It is clear beyond a shadow of a doubt based on endless case law built upon thousands of pages of legal theory that foreign nationals have no right to assert jurisdiction against the consent of the nation and its political branches of government. This issue goes well beyond the debate over birthright citizenship for illegal aliens. It stands at the nexus of the entire immigration issue, and by extension, the entire foundation of our republican form of government and status as a sovereign nation.

Contemporary courts, starting with the Warren–Brennan Court, are packed with political activists devoid of any rational jurisprudence rooted in the Constitution and our nation's history and tradition. They are bestowing all sorts of rights on illegal aliens—way beyond even the procedural due process rights to contest deportation that courts denied for almost a hundred years.

We have gone from the courts recognizing the commonsense founding principle that "over no conceivable subject is the legislative power of Congress more complete than it is over the admission of aliens" to courts mandating the release of the many violent criminal illegal aliens.[67]

For a profession that worships *stare decisis*—even when it overturns the original meaning of the Constitution—they are now reversing the most unassailable settled law of Congress's plenary power over immigration as it relates to the very foundation of our sovereignty. Nobody summed up the imperative and unassailable nature of Congress's plenary power over immigration as it relates to sovereignty like Justice Felix Frankfurter:

> As to the extent of the power of Congress under review, there is not merely "a page of history" . . . but a whole volume. . . that the formulation of these policies is entrusted exclusively to Congress has become about as firmly embedded in the legislative and judicial tissues of our body politic as any aspect of our government. . . .

We are not prepared to deem ourselves wiser or more sensitive to human rights than our predecessors, especially those who have been most zealous in protecting civil liberties under the Constitution, and must therefore under our constitutional system recognize congressional power in dealing with aliens."[68]

When studying the immigration laws and the case law from earlier in our history, even during the most open periods of immigration, some of the laws might seem a bit harsh when viewed through a modern lens, and some might even seem quite appalling and discriminatory.[69] Nonetheless, governments have the right to restrict entry of anyone for any purpose, and the reality is that these laws merely reflected the sentiment of the people through the consent given to Congress by the voters of the time. And clearly, unlike today, the government was very committed to upholding the will of the people and protecting them from security, social, and fiscal threats—even if they now seem ridiculously paranoid.

Our nation now faces an existential threat from Islamic terror from a growing population of immigrants from the Middle East—over and beyond any immigration threat our nation faced at the time of these immigration laws. Anyone endowed with a modicum of common sense would look at the mistakes of Europe, with their irresponsible immigration policies, and understand that America needs a cooling-off period of immigration from the Islamic world until there is some sort of reformation within the religion that gains steam in the broader Islamic religion.

Yet, when Donald Trump and others suggested that we place a moratorium on immigration from Islamic countries, there was near unanimity of opinion among the political leaders—from left to right—that such a move would be out of step with our values, tradition, and history. Even Republican leaders suggested that it is "unconstitutional" to bar Muslims from immigrating to the United States.

After reviewing the information presented in this chapter, it should be abundantly clear that such a move would not only be in harmony with our history and values on immigration—rooted in the principle of protecting Americans first—*it is most certainly constitutional to exclude any group of people for any reason*, and to a large extent, *even deport those here legally*.

We will always have social disagreements on immigration as a matter of policy, but to eliminate the people's ability to even debate the future membership of their society without any recourse through their elected representatives will spell the end of our country as a sovereign entity. To create an affirmative right to immigrate and remain in the country against the national will and to create a right to birthright citizenship for illegal aliens represents that most profound usurpation of a nation's sovereignty.

The politicians, legal scholars, and contemporary judges who confer full constitutional rights on illegal aliens and citizenship on their children are no longer engaging in a debate over the meaning of the Fourteenth Amendment. They are asserting that we are no longer a nation-state with any Constitution of and by *the* people—the sovereign citizens of this nation.

5

THE JUDICIAL COUP

Every society from a great nation down to a club had the right of declaring the conditions on which new members should be admitted, there can be room for no complaint.

—GOUVERNEUR MORRIS, AT THE CONSTITUTIONAL CONVENTION IN 1787

When—and how—did this impervious precedent of settled law change? How has our sovereignty transmogrified from an unassailable ideal meticulously guarded by the people's representatives to a shooting target for the judicial playground and the unelected bureaucrats? How have illegal aliens been granted equal rights to citizens, and in some cases, super rights and privileges against "discrimination" not afforded to Americans?

The answer lies in the legal ratchet phenomenon we cited in chapter 1, of course. One post-constitutional court decision blasts a hole through the parchment of our Constitution, creating an even bigger opening for subsequent judges who become even more emboldened and radicalized. This has engendered an irreversible jurisprudential velocity toward international "universal values" instead of popular and jurisdictional sovereignty of the American citizenry.

Although the courts began gradually introducing newfound constitutional rights for legal immigrants in the 1970s—rights that were previously held to only apply to citizens—the courts commenced the process of violating our sovereignty and encroaching upon the plenary power of Congress in a pair of decisions in 1982.

The real devious coup against the Constitution and our sovereignty as a nation, however, started with the infamous *Plyler v Doe* decision written by Associate Justice William Brennan.[1] The state of Texas passed a law prohibiting local school districts from using state education funds to subsidize illegal aliens in public schools. Writing for the majority in striking down the state law, Brennan created a Fourteenth Amendment equal protection right to education—even for *illegal* aliens—forcing taxpayers to foot the bill for those who had no right to be in the state. And once again, using the paradoxical post-constitutional legal tyranny theory, Brennan backfilled that right into the Fifth Amendment.

"Aliens, even aliens whose presence in this country is unlawful, have long been recognized as "persons" guaranteed due process of law by the Fifth and Fourteenth Amendments," declared a sanctimonious Brennan.[2]

Aside from the pernicious and illegal precedent he set to apply the Bill of Rights to illegal aliens, Brennan had the nerve to cite the cases from the 1800s and 1950s we explored in chapter 4 that actually repudiate his premise.[3] For example, in *Wong Wing v. U.S.* (1896), the court affirmed that Congress has the full authority to pass statutes deporting even *legal* immigrants without any judicial review, much less conferring upon *illegal* immigrants substantive rights, such as the right to send their kids to school on the taxpayer dime. The only limitation the courts made was that an alien cannot be subjected to hard labor, as was the case before them in *Wong Wing*, without a judicial process.

In a breathtaking act of brazen judicial supremacism, Brennen took an eight-five year old court opinion, which upheld the ability of the political branches to deport even legal immigrants, and used it to strike down a much-needed state law against illegal aliens. And in a decision eerily similar to what we've dissected from the marriage case in chapter 3, Brennan extrapolated from the prohibition on coerced labor and transformed it into a positive right to taxpayer-funded education. We see from *Plyler* that not only do judicial supremacists backfill their anti-constitutional sentiments into the Constitution; they also build precedents on the backs of settled case law that have preemptively repudiated their views. *Plyer* also set the precedent for violating the sovereignty of individual states and taking away the most basic tools they need to protect their residents from people who are deemed outside of their boundaries by federal law.

Writing in his dissent in *Zadvydas v. Davis* (2001), Scalia scoffed at Brennan's citation of the 1896 case and its use by the *Zadvydas* majority to mandate the release of criminal aliens into the country. "I am sure they cannot be tortured, as well—but neither prohibition has anything to do with their right to be released into the United States," wrote Scalia in the dissent.[4]

If they lack the right to be released into the country, they certainly lack the affirmative entitlement to free public education for their children. It's the old sleight of hand, conflating the *procedure* of due process for inalienable rights with the substantive right to welfare and entitlements—and applied to those here illegally. Jumping three steps from precedent and common sense in one decision is the black magic of the judicial tyrants.

The second problem with Brennan's bleeding-heart musings that illegal aliens are considered present in the United States for purposes of constitutional rights is that, well, they are not considered present in the country at all. As we noted time and again from settled law, illegal aliens are considered to be at the boundary *outside* of our jurisdiction, even if they are physically present in the country.

Ironically, it is at this point that Brennan inserted his infamous "footnote 10" in which he declared the phrase "subject to the jurisdiction thereof" in the Fourteenth Amendment to include illegal aliens. In one of the most gruesome contortions of legal mental gymnastics of all time, Brennan ignored 90 years of case law and suggested that "jurisdiction" means *geographical* status by citing the same phrase in the Fourteenth Amendment, which most assuredly meant *legal* status—for the numerous reasons we laid out before—thereby simultaneously creating the right to citizenship for illegal alien children.[5] In legal arithmetic, evidently, the right to due process before getting punished with hard labor equals the right to free education against the will of the people, which is multiplied to produce the right to citizenship without the consent of the society and in violation of the nation's sovereignty—all divided by previous settled law that explicitly states the opposite.

Brennan's naked political play is a quintessential example of how illegal and illogical the opinions of the Court have been concerning some of the most consequential issues of our time. In recent years we have witnessed the courts violate the individual sovereignty of American citizens and their property rights, such as the Obamacare and marriage decisions we explored in chapters 2 and 3. Now we are staring down the barrel of a judicial cannon about to eradicate state and national sovereignty. It was the *Plyler* decision in 1982 that led to the destruction of a century of settled law, opening the door to the end of our sovereignty as we know it.

ARIZONA AND THE ASSAULT ON STATES OVERRUN BY ILLEGALS

Sovereignty is not just the right of our whole nation to independent self-governance over our national territory. Each state has the right to self-government and the protection of its integrity as a distinct independent jurisdiction. After all, the states created the union, not vice versa. In return for ceding some of their powers to the federal government in order to create a united and secure federal union, the federal government has an obligation to protect the sovereignty of the states. The Constitution states "the United States shall guarantee to every state in this union a republican form of government, and shall protect each of them against invasion."[6]

It was a foundational principle that although each state would concede some political autonomy, anything not enumerated in the Constitution was to be reserved to the states. Madison promised during the ratification period "the States will retain, under the proposed Constitution, a very extensive portion of active sovereignty."[7] The most fundamental right to the people of a sovereign state is protection against invasion. The federal government must guarantee that protection, and if they fail to do so, it is a violation of the underpinnings of the agreement to join the union.

One of the indictments against King George listed in the Declaration was: "He has forbidden his Governors to pass Laws of immediate and pressing importance, unless suspended in their operation till his Assent should be obtained; and when so suspended, he has utterly neglected to attend to them."[8]

Certainly, when the federal government was created to replace King George as the national authority, they never intended to suppress states from passing laws to protect themselves and their taxpayers, not with a standing army, but at least with their legitimate state law enforcement and power over local issues. In fact, they guaranteed the help of the federal government to protect them from invasion. And in the case of endless illegal immigration, which has engendered a wave of violent crime, drugs, and kidnappings in states like Arizona—not to mention the unbelievable fiscal drain—the federal government explicitly passed statutes deputizing the states to enforce immigration law.[9] After all, the federal government cannot protect our sovereignty without their help and cooperation because most illegal aliens who get beyond the border are caught by state officials.

Yet, the courts have violated the Constitution and the sovereignty of the states by placing themselves in the role of Congress as it relates to regulating state immigration enforcement laws.

Following *Plyler*, in yet another clever judicial magic trick, which has been employed by subsequent judges ever since, Brennan used the plenary authority of Congress over immigration to prevent states from enforcing the will of congressional statutes. In striking down the Texas law barring state funding for education of illegal aliens, which works harmoniously with federal law, Brennan opined that because it is conceivable that the federal government might one day legalize illegal aliens, states could not enforce existing immigration law!

> [T]here is no assurance that a child subject to deportation will ever be deported. An illegal entrant might be granted federal permission to continue to reside in this country, or even to become a citizen. . . . In light of the discretionary federal power to grant relief from deportation, a State cannot realistically determine that any particular undocumented child will in fact be deported until after deportation proceedings have been completed.[10]

Brennan admitted that these people were most certainly here in contravention to our laws, but in an appalling act of impudence, he declared it incumbent upon the court to vouch for federal supremacy on immigration even more than Congress itself—even when it is opposite of congressional intent.

When the Framers indicted King George for ignoring the security of the states and governors, they could not have possibly imagined that the federal government they established—the unelected executive agencies and the courts—would collectively disenfranchise a sovereign state from following the laws passed by Congress to protect themselves from a mass illegal invasion. They certainly could never have envisioned the sheer magnitude of what Arizona is confronted with today.

Consider the following destruction wrought upon Arizona by illegal immigration and the refusal of the unelected branches to follow the plenary authority of Congress to protect them or allow the state to protect itself:

As of 2013, it was estimated that there were 630,700 illegal aliens residing in Arizona (including American-born anchor babies).[11] That is a population of foreign invaders larger than the total population of any single colony at the time of our founding.[12]

Over 10 percent of the state's public school population is composed of illegal alien children.[13] When coupled with the fiscal strain of health care and incarceration, the total cost of illegal immigration is $2.4 billion a year.[14]

The Arizona Department of Corrections estimates that illegal aliens comprise 17 percent of its prison population and 22 percent of all felony defendants in Maricopa County.[15]

Arizona has become the drug-smuggling capital of the country. From 2010 to 2015, heroin seizures in Arizona have increased by 207 percent, while methamphetamine seizures grew by 310 percent.[16] In fiscal year 2014, there were more pounds of marijuana seized in the Tucson corridor than every other border sector combined.[17]

Arizona has completely been deprived of sovereignty. A number of state and federal parks, as well as private lands, are overrun by violent drug cartels.[18] Their education, health care, welfare, and criminal justice systems are drained beyond capacity. What happened to their guarantee of protection?

The reality that Arizona must confront in terms of violent crime and public charge from foreign infiltrators is not only appalling; it is an anathema to the core values of the republican form of government expressed in so many court decisions before the judicial tyrants hijacked that branch of government.

Yet, when Arizona passed its famous SB 1070 law to clamp down on illegal immigration, President Obama directed the unelected bureaucrats at the Justice Department to sue Arizona for thwarting his illegal amnesty program. Arizona merely mimicked federal law and required, among other things, that local law enforcement make a "reasonable attempt" to ascertain the immigration status of an individual during a lawful stop, such as a traffic violation, if the officer has "reasonable suspicion" to believe the person is an illegal alien.[19]

After being struck down by the Ninth Circuit, the Supreme Court upheld the aforementioned core provision of SB 1070, but opened the door for future legal action with a wink and nod to the powerful illegal alien legal lobby to sue for discrimination once the lawful stops were implemented.[20] Moreover, the court struck down three other provisions of the Arizona law, which shadowed and reinforced federal law by making it a state crime not to follow federal registration statutes, a state crime for an illegal alien to work in the state of Arizona, and to empower local law enforcement to conduct warrantless arrests of illegal aliens if the officer had "probable cause" to believe the alien committed a removable offense.[21]

In this decision, the Supreme Court upheld the growing legal sentiments from the lower courts, inspired by Brennan's opinion in *Plyler*, that states have no authority to deny benefits and keep out those who have no right to be in the state—pursuant to *federal* law.

Let's consider the magnitude of this decision. The courts have decided that even when states are acting in accordance with congressional statutes, they are precluded from defending their sovereignty . . . because the courts said so. With this decision, the Supreme Court has codified the notion that the judiciary, which lacked any jurisdiction over immigration at the founding of our country, now has full power over the states—even as it relates to repelling illegal immigration.

Undoubtedly, states can't override Congress by making their own rules on admissions to the country or naturalization. That is within the complete domain of Congress. But as Scalia wrote in his dissent, "the naturalization power was given to Congress not to abrogate States' power to exclude those they did not want, but to vindicate it."[22] The great early constitutional scholar Justice Joseph Story made it clear that immigration was federalized in order to protect the states from mass migration, not saddle them with its most harmful effects. "If aliens might be admitted indiscriminately to enjoy all the rights of citizens at the will of a single state, the Union might itself be endangered by an influx of foreigners, hostile to its institutions, ignorant of its powers, and incapable of a due estimate of its privileges," wrote Story.[23]

Federalizing immigration was a way of preventing states with *lax* immigration laws from ruining the sovereignty of the other states with undesirable inhabitants. The federal legislature's job was to protect states from illegal or undesirable migration, and Congress has passed laws since 1790 to do just that. In fact, one of the reasons there were no official regulations on entry (only naturalization) before 1875 and 1882, even though the federal government had the power to enact them, is precisely because the states passed numerous laws keeping out undesirable or illegal immigrants for the first one hundred years of the republic.[24]

Federalism, as it relates to immigration, has been flipped on its head by the legal profession. At the same time states like Arizona were working harmoniously with federal law to enforce the sovereignty of the people, as originally envisioned by our Founders, other states and localities were flagrantly violating federal immigration law in order to encourage illegal immigration.

In 2013, California and Connecticut passed laws prohibiting local law enforcement from cooperating with ICE to detain criminal aliens as required by federal regulations.[25] In total, there are at least 340 sanctuary jurisdictions in the country that refuse to cooperate with federal immigration officials, and as a result, have recently released more than ten thousand criminal aliens into our population.[26] Yet, the Obama administration and the legal profession had nothing to say about it.

This is exactly what Justice Story meant when he observed that federal power over immigration was designed to prevent individual states from endangering the Union. What's worse, as I will explain in chapter 8, the states that thwart federal immigration law by encouraging more illegal immigration stand to benefit from the increased population in the form of more congressional representation.

But once again, the majority opinion of the Court in the Arizona case flipped the Constitution on its head to deny a state its own sovereignty and security guaranteed by Congress. Worse, in the ultimate betrayal of a state's sovereignty, and in a disturbingly growing trend of factoring in international law and foreign sentiments, Kennedy invoked the foreign country's concerns "about the status, safety, and security of their nationals in the United States" resulting from Arizona's law to protect its residents and Americans at large.[27]

The message to the states emanating from this decision was essentially that even though Congress has exclusive authority over immigration, given that the executive branch is illegally refusing to enforce the laws of Congress and foreign countries hate those laws, you are arrested from doing anything to protect the people of your state.

Think for a moment: is this appalling lawlessness the "law of the land," as many pseudo-conservatives are wont to say following any Supreme Court opinion that flips the Constitution upside down and inside out? Is the Constitution and its guarantee of sovereignty against foreign invaders unconstitutional? As Scalia asked rhetorically at the end of his dissent, "[W]ould the States conceivably have entered into the Union if the Constitution itself contained the Court's holding?"[28]

As early as 1823, Thomas Jefferson warned about the involvement of federal courts in state criminal laws, even pertaining to white-collar crimes. "Can it be believed, that under the jealousies prevailing against the General Government, at the adoption of the constitution, the States meant to surrender the authority of preserving order, of enforcing moral duties and restraining vice, within their own territory?" asked Jefferson in a letter to Justice William Johnson.[29] One can only imagine Jefferson's anguish were he to see federal courts constrain states from enforcing federal laws against violent foreign invaders at the behest of foreign governments and a lawless administration—all in violation of the life, liberty, property rights, and sovereignty of the people.

THE HANDCUFFING OF ARIZONA

The judicial war on Arizona's sovereignty, engendered by unconstitutional and hypocritical legal analysis, gets even worse. After Obama illegally granted amnesty to young illegal immigrants as part of the DACA, or Deferred Action for Childhood Arrivals, program, Arizona refused to grant driver's licenses to these illegal aliens. Arizona was upholding the federal laws on the books, which require ICE agents to place all illegal aliens into removal proceedings.[30] Obama was in clear violation of congressional statutes and is preempted from making his own laws. Congressional preemption was the entire rationale the courts used to toss out parts of SB 1070. Yet, some of the same district and appellate judges used the exact *opposite* logic to coerce Arizona into providing illegal aliens with driver's licenses. They held Arizona in violation of Obama's royal edict, which itself was the most egregious violation of Congress's plenary power over immigration.

Instead of applying the Constitution on this critical issue of sovereignty and security of a state, Judge Harry Pregerson, a Ninth Circuit Judge appointed by Jimmy Carter, used political arguments and accused Arizona of being racist. "Nothing horrible has happened on the highways of Arizona," said Pregerson during oral arguments in July 2015. He then badgered Arizona Assistant Atty. Gen. Dominic Draye, asking him, "Does it come down to racism? Does it come down to discrimination against these people? What else does it come down to?"[31]

Well, if Judge Pregerson wants to focus on political arguments instead of constitutional arguments, maybe he ought to speak to the mom of Brandon Mendoza, a promising young police sergeant, who was killed by a drunk-driving illegal alien who was traveling the wrong way on the highway.[32] Or what about Tricia Bracho and her children, who were injured on July 4, just two weeks before oral arguments, when an illegal alien high on drugs slammed into their car head-on?[33]

Maybe the judge ought to check out the data showing how almost 30,000 driving offenses have been committed just by the 30,558 criminal aliens Obama released in fiscal year 2014.[34] Yes, it must be racism. That's the only reason a state would care about clamping down on illegal immigration in the polluted minds of the legal profession.

But even if Arizona didn't have a good *policy* reason to deny them driver's licenses, what happened to federal law which requires ICE to place aliens who are not "clearly and beyond a doubt entitled to be admitted" to the United States into removal proceedings?[35] What happened to the sovereign authority of a nation and a state to keep out illegal immigrants? Now illegal aliens have a right to a driver's license? How can we the people allow this injustice and tyranny emanating from the bench to stand for even one day?

In November 2014, the Tenth Circuit Court of appeals struck down laws in Arizona and Kansas requiring those who register to vote with federal forms to show proof of citizenship in order to vote. Overturning a district judge's opinion, the appeals court denied requests from those states that the federal government alter their forms to require the additional proof and protect the integrity of state elections.[36] The Supreme Court refused to hear the case.[37]

Step back for a moment and ponder the following thought. In chapter 3, we discussed how the court praised the Arizona voters for passing a ballot initiative creating a redistricting commission in clear violation of the Constitution. Yet, when the state's voters sought to protect their elections from the hundreds of thousands of illegal aliens in their state, the courts struck down the will of the people, even though the Constitution clearly grants the states control over regulating elections.[38]

Although the Constitution does allow the federal government to "alter such regulations," Alexander Hamilton promised that federal interposition would only be under "extraordinary circumstances."[39] Further, he made it clear that the federal government's role in regulating elections was only for the purpose of its self-preservation. "Every government ought to contain within itself the means of its own preservation," wrote Hamilton in defense of the Constitution. How sorrowful it must be for Hamilton in his grave, watching unelected judges use this very clause of the Constitution as the "extraordinary circumstance" to violate the sovereignty of the state, the franchise of the people, and the preservation of both our state and federal governments.

Once again, in the eyes of the courts, the Constitution is unconstitutional—what is in the document is erased and what's not in it is added in. The common denominator is that the citizenry is disenfranchised and stripped of their sovereignty. That states are prevented from even upholding the integrity of their elections from illegal votes of foreign invaders violates the very essence of popular sovereignty, the social contract, and the social compact expressed in the preamble of the Declaration.

In 2006, 77 percent of voters approved Arizona Proposition 100, which denied bail to illegal aliens charged with "serious felony offenses."[40] After being struck down by the Ninth Circuit, the Supreme Court refused to grant Arizona cert[41] to have their voices heard.[42] Evidently, even Chief Justice Roberts joined with the liberals to deny Arizona the requisite four votes to hear the case. In dissenting from the denial of cert, Thomas and Scalia were furious. "Our indifference to cases such as this one will only embolden the lower courts to reject state laws on questionable constitutional grounds," wrote Thomas.[43]

Hence, the Supreme Court could not even be relied on to review a lower court ruling striking down the last remaining act of Arizona to prevent illegal alien murderers and rapists from absconding from trials when let out on bail. Ignoring one hundred years of settled case law on deportation of legal immigrants, courts are now granting *illegal* alien murderers the right to bail, denying the people of a sovereign state through a citizen's initiative the ability to protect themselves from foreign invaders.

Of course, the problem of violent illegal aliens jumping bail is not limited to Arizona. The courts are violating our *national* sovereignty as well. In July 2015, Francisco Javier Chavez, an illegal alien from Mexico who repeatedly reentered the country illegally, was arrested in California on charges of brutally beating a toddler to within an inch of her life. Despite the fact that Chavez had a lengthy rap sheet of numerous violent crimes, including cruelty to a child, he was set free by a liberal judge after he posted $10,000 for bail. Needless to say, he never showed up for his arraignment and is still at large in the country to this day.[44]

In October 2015, the Second Circuit Court of Appeals ruled that a number of criminal aliens cannot be held for longer than six months without a bail hearing. This ruling essentially codifies the policy of releasing dangerous aliens who will never return for their trial.[45] Once again, two of the three judges in that case were Republican appointees.[46] So much for the federal government having full control over immigration enforcement. The courts only used that as an excuse to screw over the states.

A recent report from the US Customs and Border Protection revealed that the lack of enforcement and the understanding that illegals will never be deported is largely contributing to the incentive for new illegal aliens to arrive and overwhelm the states.[47] Accordingly, we now have endless waves of illegal immigration, including a large contingent of violent offenders and drug traffickers, yet our own laws and openness as a society are being used against us in a commonsense effort to protect the people of this country.

These are the type of judges we have serving on the bench. The voice of the people—both on a state and a federal level—have been silenced in favor of the most violent criminals, who have no right to be in Arizona or any other state in America in the first place. If this is not enough to wake Americans up to judicial tyranny, we deserve the judicial oligarchy we have.

GUN RIGHTS FOR ILLEGALS

We already see that illegal aliens are illegally granted an assortment of rights, privileges, and benefits by the courts. How about gun rights at the expense of the safety of American citizens?

Writing a unanimous opinion in *United States v. Meza-Rodriguez*, chief judge Dianne Wood, a radical liberal appointed by Bill Clinton and often hyped as the next Democrat nominee for the Supreme Court, opined that illegal aliens have the fundamental right to bear arms. "We see no principled way to carve out the Second Amendment and say that the unauthorized (or maybe all noncitizens) are excluded," wrote Judge Wood in a unanimous opinion of the three-judge panel. She brazenly continued, "[N]o language in the Amendment supports such a conclusion, nor, as we have said, does a broader consideration of the Bill of Rights."[48]

What's worse, a prominent GOP-appointee, Frank Easterbrook, signed onto Wood's opinion.[49] Easterbrook is the same judge who later in 2015 wrote an opinion upholding Illinois's sweeping ban on "assault" weapons using an embarrassing justification that it "may increase the public's sense of safety."[50] The Second Amendment be darned. Once again, we see the most radical contortion of fundamental rights on display—granting citizen rights to those here against the national will while infringing on the most foundational rights of citizens. And this was all done by Republican-appointed judges.

SUBSIDIZING THE STEALING OF OUR OWN SOVEREIGNTY

After using the federal government against the states in order to violate their sovereignty, now the courts are directly challenging the federal government's control over immigration, most prominently, by forcing them to release criminal aliens into our communities.

On July 24, 2015, Central California district judge Dolly Gee essentially ruled that the federal government must release from detention all illegal aliens who come here with a minor child.[51] Americans are forced to foot the bill for thousands of indigent illegal immigrants flooding the southern border from Central America who are now able to use our own court system against us. Even though 84 percent of family units from Central America that received a notice to appear before an immigration judge absconded and disappeared into the population, the court feels that none of them can be detained.[52]

This same federal judge issued a ruling allowing nine hundred illegal aliens who were already deported to force immigration officials to reopen their cases because they may not have been mentally competent during their deportation proceedings. In 2013, Judge Gee found a new fundamental right for those illegal aliens with mental disabilities to avail themselves of taxpayer-provided attorneys and is now forcing the taxpayers to pay for the transportation of these individuals back into our country.[53]

Think about how careful our forefathers were to protect the country from public charge. Now we have unelected judges demanding taxpayer-funded counsel and transportation for illegal aliens with mental disabilities who have *already* been deported. This is in direct violation of federal laws passed by Congress, which protect taxpayers from funding counsel to those in deportation proceedings.[54] The Obama administration has pledged an additional $9 million in taxpayer funds to enrich the anti-sovereignty legal profession and represent illegal alien minors on the public dime.[55] The citizenry is not only disenfranchised and denuded of their sovereignty, security, and public safety; they are forced to subsidize it as well.

We are often lectured by the political elites with pomp and sanctimony that being open to "immigrants" was always a part of our values and traditions. The reality is the exact opposite. How far we have come from the 1891 immigration law, which not only barred the entry of those who would constitute a public charge (still the law on the books), but ordered the owner of the vessel that transported those aliens liable for the cost of their return trip and their temporary stay on American soil.[56] Now, unelected judges are ordering the *return* of impoverished, and often violent, illegal aliens and demanding that taxpayers pay the cost of the return, legal fees, and the full smorgasbord of privileges, including driver's licenses, health care, and education.

How far our judicial oligarchy has strayed from their predecessors who brusquely denied illegal aliens any opportunity to assert rights to remain in the country and enjoy privileges of citizens. "To appeal to the Constitution is to concede that this is a land governed by that supreme law, and as under it the power to exclude has been determined to exist, those who are excluded cannot assert the rights in general obtaining in a land to which they do not belong as citizens or otherwise," declared Chief Justice Fuller in 1904.[57]

In a further free-for-all, illegal aliens in Georgia are now suing for the right to obtain a driver's license under—you guessed it—the equal protection clause of the Fourteenth Amendment.[58] There is a similar lawsuit pending in Oregon.[59] Despite being outspent ten to one by the open borders lobby, the people of liberal Oregon struck down a ballot measure in 2014 granting illegal aliens driver's licenses by a margin of two to one.[60] Even if the state and federal governments ultimately win these lawsuits on behalf of the people, the legal profession has created so much precedent giving legitimacy to these anti-sovereignty and anti-constitutional lawsuits that they serve as a deterrent to those states that wish to enact laws protecting themselves against illegal immigration.

SUPER RIGHTS FOR ILLEGALS

If your blood is already boiling, stop right here, because the following is going to make your blood pressure skyrocket.

What happens when you combine the citizen rights the courts are now granting to illegal aliens with the super rights they are bestowing upon homosexuals? You get a de facto super-duper right for any foreign national who claims to be homosexual or transgender to immigrate to our country, even if he violated our laws and sovereignty to get here.

On September 3, 2015, the very same day a court ordered the arrest of Kim Davis for refusing to sign a marriage license for homosexual couples, the Ninth Circuit Court of Appeals ordered federal immigration officials to stop the deportation of a transgender illegal alien. Edin Carey Avendano-Hernandez, who had previously been deported back to Mexico but reentered the country illegally a second time, was arrested twice for drunk driving offenses.[61]

Judge Jacqueline Nguyen, an Obama appointee, ruled that because he was transgendered and would likely be tortured in Mexico, the deportation was in violation of the U.N. Convention Against Torture (CAT). The fringe judge further went on to rebuke the immigration official for failing to "recognize the difference between gender identity and sexual orientation, refusing to allow the use of female pronouns because she considered Avendano-Hernandez to be 'still male.'"[62]

Let's review what happened on that dark day in September. All in one case, we had a circuit judge applying international law, creating new transgendered rights, deciding a controversial societal issue over something universally regarded as a mental disorder until recently, and granting a dangerous illegal alien the right to remain in our country in contravention to the plenary power of Congress over immigration, our national sovereignty, and the very essence of the social contract. In other words, on the same day a citizen was stripped of the most inalienable right to religious freedom, an illegal alien was granted constitutional rights—and even super rights simply for asserting that he was really a she.

The granting of wholesale amnesty for illegal aliens by liberal judges, especially for those who claim to be homosexuals, is a growing phenomenon. In December 2015, a Florida federal district judge appointed by George H. W. Bush, unilaterally granted asylum to Jose Crespo-Cagnant, a Mexican national who entered the country illegally numerous times since 2002 and committed identity fraud. Even though this alien had attempted to enter the country on a number of occasions and never mentioned a credible fear of persecution in Mexico, on advice from his sleazy attorney, Crespo-Cagnant alleges that in 2012 he told the border agent he feared persecution back home for being gay.[63]

Despite the fact that the border agent denied ever hearing such an expression from Crespo-Cagnant when he was apprehended, and despite no specific evidence of persecution, Judge Ursula Ungaro granted this career criminal full amnesty and set him on what will be an eventual path to citizenship. We are rapidly reaching a point when the judiciary will grant blanket legal status to anyone claiming to be gay who wants to emigrate from a third world country.

This is also part of a growing trend in which judges also second-guess the word of immigration officials, even in cases where illegals had previously violated our law, are convicted criminals, and are clearly inadmissible to begin with. It's a violation of long-standing precedent of taking the word of immigration officials as due process and placing the burden on the alien to show that administration officials violated statutes.[64]

Last October, the Ninth Circuit invalidated a deportation order against a criminal alien who was charged for aggravated burglary on two occasions.[65] The court went a step further by declaring the *congressional* statue, which orders the deportation of any legal immigrant convicted of an "aggravated felony," unconstitutionally vague.[66] It's becoming clear that if the courts are not stripped of their power over immigration, they will prevent a future conservative administration from following the law, even to protect our sovereignty from criminal aliens.

In another pending case at the time of this writing, Arizona federal district judge David Bury, a George W. Bush appointee, has agreed to hear a class action suit from illegal aliens alleging that the border patrol is denying them "adequate sleep, sanitary conditions, medical care, food and water, and warmth at holding centers."[67] If the plaintiffs win, which this leftist judge seems to indicate they will, it could single-handedly force the border patrol to release hundreds of thousands of illegal aliens. Meanwhile, our brave agents are working overtime in the Tucson sector to stop the flow of violent crime and drugs, yet they are stymied by the reprehensible liberal legal profession and a single unelected judge!

Looking ahead, there is a truculent army of immigration lawyers with the ability to bankrupt states and localities that want to enforce the law or encumber federal law enforcement measures in court for years. The fears of lawsuits are so bad that even though employers are required by federal law to verify the legal status of employees, they are being threatened with lawsuits if they check the legal status of workers who were caught providing fraudulent identification.[68]

Folks, the inmates are now running the asylum.

At this point it's appropriate to take a trip back in a time machine and view this dyslexic and immoral usurpation of power through the lens of Justice Samuel Chase, one of the earliest judicial activists. Chase was impeached, at the behest of President Jefferson, for using the court to advance his political agenda. When advancing the original rationale for the power of judicial review against laws passed by legislatures, Chase declared, "an act of the Legislature contrary to the great first principles of the social compact, cannot be considered a rightful exercise of legislative authority."[69] Chase believed the Court could strike down laws passed by Congress that violated the essence of the social compact and fundamental natural rights.

Fast-forward two centuries and we have unelected judges, not the legislature, violating the essence of the social compact by redefining marriage and gender itself (the ultimate natural law) and the popular and jurisdictional sovereignty of our states and federal union in hamstringing the elected representatives from protecting us against those who come here without our consent and harm our society.

COURTS AS A DEAD-END FOR CONSTITUTIONALISTS

In observing the degree of illogical, illegal, and immoral decisions emanating from the court system, it's important to discuss the dyslexic dichotomy as it relates to standing to sue in court. As we noted, federal judges are now granting illegal aliens standing to sue not only against imprisonment, fines, or even deportation, but also for affirmative government benefits, such as driver's licenses, education, and gun rights. This in itself is an inexcusable departure from years of settled law making it clear that illegal aliens lack any right to judicial review over deportation, much less a right to live freely in the country with free stuff.

But perhaps you think there is some redeemable quality of having such easy access for standing to sue in the court system. Perhaps we should not embark on this effort to strip the courts of their power over immigration, as we propose in chapter 9, because we can use the liberal standard for standing in our favor when we need to sue a runaway executive that refuses to enforce immigration laws. Wrong! This is where the nakedly duplicitous political motivations supplant any semblance of consistent jurisprudence—even post-constitutional jurisprudence.

In August 2012, ten ICE agents, led by ICE Union president Chris Crane, filed suit in the US District Court for the Northern District of Texas against the administration's policy of suspending deportations against those illegals who would qualify for the Dream Act—a law that never passed Congress. Judge Reed O'Connor, a Bush appointee, affirmed the plaintiffs' argument on the merits of the case—that Obama had plainly violated our immigration laws—but he denied these agents standing to sue Obama.[70] In April 2015, a three-judge panel of the Fifth

Circuit Court of Appeals reaffirmed that "neither the Agents nor the State of Mississippi has demonstrated the concrete and particularized injury required to give them standing to maintain this suit."[71]

Let's consider this for a moment. ICE agents were directly threatened with reprisal for upholding the laws passed by Congress and not the illegal abrogation promulgated by Obama's executive edict.[72] A state that is flooded with violent illegal aliens and saddled with a fiscal strain on their education and public services was denied standing to sue Obama for one of the most egregious power grabs of all time. Two of the three judges were Republican appointees.[73]

In August 2015, the D.C. Circuit Court of Appeals affirmed a lower court's ruling that Sheriff Joe Arpaio, the lead law enforcement officer of a border county, Maricopa County, Arizona, lacked standing to sue Obama for the DACA amnesty because his grievances were "speculative."[74] Once again, illegals can obtain standing to sue for any privilege they desire, but Arizona county law enforcement cannot sue when the federal government is flooding their jurisdiction with crime, drugs, and anarchy.

And there you have it. The same branch of government that was supposed to have neither force nor will now has the force to side with foreign invaders and the will to deny our law enforcement officials their constitutional right to defend their own borders.

It's clear that the radical courts are a one-way street and a dead-end for constitutionalists. Illegal aliens have standing to sue for gun rights, but law enforcement has no standing to block lawlessness. Clearly, the courts will never serve as an avenue for restoring our sovereignty even with more GOP judges, given the malignant precedent that has been set over the past few decades.

What a tragic end to our constitutional system of governance as unelected judges are now violating the sovereignty of our nation by granting illegal immigrants all the benefits ascribed to "the people" in the Constitution. How ironic that the preamble of the Constitution, declaring "we the people," was authored by Gouverneur Morris, an early advocate for American sovereignty and consent-based immigration.[75] It could truly be said that the lawlessness of the modern courts could not possibly drift further from the intent of the Founders than it already has in respect to immigration.

6

OUR FOUNDERS' COMMITMENT TO AMERICAN SOVEREIGNTY

As a nation, our first duty must be those who are already our inhabitants, whether native or immigrants.

—CALVIN COOLIDGE

The judicial assault on the legal aspects of sovereignty is actually a reflection of the bureaucratic departure from our founding values related to immigration.

From the time of our founding, the political leaders understood that, much like the head of a household, whose first responsibility is to care for his family, their first and only solemn duty was to protect the well being of Americans and their sovereignty over this great land. As such, Congress (or states, before 1875) passed laws that reflected the values of the people, and the executive branch faithfully executed those laws without exception. As I explained in chapter 4 with regard to the Chinese exclusion acts, the executive officials scrupulously carried out the letter of the law even in the overly harsh application of retroactive deportations.

That has changed over the past generation as the political elites in both parties have given preference to multiculturalism and political correctness over national sovereignty. This schism within the political branches of government has enticed the judiciary to also lay its claims on the issue of immigration.

But all of our Founders and great leaders—who lived before and after the ratification of the Fourteenth Amendment—have taken a very different view. Our Founders and early political leaders always understood that immigration must be governed by common sense and with the principle that we must only have immigrants to the extent that they enrich the country and become a net benefit for our society. They followed Gouverneur Morris's maxim that "we should not be polite at the expense of prudence."[1]

Immigration is the most powerful transformative tool in a country. When done responsibly and gradually with the best interests—first and foremost—of those already here in mind, it can enrich society. But when sanctioned with political motivations and in a precipitous fashion—with no regard for the fiscal, cultural, employment, and security concerns of those already here—nothing is more destructive to a republic. The Islamization of Europe should serve as a stern warning to anyone who believes unqualified and boundless immigration is categorically virtuous for a nation.

Consider for a moment the sophomoric nature of the unqualified bromide that "immigration is good for the country." It's like declaring that high-calorie food is good for the body. Any thinking person would immediately ask, "What type and how much and over what period of time?" Yes, a certain amount is absolutely necessary for the body to function. A further increase in calorie intake might be innocuous in its effects. However, overindulgence in calorie consumption is inimical to the body. Furthermore, if the calories come from certain things, like trans fats, they can be harmful even in smaller quantities. Just ask Michelle Obama and Mike Bloomberg.

The same principle applies to immigration, which is as consequential and powerful to a country as fat and calories are to the body. A reasonable amount of immigration over a manageable period of time, with a focus on those who will assimilate into our culture and values, while shunning those who represent a public charge, helps enrich our civil society. But endless waves of immigration, with a focus on those from indigent and low-skilled regions, are harmful to a country in large quantities, especially over a short period of time. Criminals and Islamic terrorists or those who will adhere to sharia law and have disdain for our Constitution should never be let in. Those are your trans fats—to continue the analogy.

While our Constitution mandates equal inalienable rights for citizens and—to a certain extent—legal permanent residents who were consensually admitted to the society of citizens, no such right exists among those who seek entry to our country. As a society we have the impregnable right to pick and choose the type or numbers of immigrants we admit, unencumbered by the court system. The delegates at the Constitutional Convention, including James Madison, spoke of the need to bring in only "meritorious" immigrants.[2] In this chapter I discuss the importance of exercising that right and how our Founders believed it was a solemn duty of the political leadership to only admit those who would enhance the character and economy of the nation.

THE FOUNDERS AND IMMIGRATION

There is no greater decision a society makes than those pertaining to admitting new members to that society. At the foundation of the social compact and the idea of popular sovereignty is that new members can only be added with the consent of the existing society. And in a republican form of government that must necessarily be done through majoritarian decision making of the representatives chosen by those who formed the social compact. As Madison wrote toward the end of his life, in his essay titled "Sovereignty," "[I]n the case of naturalization a new member is added to the Social compact, not only without a unanimous consent of the members but by a majority of the governing body deriving its powers from a majority of the individual parties to the social compact."[3]

When discussing why the Constitution moved the power over naturalization from the states to the federal government, it is clear that Madison was not concerned about some states being too *strict* on enforcement. Quite the contrary, he wanted the power to initially admit those to the society vested in the power of the people as a whole—through the federal union—to prevent some states from flooding the rest of the country with undesirable immigration affecting the rest of the nation.[4]

Roger Sherman, among the greatest of all the Founders, noted during the House debate on the Naturalization Act of 1790 that "it was intended by the Convention, who framed the Constitution, that Congress should have the power of naturalization, in order to prevent particular States receiving citizens, and forcing them upon others who would not have received them in any other manner." Sherman was emphatic that federal control was designed to "guard against an improper mode of naturalization," and prevent individual states from flooding the country with immigrants based on "easier terms."[5]

The reason it is of upmost vitality to a nation-state to have the people directly decide questions concerning immigration, and that immigration not be encouraged in mass numbers, is not only to maintain the obvious need for security and territorial sovereignty, but to preserve the values of the society. It was a no-brainer to our Founders and all subsequent generations that the society they created should not be diluted by those who would pose a security threat or fiscal burden. But they were also concerned about changing the orientation of the country too quickly with those who didn't share their *political* ideals of a constitutional republic built upon the values of the Declaration.

Remember, the uniqueness of America's system of government at the time, even relative to other democracies in this era, was something they wanted to preserve. They understood there is no surer way to countermand the very society they created than by making bad choices on citizenship and creating a permanent majority against the values that helped conceive the original social compact.[6]

In the early 1780s, Thomas Jefferson penned a rhetorical discussion on the population of Virginia and the colonies at large—a discussion that reveals how foreign the immigration views of the contemporary elites would be to our Founders. Writing in *Notes on the State of Virginia*, Jefferson observed the obvious desire to fill up the new country and bring in as many new people as possible, but he then rhetorically asked, "but is this founded in good policy?"[7]

While noting the advantage of filling up the sparsely populated frontiers of the inchoate nation-state, Jefferson opined that the disadvantages would far outweigh the decision:

> But are there no inconveniences to be thrown into the scale against the advantage expected from a multiplication of numbers by the importation of foreigners? It is for the happiness of those united in society to harmonize as much as possible in matters which they must of necessity transact together. Civil government being the sole object of forming societies, its administration must be conducted by common consent.

Jefferson went on to speculate about what such a society of mass, precipitous immigration would look like and how that would affect the government:

> They will bring with them the principles of the governments they leave, imbibed in their early youth; or, if able to throw them off, it will be in exchange for an unbounded licentiousness, passing, as is usual, from one extreme to another. It would be a miracle were they to stop precisely at the point of temperate liberty. These principles, with their language, they will transmit to their children. In proportion to their numbers, they will share with us the legislation. They will infuse into it their spirit, warp and bias its direction, and render it a heterogeneous, incoherent, distracted mass.

Sound familiar? There is a reason why mass migration, balkanized from a number of third world countries, has helped create a permanent Democrat majority in states like California and is threatening to do so in large swaths of the country. There's nothing wrong with immigration, when done gradually, allowing immigrants to assimilate into our values and system of government. But mass migration brings foreign values and concepts of government to America rather than inculcating the immigrants with American values.

Keep in mind Jefferson was not anti-immigrant across the board. Indeed, he opposed the Alien Act of 1798 and other more restrictive measures promoted by Alexander Hamilton's Federalists, although that was primarily due to party politics and foreign policy disagreements over the French Revolutionary Wars. Like the other Founders we will cite, he clearly felt that individuals who come here of their own volition and assimilate into our culture should be welcomed.

However, he also echoed the view of the other Founders that individual *immigrants* should be embraced, but *immigration* as a systemic institution should not be encouraged. "If they come of themselves, they are entitled to all the rights of citizenship: but I doubt the expediency of inviting them by extraordinary encouragements," wrote Jefferson in that same essay. This feeling coincides with his assertion in another essay that "a foreigner of any nation, not in open war with us, becomes naturalized by removing to the state to reside, and taking an oath of fidelity; and thereupon acquires every right of a native citizen."[8]

The rationale behind this founding view of immigration is pragmatic and rooted in common sense. Jefferson understood that he and his colleagues were crafting the greatest system of governance of all time, built upon the most moral and ordered civil society known to man. By definition, they believed every other system was at least somewhat inferior to their own. Why would they, then, desire to dilute that society with other inferior societies?

This is where the distinction between immigration and individual immigrants of merit is important. Immigration as an institution would import the values of the inferior cultures and systems of governance. On the other hand, individual immigrants of merit who craved to share in our values would be useful additions and enhancements to our society. This is why they were so ardently opposed to *encouraging* immigration but still welcomed individual immigrants.

Jefferson concluded that it would be more prudent to wait to gradually fill up the country and preserve its character and make it "durable" rather than populate the country precipitously and lose its moral fiber altogether.

Keep in mind that during colonial times, they were still initially forming their society, especially before they had a formal country. Any country, especially so large and vast, that is initially forming must bring in many immigrants to "get off the ground," so to speak. In fact, to the extent they wanted more immigrants, it was to unite as a common nation in expanded numbers to *protect* their sovereignty against the Indian raids on the frontiers. They certainly never envisioned immigration as a tool to *transform* the existing society and sovereignty from within.

Moreover, almost all of the immigrants at the time were largely homogeneous and coming from similar if not the same backgrounds and ancestry as the existing colonists. Most of the immigrants before the first large-scale wave in the 1830s were Protestants from the British Isles and northern Europe, who were entering a newly founded country with many natives from the same background who were only on the continent themselves for a few generations. Even from 1820 to 1865, when roughly 5.85 million immigrants settled in America, 95 percent hailed from the British Isles and northwest Europe. The other 5 percent were mainly from Canada and southern and eastern Europe.[9]

What would Jefferson think of taking a mature country with 320 million individuals and flooding it with endless waves of the most eclectic values and cultures, in conjunction with a fully stocked welfare state, the threat of Islamic terror and sharia, and a boundless array of anti-assimilation agitation groups—at a time when much of the existing population has turned away from founding values?

During the debate over the Naturalization Act of 1790, Rep. Theodore Sedgwick of Massachusetts warned of the effects of mass migration, even from Europe, where the prospective immigrants likely shared a similar ancestry to the existing American population. "The citizens of America preferred this country, because it is to be preferred; the like principle he wished might be held by every man who came from Europe to reside here; but there was at least some grounds to fear the contrary; their sensations, impregnated with prejudices of education, acquired under monarchical and aristocratical Governments, may deprive them of that zest for pure republicanism, which is necessary in order to taste its beneficence with that gratitude which we feel on the occasion."[10]

Notice how Sedgwick recognized how individual immigrants could easily appreciate our values and assimilate into them. Like all Founders, he wished to invite "reputable and worthy characters," but only those who were "fit for the society into which they were blended." But he was clearly concerned that, on average, when brought in on a large scale, there was "at least some grounds to fear" that they would bring the anti-republican prejudices of the countries they'd just left.

Pure common sense.

Once again, we must ask what Sedgwick would think of mass migration from the third world, including 680,000 immigrants from predominantly Muslim countries in just five years—countries that hate Jews, subjugate women, and live by an ethos—sharia law—that is antithetical to republican values?[11] Most likely, our Founders would have a lot more than "some grounds to fear" the subversion of our culture.

EARLY AMERICAN IMMIGRATION POLICY

The Founders, and most political leaders thereafter, understood that America served as the beacon and envy of the world. They understood, as any student of Economics 101 learns, that supply and demand dictate the price of a commodity. Given that the supply of new immigrants was always large relative to the size of the world and that the demand for our exceptional republic was so great, and further, that immigration and expansion of a society is an elective decision at the discretion of the existing populace, logic dictates that we would use that discretion to bring in only the best and the brightest.

That is the only conclusion at which anyone with true compassion and virtue could arrive because true compassion and virtue in immigration is looking out for the interests of the existing citizenry—those who form and uphold the compact and elect its government—before the interests of those seeking to come. This is not to cast aspersions on other cultures or countries. Provided that they are not criminals or terrorists, the fact that they are unlikely to assimilate or are likely to be a public charge doesn't make them bad people or make our civilization superior *per se* (although that is something we should believe anyway). It's just that mass importation of those individuals is inimical to the interests of those already here and when the two competing interests come into conflict, the only prudent, moral, and legitimate course of action for a democratically elected government is to err on the side of protecting its citizens. Prudence before politeness, as Gouverneur Morris put it.

As Jefferson rhetorically asked in that same essay on population, "Suppose 20 millions of republican Americans thrown all of a sudden into France, what would be the condition of that kingdom? If it would be more turbulent, less happy, less strong, we may believe that the addition of half a million of foreigners to our present numbers would produce a similar effect here."[12]

There was clearly an understanding at the time there was a new, sparsely populated country to fill up, and that before telegrams and telephones and modern transportation, most immigrants just showed up on the shore. As noted, most immigrants at this time hailed from a few countries. And that is, in part, why there were no formal federal regulations on immigration until the 1870s when western states grew concerned about large numbers of immigrants and laborers from Asia.

This notion that the lack of formal federal regulations during the first one hundred years proves the values or legal imperative of open borders is ludicrous. They always had the prerogative as a sovereign nation to regulate immigration, though they opted not to for a number of practical reasons. To begin with, before the 1830s and especially the 1845 Great Potato Famine in Ireland, there was no need to regulate immigration because there was no mass immigration and the trickle of immigrants who arrived had similar backgrounds as the natives. In 1823, toward the end of his seventh annual message to Congress, President James Monroe observed that since the country's founding, "the immigration from other countries has been inconsiderable." He seemed to consider it "extraordinary" in a positive sense that almost all of the nation's growth from 3 million to 10 million inhabitants was "almost altogether native."[13]

The early political leaders also didn't want to upset the delicate balancing act involving slavery and the Southern states because any discussion of immigration inevitably involved the slave trade. It also interfered with the tinderbox of pre–Civil War state's rights issues and representation in Congress.[14] But the Founders were clear that they had no desire to *encourage* immigration beyond those who would be "a cut above," and they clearly laid this out in the first naturalization laws when they required people to be living here in "good character."[15]

Given the geopolitical realities, transportation, and communication of the time, before the 1830s—and to a large part even until the 1870s—not *encouraging* immigration was their version of *restricting* it and ensuring that for the most part those migrants who did come here were productive individuals who yearned to join the common cause.[16]

Also, as we noted, given that this was a newly formed country, the restrictions on naturalization were viewed as the primary tool to ensure proper assimilation—with the five-year residency requirement and renunciation of any allegiance or fidelity to foreign powers.[17] Beginning in 1795, after fulfilling the requisite residency requirements, immigrants had to declare their intention to renounce their previous allegiance three years before being awarded citizenship.[18]

Even during the colonial days, the colonists were very adamant that those who would come and settle the new land be net contributors.

They strongly discouraged the landing of those who were alleged convicts, paupers, or thought to be carrying contagious diseases. When the British Parliament passed a law in 1717 sending thousands of convicts to exile in the American colonies, a number of individual colonies levied punitive taxes on ship captains transporting undesirable "immigrants." Massachusetts passed laws denying admission to those deemed a public charge or forced shipmasters to guarantee their economic security.[19]

Despite the enormous need for more labor and population in general during the colonial era, the colonies vigilantly guarded against harmful immigration and societal transformation. As the great American immigration historian Maldwyn Allen Jones concluded, "[S]ide by side with laws designed to promote and encourage immigration, there existed others whose purpose was to exclude or restrict it." What factors did the colonists consider when crafting immigration policy? Jones explained: "Religious affiliation, economic status, and moral standing were the yardsticks by which the desirability of immigrants was measured."[20] That we were always an unconditional open-door nation is clearly disproven by the laws and traditions in place even before we became a nation!

States continued to regulate the landing of undesirable migrants until Congress began restricting immigration at a national level in 1875 and 1882, and completely took over the policy of immigration inspections at ports of entry in 1891. Even after the Constitution was already signed but still in the process of being ratified, the Continental Congress passed a law in 1788, pursuant to the articles of Confederation, urging states to pass laws "preventing the transportation of convicted malefactors from foreign countries."[21] A number of states followed suit and banished those viewed as criminals or even impoverished.[22]

All of these factors combined contributed to why the Founders viewed the lack of encouraging immigration as a means of limiting it to only those who yearned to be free, independent and republican minded. It wasn't until after the Civil War, when the federal government was fully empowered to act on national sovereignty and there was a need to restrict immigration, that Congress began regulating it. Until that point, they didn't even want to *recognize* immigration as an official policy.

In a letter to an immigrant friend in 1813, then President Madison made it clear that they would always warmly welcome immigrants "who are attached to our Country by its natural and political advantages." He was emphatic about his views that mass immigration as an end to itself beyond those with particular skills was not to be encouraged. "I am obliged, at the same time, to say, *as you will doubtless learn from others*, that it is not either the provision of our laws or the practice of the Government to give any encouragement to emigrants, unless it be in cases where they may bring with them some special addition to our stock of arts or articles of culture."[23]

The context of this letter is even more revealing. The letter was written to Morris Birkbeck, an English immigrant living in the Midwest frontier at a time when the country was underpopulated and was in need of more people to defend the frontier. Birkbeck was regarded as "one of the most scientific and best practical agriculturalists of England," before he emigrated.[24] Yet, even among those of similar ancestry, Madison had no desire to categorically encourage their migration and communicated that to Birkbeck.

Imagine the expression on Madison's face were he to be informed that the government has created special taxpayer-subsidized subprime loans tailored to Hispanic immigrants who don't qualify for non-risk mortgages?[25] After all, Madison informed Birkbeck that immigrants cannot expect special land deals from his administration because "it is not in the power of the Executive to dispose of the public land in a mode different from the ordinary one."

This was the same sentiment Madison had expressed twenty-six years earlier during the Constitutional Convention when he stated a desire to invite only "foreigners of merit & republican principles among us."[26] During the debate over the Naturalization Act of 1790, Madison declared, "I do not wish that any man should acquire the privilege [citizenship], but such as would be a real addition to the wealth or strength of the United States."[27]

These views coincide with those of other Founders. In Jefferson's essay on immigration, he made exceptions for "useful artificers" against his general principle of not encouraging mass migration.[28]

In 1794, President George Washington expressed his views on immigration to his vice president, James Adams, as follows:

> My opinion, with respect to emigration, is, that except of useful mechanics, and some particular descriptions of men or professions, there is no need of encouragement; while the policy or advantage of its taking place in a body (I mean the settling of them in a body) may be much questioned; for by so doing they retain the language, habits, and principles, good or bad, which they bring with them.[29]

This was clearly a deeply held conviction for Washington. He always welcomed those who would contribute to the country and assimilate not just into the culture but into the nation's political values of the country, which he viewed as the most important element of culture. But there was always an understanding that immigration would never transform the orientation of the country. And like all the Founders, Washington was very firm about his conviction not to explicitly invite or encourage immigration. Writing in a letter to Sir John Sinclair of England, Washington was emphatic: "I have no intention to invite immigrants, even if there are no restrictive acts against it. I am opposed to it altogether."[30]

Washington obviously felt that, given the circumstances of the time, not inviting immigration had the same result as restricting it, albeit leaving the door open for those who would be net contributors and assimilate into America's novel political culture. And indeed during the first few decades of our national history, immigration was composed of a trickle of independent-minded Europeans seeking the American dream and yearning for American values.[31]

When the country was founded, George Washington always spoke of a nation of citizens united behind a common culture and a common cause in pursuit of liberty. This desire was punctuated by a series of letters Washington wrote to religious minority groups (Catholics, Jews, and some Protestant denominations), culminating with his 1790 letter to the Hebrew Congregation in Newport, Rhode Island, when he noted that all citizens of the United States "possess alike liberty of conscience and immunities of citizenship."[32] There were no second-class citizens in the eyes of our founding president.

With an ideal antithetical to the multiculturalism and balkanization of today's progressive America, Washington laid out a vision of American citizenship and pride of patriotism as follows in his farewell address:

> Citizens, by birth or choice, of a common country, that country has a right to concentrate your affections. The name of American, which belongs to you, in your national capacity, must always exalt the just pride of Patriotism, more than any appellation derived from local discriminations. With slight shades of difference, you have the same religion, manners, habits, and political principles. You have in a common cause fought and triumphed together; the Independence and Liberty you possess are the work of joint counsels, and joint efforts, of common dangers, sufferings, and successes.[33]

Notice how Washington spoke of "common cause" and presumed only "slight shades of difference" among the people—and considered that a necessary positive. It's not that he was intolerant of non-Christians or people from other backgrounds who wanted to share in American values. As witnessed by Washington's very warm letter to a Jewish synagogue, he fully accepted those of different faiths or backgrounds who wanted to unite under that common cause. He famously spoke of a government "which gives to bigotry no sanction, to persecution no assistance, requires only that they who live under its protection should demean themselves as good citizens in giving it on all occasions their effectual support."[34]

Nonetheless, he clearly envisioned that the character of the nation would not be fundamentally altered by multiculturalism and balkanization. At the end of his presidency he wrote to Patrick Henry that it was his fervent wish that America "*may be* independent of all, and under the influence of *none*. . . . In a word, I want an American character, that the powers of Europe may be convinced we act for *ourselves* and not for *others*; this in my judgment, is the only way to be respected abroad and happy at home."[35]

What would Washington think of foreign governments having standing in our own courts to sue for citizenship rights on behalf of those who violated our sovereignty and irrevocably altered the character of our nation? What would he think of courts applying international law to bring in immigrants against the consent of the people? Watching the endless scores of Middle Eastern immigrants being arrested on terror charges or Mexican immigrants cheering against the US soccer team in a Los Angeles stadium, one can only shed tears for an American character and a common cause that is lost—the very cause for which Washington's men risked their lives, fortunes, and sacred honor at Valley Forge.[36]

Alexander Hamilton also homed in on this point in 1802 when he debated Jefferson over the repeal of the Alien Laws. "The safety of a republic depends essentially on . . . a common national sentiment; a uniformity of principles and habits; the exemption of the citizens from foreign bias and prejudice; and . . . love of country."[37]

Could our Founders have ever envisioned a scenario in which we'd bring in a population that hates our country and celebrated on American soil when we were attacked on 9/11? Could they have even imagined the entitlement mentality that is bestowed on many of today's immigrants, or the sharia law from the Middle East and liberation theology from Latin America? Even speaking of European immigrants, Hamilton presciently asked, as a "general rule," "how extremely unlikely is it that they will bring with them that temperate love of liberty, so essential to real republicanism?"[38]

Of course, he recognized that "particular individuals" and "at particular times" there would be exceptions to this general suspicion.[39] But this is where numbers and origin matter in determining whether we have meritorious individuals assimilating into the American melting pot or immigration as a heterogeneous institution within the nation to undermine the common cause of ordered liberty and republicanism.

In 1819, John Quincy Adams, then secretary of state under President James Monroe, wrote a letter to a prospective German immigrant who wanted to know if he'd be granted a job upon entry into the country. What Adams told him would shock the consciousness of all modern elites who worship multiculturalism. First, he reiterated what Washington, Jefferson, and Madison said about it being the policy of the country, even in its early, sparsely populated days, not to encourage immigration. Then he affirmed his support for equal rights and welcoming of all those who chose to immigrate. But he made it very clear what is expected of those who come:

> They come to a life of independence, but to a life of labor—and, if they cannot accommodate themselves to the character, moral, political, and physical, of this country, with all its compensating balances of good and evil, the Atlantic is always open to them, to return to the land of their nativity and their fathers. To one thing they must make up their minds, or, they will be disappointed in every expectation of happiness as Americans. They must cast off the European skin, never to resume it. They must look forward to their posterity, rather than backward to their ancestors;—they must be sure that whatever their own feelings may be, those of their children will cling to the prejudices of this country, and will partake of that proud spirit, not unmingled with disdain, which you have observed is remarkable in the general character of this people, and as perhaps belonging peculiarly to those of German descent, born in this country.[40]

Adams went on to explain why they didn't encourage immigration at the time. Contrary to the thesis of the open borders crowd—that our Founders were willing to welcome anyone and everyone until the late nineteenth century—the federal government didn't regulate immigration because they didn't want to *encourage* it. They didn't want to recognize immigration as a fixed policy and phenomenon. At the same time, they respected those *individuals* who came of their own will with a pioneer spirit of rugged individualism who would assimilate into American values and cast off the European culture, something that would not have happened were they to streamline and institutionalize immigration.

These sentiments were also expressed by his father, John Adams, in a letter to John Wooddrop in 1786. Adams appears to express the bifurcated view of not encouraging immigration even before the Constitution was ratified, offering no "rewards or assistance" to immigrants, yet keeping the country open to those who will benefit the nation as a whole. "Those who love liberty, Innocence And Industry, are sure of an easy, comfortable Life, but they must go there to obtain it at their own Cost & Risque," wrote Adams.[41]

Benjamin Franklin wrote a long-winded open letter at the end of the Revolutionary War to prospective European immigrants, echoing the Founders' ideals with regard to immigration: rugged individualism, hard work, independence, and respect for America's political, religious, and cultural values. He also made it clear that the only "encouragement" of immigration at the governmental level was the very existence of "good Laws and Liberty."[42]

Most of the Founders were by no means "anti-immigrant" or discriminatory toward other Europeans. That is why they never attempted to limit immigration only to Protestants from England and Scotland. They welcomed other nationalities as well as Catholics and Jews. However, they wagered that by not encouraging immigration, the natural factors would ensure that, for the most part, the immigrants who did come would benefit society, not harm or transform it.

Most importantly, they always viewed immigration as a powerful tool that should only be turned on to benefit those already in the society and turned off when it is perceived as harming the society. This sentiment was best captured during the nascent days of the Founding by the words of leading political economist Tench Coxe. Reading his essay before a political group in the house of Benjamin Franklin on April 20, 1787, Coxe observed the benefits of filling up the empty frontier at the time while also noting the need to weigh against any deleterious effects of mass migration. "It is clear, that the present situation of America, renders it necessary to promote the influx of people; and it is equally clear, that we have a right to restrain that influx, whenever it is found likely to prove hurtful to us," wrote Coxe.[43]

At this very gathering during the founding year of our constitutional republic, Coxe observed the importance of sovereignty and the ability of the society to weigh such decisions of future immigration, perhaps the most important decision any society will make.[44] Along with the foundational value of religious liberty they earned through their victory, the new Americans had also earned the right to popular sovereignty and the ability to decide who enters their country.

* * *

How far we have drifted from our founding values as the Obama administration is moving heaven and earth to entice immigrants to become citizens, including using taxpayer funds to establish programs mollycoddling immigrants and holding their hands right up to the day of naturalization and straight into the Democrat Party voter registration rolls.[45] What's worse, the US government is now spending taxpayer funds on ads inviting in illegal aliens who were already deported. In chapter 5, we detailed how the courts are violating our sovereignty by granting nine hundred illegal aliens who allegedly lack mental competency the right to return to the United States. Our government is now running Spanish language ads in Mexico—in print, on billboards, and on radio stations—to inform them of the court decision.[46] What a departure from the late nineteenth century when our government prohibited private companies from encouraging immigration through advertisements!

OPRIMA EL DOS

The same values expressed by our Founders with regard to immigration was carried on by twentieth-century leaders. In 1919, former president Roosevelt said:

> We should insist that if the immigrant who comes here does in good faith become an American and assimilates himself to us he shall be treated on an exact equality with every one else, for it is an outrage to discriminate against any such man because of creed or birth-place or origin.

However, he made it very clear what America expected of immigrants:

> But this is predicated upon the man's becoming in very fact an American and nothing but an American. If he tries to keep segregated with men of his own origin and separated from the rest of America, then he isn't doing his part as an American. There can be no divided allegiance here. . . . We have room for but one language here, and that is the English language, for we intend to see that the crucible turns our people out as Americans, of American nationality, and not as dwellers in a polyglot boarding-house; and we have room for but one soul loyalty, and that is loyalty to the American people.

This was Roosevelt's final public message before he passed away the very next day.[47] What would he think of the new practice in which even the Republican Party now delivers a response to the annual State of the Union Address in Spanish? What would he say about the fact that as much as 20 percent of Californians are considered "Limited English Proficient"?[48] Could Roosevelt or any of our early leaders have ever envisioned presidential candidates and sitting US senators delivering major policy speeches in foreign languages? Did they intend for entire counties and school districts to be overrun by the Spanish language instead of our native English language?

There was no greater champion of true equality, not just in its strict legal sense, but in the sociological sense, than Teddy Roosevelt. He was ahead of his time in that respect. In his 1906 State of the Union Address, Roosevelt lambasted those who discriminated against legal Japanese immigrants.[49] Here is what he wrote in his 1905 State of the Union Address:

> We cannot afford to consider whether he is Catholic or Protestant, Jew or Gentile; whether he is Englishman or Irishman, Frenchman or German, Japanese, Italian, Scandinavian, Slav, or Magyar. What we should desire to find out is the individual quality of the individual man.

Roosevelt considered all citizens equal. But in choosing who would become a citizen, he was unambiguous. "The prime need is to keep out all immigrants who will not make good American citizens. The laws now existing for the exclusion of undesirable immigrants should be strengthened," he declared in the same 1905 address. He wagered that "it will be a great deal better to have fewer immigrants, but all of the right kind, than a great number of immigrants, many of whom are necessarily of the wrong kind." What was his definition of the "wrong kind"? "[A]ll violent and disorderly people, all people of bad character, the incompetent, the lazy, the vicious, the physically unfit, defective, or degenerate should be kept out. The stocks out of which American citizenship is to be built should be strong and healthy, sound in body, mind, and character."[50] Notice he made no mention of race or nationality; it was all about one's qualities.

To achieve this desired goal of admitting "the right sort" of immigrant and excluding the "wrong sort," Roosevelt called for a tightening of the laws against those who advertise and encourage immigration through commerce.[51] He also called for education and economic litmus tests as well as the "absolute exclusion" of those with "low moral tendency or of unsavory reputation."[52] Roosevelt must be happy he didn't live long enough to see the reality of 2.1 million known criminal aliens in the country.

There is perhaps no American leader whose values on immigration relate more to the time we live in than President Calvin Coolidge. Even after several decades of mass immigration in the early twentieth century, Coolidge continued to espouse the same values of our Founders—putting Americans first, welcoming all who become American who add to this country, while keeping out those who are not a net positive to this country's future. The reason Coolidge is such a good source to draw upon for policy makers seeking guidance on immigration principles is that, unlike other leaders during his time, he was not discriminatory or hostile to those with different backgrounds. Yet, he still enthusiastically signed the Johnson–Reed Act in 1924, shutting off most immigration.

Coolidge embraced people of all backgrounds. He said at the time that had the Japanese provision been sent to him in a standalone bill he would have vetoed it. But on net, he felt the immigration cooling-off was worth it.

In 1925, he delivered an enthralling tribute to American Jews at the groundbreaking of a Jewish Community Center in Washington. Coolidge noted their great civic work and the "genius of the Jewish people" and that "Hebraic mortar cemented the foundations of American democracy."[53]

As you can see from this and his opposition to punitively banning immigration from Japan simply because of their race, Coolidge embodied the true values of equality expressed in the Declaration. And he extended this to immigration policy as well. He was quite evidently not anti-immigrant, even to nonwhites or non-Christians.

At the same time, Coolidge made it clear that from a legal standpoint, there is no affirmative right for any class of people or individual to immigrate. In his 1925 State of the Union Address, Coolidge said that any ideals of compassion for immigrants must always work "in accordance with the principle that our Government owes its first duty to our own people and that no alien, inhabitant of another country, has any legal rights whatever under our Constitution and laws."[54]

While Coolidge disagreed with the discriminatory sentiments of some supporters of the immigration shutoff, he generally supported it because after so many years of new immigration, this was the only way to help both natives and immigrants adjust to American culture and not become a fiscal burden.[55]

> New arrivals should be limited to our capacity to absorb them into the ranks of good citizenship. *America must be kept American.* For this purpose it is necessary to continue a policy of restricted immigration. It would be well to make such immigration of a selective nature with

> some inspection at the source, and based either on a prior census or upon the record of naturalization. . . . Those who do not want to be partakers of the American spirit ought not to settle in America.[56]

In defense of the 1924 law, Coolidge said that while he would have loosened a few provisions, "this law in principle is necessary and sound, and destined to increase greatly the public welfare. We must maintain our own economic position, we must defend our own national integrity."[57]

Accepting the GOP nomination at the convention on August 14, 1924, Coolidge revealed his motivations behind supporting the shutoff:

> Restricted immigration is not an offensive but purely a defensive action. It is not adopted in criticism of others in the slightest degree, but solely for the purpose of protecting ourselves. We cast no aspersions on any race or creed, but we must remember that every object of our institutions of society and government will fail unless America be kept American.

In a speech before a group of immigrants several months later, Coolidge again defended the idea of reducing immigration after such a period of expansion as pro-American and pro-immigrant in every sense of the word. He then punctuated the speech with a maxim that, until recently, long guided American immigration policy: "As a nation, our first duty must be those who are already our inhabitants, whether native or immigrants."[58]

At the time of his final State of the Union Address in December 1928, he barely dedicated any space to the issue of immigration, blithely noting what was clearly a consensus at the time:

> The policy of restrictive immigration should be maintained. Authority should be granted the Secretary of Labor to give immediate preference to learned professions and experts essential to new industries. The reuniting of families should be expedited. Our immigration and naturalization laws might well be codified.[59]

The principle that immigration policy must be centered around the needs of the existing population is rooted in our existing immigration law. While Congress has full power over immigration and has clearly never delegated any discretion to the president to expand immigration unilaterally, as President Obama has attempted to do on so many occasions, existing statute grants the president complete power at will to cut off any category of immigration for any reason. Section INA § 212(f) of the Immigration and Naturalization Act (INA) unambiguously grants the president power in a time of great security concerns to immediately, swiftly, and categorically ratchet down immigration "whenever the President finds that the entry of any aliens or of any class of aliens into the United States would be detrimental to the interests of the United States."[60]

To this very day, our immigration laws reflect the maxim that the federal government's job is to protect the people first and that the elected branches of government may always reduce immigration but can never expand it without the consent of the people—through new laws passed by Congress.

After dissecting the views of our Founders and great political leaders of the past on immigration, consider the philosophy of our forty-fourth president. In an effort to actively entice eligible immigrants into becoming naturalized, Obama said we no longer require immigrants to assimilate. "It's not about changing who you are, it's about adding a new chapter to your journey . . . and to our journey as a nation of immigrants."[61] John Quincy Adams is shedding tears in heaven.

That we have deviated from these founding values by transforming the very essence of our country, ideals, government, culture, language, fiscal solvency, and security through endless and irresponsible illegal and legal immigration is bad enough. But what would appall the Founders beyond their worst imagination is that these transformations have occurred without the consent of the people. It has evolved surreptitiously by a feckless Congress that has devolved its power to unelected bureaucrats on one of the most essential enumerated powers, as we will explore in the next chapter.

7

TRANSFORMATION THROUGH IMMIGRATION: REMAKING AMERICA WITHOUT CONSENT

We reflect on no one in wanting immigrants who will be assimilated into our ways of thinking and living. Believing we can best serve the world in that way, we restrict immigration.

—CALVIN COOLIDGE

"We propose a five-word constitutional amendment: There shall be open borders."[1] As absurd and harmful as this 1984 idea from the *Wall Street Journal* sounds to ordinary Americans, they deserve points for honesty. At least they were candid about their agenda and correct in the process required to implement their utopian view. Indeed, we did need the ratification of a new constitutional amendment to uproot the foundation of our country and declare open borders. Even the open border zealots at the *Wall Street Journal* understood that you cannot disenfranchise the existing citizenry and steal their sovereignty without their consent.

Unfortunately, the unelected bureaucrats, cheered on by the courts and the insidious legal profession, have already transformed America through *de facto* open borders. And thanks to lax oversight from Congress and deceptively written statues, open borders became the policy of our country without ever so much as passing a bill, let alone amending the Constitution.

So how did this happen? Who voted for this? When did the people decide to transform their country like never before in our history?

Answer: They never did.

Even the perpetrators of this transformation never campaigned on a platform of mass immigration. Yet, over the past three decades, they permanently remade America's culture, society, and language through endless chain migration from the third world. This has strained our education system, welfare, and infrastructure with people who represent a public charge.

Thanks to loosely written statutes and feckless leaders in Congress whistling past the graveyard, the bureaucracies of the executive branch have been able to stage a silent coup against the membership of the civil society.

To fully appreciate the shocking disconnect between modern immigration policy, which was never ratified or supported by the people with a democratic mandate, and our traditional values on immigration, it's important to observe one final quote from President Coolidge:

> We have certain standards of life that we believe are best for us. We do not ask other nations to discard theirs, but we do wish to preserve ours. Standards, government and culture under our free institutions are not so much a matter of constitutions and laws as of public opinion, ways of thought and methods of life of the people. We reflect on no one in wanting immigrants who will be assimilated into our ways of thinking and living. Believing we can best serve the world in that way, we restrict immigration.[2]

These precious pearls of common sense, as noted in the last chapter, guided our Founders and all respected political leaders for most of our history. There might have been some minor disagreements over particular policies, but everyone agreed with the principle that immigration should only enhance Americanism as it existed, not alter, harm, undermine, or overwhelm it—culturally, economically, politically, or security-wise.

Coolidge's point was that we love America the way it is and we seek to preserve it, and we welcome immigrants to share America's greatness. But increased levels of immigration could irrevocably transform the America we know and love. As president, Coolidge succeeded in preserving this America for both natives and newly arrived immigrants.

That has all changed, and without consent of the governed.

THE GREATEST SOCIETAL TRANSFORMATION OF ALL TIME

Bureaucrats both expanded upon legitimate loopholes in statutes and violated the spirit of the laws passed by Congress to engender this change. Few Americans or members of Congress would have voted for bills, such as the 1965 immigration act or the 1980 refugee act, had they known they would prompt a transformative and irrevocable remaking of America.

These numbers show the sheer magnitude of the second great wave of immigration:

- We take in 20 percent of all international migrants, even though the United States comprises just 4 percent of the global population.[3]
- Aside from the millions of illegal immigrants, the United States admitted 25.3 million legal immigrants over the twenty-five-year period from 1989 to 2013. During a comparable twenty-five-year period at the height of the Great Wave, from 1900 to 1924, only 16.8 million green cards were issued.[4] In total, almost 59 million immigrants have come to America since passage of the 1965 bill.[5]

- As of 2015, there were 45 million immigrants in this country, more than at any other time in history.[6] The immigrant population is expected to rise to over 58.2 million by 2022.[7]

- As of 2015, 13.5 percent of the US population was foreign born, more than at any other time since the peak of the great wave. We will soon surpass that level of foreign born and by 2060 we are projected to have 78.8 million immigrants in the country, representing 18.8 percent of the population.[8] When combined with children of immigrants, immigrant families already represent 26 percent of the population and will rise to 36 percent of the population in 2065.[9]

- The foreign-born population of a number of states has already surpassed 18 percent of the state's population, with California topping 27 percent.[10] Some of these states could possibly become *majority* foreign-born by 2060.

- In our tradition as a melting pot, we've never balkanized our country by tilting our immigration system tendentiously toward one region as much as we've done with Mexico and Latin America over the past few decades. Fifty percent of all immigrants since 1965 have come from Latin America—29 percent from Mexico alone.[11]

- More people have come from Mexico than from any other country in our modern history. Over the past forty-four years, 6.65 million people have emigrated from Mexico legally (not including the 6 million or so illegal immigrants) compared to 4.5 million who emigrated from Italy—the previous record-breaking country of origin—from 1880 to 1929.[12]

- The Hispanic share of the American population grew from just 3.5 percent in 1960 and 8.8 percent in 1990 to 17.6 percent in 2015, topping out at 567 million in raw numbers.[13] According to the census, by 2060 that number will reach 28.6 percent of the population—a total of 119 million. Among those under age eighteen, Hispanics will then account for 33 percent of youth. That is one out of every three individuals.[14]

- Hispanics already comprise 38 percent of California's population and are expected to become an absolute majority between 2050 and 2060.[15]

- From 2000 to 2013, seventy-eight counties in nineteen states, from California to Kansas and North Carolina, became majority-minority.[16]

- A record 63.2 million, or one in five US residents, speak a language other than English at home.[17] In six states that number exceeds 30 percent and is as high as 44 percent in the state of California.[18] Thirty-four of the major metropolitan areas in the country have a third or more of its residents who speak foreign languages at home; sixty-seven metropolitan areas top 25 percent population of foreign language speakers.[19]

- Thirty-seven million residents speak Spanish at home, and there are 708 counties where more than 10 percent of the population speaks Spanish at home. That is almost one in four counties. There are now more Spanish speakers in America than in Spain.[20]

- In 17 states Latino children account for over 20 percent of the kindergarten enrollment in public schools.[21] California governor Jerry Brown claims that 30 percent of schoolchildren in his state are either "undocumented or don't speak English."[22]

- Almost half of California driver's licenses went to illegal immigrants in 2015.[23]

- In one Wichita, Kansas school district, 81 languages are spoken as a result of the massive influx of immigrants and refugees.[24] In south Seattle schools, 167 languages are spoken.[25]

We are a welcoming and pluralistic society, but when did the American people decide to radically transform our country in a way that has never occurred in our nation's history? And these figures, for the most part, are predominantly due to *legal* immigration. Illegal immigration is merely the gravy on top. As such, what could possibly possess the political elites to call for an even larger increase in legal immigration and legalization of illegal immigrants?

These are obviously rhetorical questions. Nobody has voted for these policies, and few Americans would have ever supported these ideas. Not surprisingly, according to a recent Gallup poll, only 7 percent of respondents feel we need to increase our overall level of immigration.[26]

In fact, the transformative "Kennedy" immigration bill passed in 1965 and the subsequent act in 1976 were sold to the American people as pathways to stable and gradual immigration.[27] Sadly, what they really did was put the keys to our immigration system in the hands of the bureaucrats, and through the inevitability of chain migration, into the hands of the immigrants themselves. These harmful policies have been placed on autopilot—taken out of the hands of the citizenry and their elected representatives. Members of Congress turned a blind eye to this growing phenomenon beginning in the '80s and declined to reassert control over the process ever since.

If Calvin Coolidge and the overwhelming majority of the American people felt that America was changing too rapidly and was in need of an immigration cool-off period in the 1920s, what would they say now? Even the most ardent champions of the largely successful great wave would be appalled by what has happened this past generation. Consider these differences:

1. As noted previously, the first great wave, although larger than the immigration of our early history, was much smaller in sheer numbers than the existing wave.
2. Even though the great wave immigrants were diverse and divergent in culture from many of the original Americans, they were almost

all from Europe. The great wave never fundamentally changed the orientation of America. The racial composition of the country was almost identical in 1924 to where it was in 1980. Contrast that to this great wave, where most of the immigrants came from vastly different cultures, with half of the immigrants coming from Latin America and Mexico. Instead of a melting pot, this wave has created a dynamic where one immigrant group is so dominant that it has permanently supplanted the existing culture in large swaths of the country. Just to use the measure of racial composition (by no means the only or most important measure), the white share of the population went from 81 percent in 1980 to 62.2 percent in 2014, and is projected to dip to 43.6 percent by 2060 under the current trajectory.[28] Whites are already a minority among those under the age of five.[29] In a number of counties, whites have become the minority, and in California whites have long been the minority, while Hispanics are a plurality and headed toward majority status.

3. There were no ethnic and counter-assimilation agitation groups that fought against Americanization.[30] The prevailing pressure on immigrants was to become as American as possible. That dynamic has been completely flipped during this great wave

4. There was no formal welfare state during the first great wave, and as we've seen, they were extremely careful not to admit those who would be a public charge. Now we have a formal welfare state, and the largely low-skilled immigrants that have dominated our immigration system have flooded the welfare system.

5. Around the turn of the twentieth century, we were still a relatively young and underpopulated country in need of people to fill up the vast frontiers. We are now a fully mature country and thus we do not need the mass numbers of immigrants.

6. Modern communications, culminating with the advent of the Internet, has made it much harder for recent immigrants to make a clean break from their countries of origin. This is especially true of immigrants from the Middle East, who are radicalized by anti-American Islamic propaganda on the Internet and through satellite TV.[31]

7. During the great wave, the courts humbly understood their non-existent role in immigration policy: none at all Nowadays, there is a voracious immigrant legal defense movement with enough resources to bankrupt any state and locality seeking to control immigration.[32]

Finally, there is one overarching factor that distinguishes the great wave of immigration from Coolidge's time. After bringing in so many new immigrants at the beginning of the twentieth century, the government decided to almost completely shut off immigration. What few elites bother to tell you is that this is a predominant factor in the success of the great wave.

While most in hindsight would say we should have permitted more refugees escaping Hitler's reign of terror in the '30s, that doesn't countermand the main point that, in general, it was time to shut off broad-based immigration. We could have easily made an exception for the Jews of Europe in subsequent legislation without undermining the spirit of the 1924 legislation. The cool-off period gave those immigrants time to assimilate and become absorbed into American society without endless subsequent waves that would undermine the melting pot dynamic.

Instead of talking about a cooling-off period, the elites are demanding that we double or even triple legal immigration while granting green cards to all of the illegal immigrants, thereby enabling them to bring in millions more through chain migration.[33] And yet, according to the census data, the full magnitude of the current wave has not even crested.[34] In fact, under current law and the present trajectory, immigration is going to explode through 2060—all without the open borders lobby passing any new legislation. Thus the public has not consented to this societal transformation.

JEFFERSON'S WORST NIGHTMARE COME TRUE

Most potently, in our departure from traditional immigration policy, this mass wave has irrevocably changed the political values of our country. The current wave of immigration has resulted in a torrent of new citizens beyond anything seen even during the greatest periods of immigration expansion. Although several years during the first two decades of the twentieth century approached the level of current annual *immigration admissions* in raw numbers, the resulting *naturalizations* from the earlier wave were but a fraction of the current rate of naturalization.

Let's explore the numbers.

In 2013, almost 770,000 immigrants became US citizens, a level of naturalization that has persisted almost every year over the past two decades.[35] From 1996 to 2013, over 12.6 million new immigrants became citizens. Contrast that to the period of the great wave and the ensuing years, when only roughly 50,000–250,000 immigrants were naturalized per year. The highest rate of naturalizations during the pre-'65 immigration regime appears to have occurred from 1928 to 1945 (a lagging effect of the great wave). During that eighteen-year period, approximately 3.8 million immigrants were naturalized, a little more than one-fourth of the naturalization that has occurred over the past eighteen years.[36]

In other words, while the immigration wave of the modern era thus far was 66 percent larger than the great wave, the "naturalization wave" was 329 percent greater.[37]

Not only was the wave of naturalizations resulting from the first great wave much smaller, but it coincided with the "shutoff" on new immigration. The '30s and '40s, when the highest numbers of great wave immigrants were becoming voting members of society, was the nadir in our immigration levels. As noted immigration historian

Maldwyn Allen Jones observed, "With reinforcements no longer arriving from across the ocean, ties with Europe were gradually weakened and memories of the old life grew dimmer with each passing year." This dynamic "accelerated the Americanization of those groups which had come earlier."[38]

Although immigration spiked between 1880 and 1920, the shutoff created a dynamic in which, on net, the foreign born population in the country went down so that by 1970—ninety years after the beginning of the great wave—the immigration population had only increased 44 percent in raw numbers. Over that same time period, the native-born population increased by 306 percent.[39]

Contrast this to the current wave of naturalization, which is already three times larger than the peak wave in the '40s, and it is coinciding with an even larger wave of *new* immigrants coming to reinforce the new citizens, anchoring them back to their old culture and values. By 2060, ninety years after that benchmark in 1970, the immigrant population is projected to be 715 percent larger in raw numbers. Over the same period the native-born population is projected to increase by just 77 percent.[40]

And unlike during the great wave, when most immigrants came from Europe, today's immigrants come from countries in Asia, Africa, and Latin America, countries that have political values very different from the constitutional republicanism we seek to preserve.[41]

PERSONS NATURALIZED BY REGION AND COUNTRY OF BIRTH: FISCAL YEARS 2011 TO 2013

(Countries ranked by 2013 persons naturalized)

	2013		2012		2011	
COUNTRY	**Number**	**Percent**	**Number**	**Percent**	**Number**	**Percent**
Total	779,929	100.0	757,434	100.0	694,193	100.0
Mexico	99,385	12.7	102,181	13.5	94,783	13.7
India	49,897	6.4	42,928	5.7	45,985	6.6

Philippines	43,489	5.6	44,958	5.9	42,520	6.1
Dominican Republic	39,590	5.1	33,351	4.4	20,508	3.0
China	35,387	4.5	31,868	4.2	32,864	4.7
Cuba	30,482	3.9	31,244	4.1	21,071	3.0
Vietnam	24,277	3.1	23,490	3.1	20,922	3.0
Haiti	23,480	3.0	19,114	2.5	14,191	2.0
Colombia	22,196	2.8	23,972	3.2	22,693	3.3
El Salvador	18,401	2.4	16,685	2.2	13,834	2.0
Jamaica	16,442	2.1	15,531	2.1	14,591	2.1
Korea, South	15,786	2.0	13,790	1.8	12,664	1.8
Pakistan	12,948	1.7	11,150	1.5	10,655	1.5
Peru	11,782	1.5	11,814	1.6	10,266	1.5
Iran	11,623	1.5	9,627	1.3	9,286	1.3
Bangladesh	9,571	1.2	8,417	1.1	7,325	1.1
Brazil	9,565	1.2	9,884	1.3	10,251	1.5
Nigeria	9,545	1.2	9,322	1.2	9,344	1.3
Guatemala	9,530	1.2	8,797	1.2	7,285	1.0
Ecuador	9,470	1.2	8,783	1.2	6,929	1.0
All other countries	277,083	35.5	280,528	37.0	266,226	38.4

Figure rounds to 0.0; Source: U.S. Department of Homeland Security, N-400 naturalization data for persons aged 18 and over, Fiscal Years 2011 to 2013.

Perhaps the most glaring contrast between this great wave and the early wave of immigration is the difference in character of the America to which they were emigrating. During the first half of the twentieth century, America had a very strong culture and an unflinching sense of patriotism and Americanism permeating every facet of society. Nobody expressed this dichotomy better than Ronald Reagan toward the end of his farewell address in 1989:

> Those of us who are over 35 or so years of age grew up in a different America. We were taught, very directly, what it means to be an American. And we absorbed, almost in the air, a love of country and

> an appreciation of its institutions. If you didn't get these things from your family you got them from the neighborhood, from the father down the street who fought in Korea or the family who lost someone at Anzio. Or you could get a sense of patriotism from school. And if all else failed you could get a sense of patriotism from the popular culture. The movies celebrated democratic values and implicitly reinforced the idea that America was special. TV was like that, too, through the mid-sixties.[42]

This America was the country that absorbed the immigrants of the great wave. The cultural pressure to assimilate and Americanize was too impervious for any ethnically motivated subversion and counterculture to successfully dilute the character of the country in a negative way.

Contrast that to the American culture to which the modern wave of immigrants has emigrated, and you get a sense of why this wave has permanently transformed this country. As far back as 1989, when the counter-culture to Americanism and patriotism was far less potent than it is today, Reagan was already ominously warning the public: "But now, we're about to enter the nineties, and some things have changed. Younger parents aren't sure that an unambivalent appreciation of America is the right thing to teach modern children. And as for those who create the popular culture, well-grounded patriotism is no longer the style."[43]

Remember, as we noted in chapter 6, even when immigration was relatively "open" in our early years, policy makers carefully guarded citizenship and the right to vote as the second line of defense against radical societal transformation. Now the number of immigrants receiving voting rights is growing at such a rapid rate that we've actualized Jefferson's worst nightmare of flooding the country with millions of new voters who "will bring with them the principles of the governments they leave."[44]

And what are these principles? In 2010, when Obamacare was passed, 69 percent of immigrants supported the government takeover of health care. Just 18 percent of Asian immigrants disapproved of Obamacare.

Seventy percent of Asian immigrants consider themselves environmentalists, compared with 41 percent of the general population.[45] The majority of immigrants support affirmative action, including 63 percent of Hispanic and 64 percent of Asian immigrants.[46] Seventy-five percent of Hispanic immigrants prefer a "bigger government providing more services," compared to 41 percent of the general population.[47]

Even with regard to bedrock patriotism and sovereignty, ideals embraced by most American voters across the spectrum, the current wave of immigrants do not share the sense of American pride as they have in the past. According to a 2013 Harris Interactive Survey, only 50 percent of naturalized citizens think "schools should teach children to be proud Americans," compared to 81 percent of native-born. Just 37 percent of naturalized citizens think "the U.S. Constitution is a higher authority than international law," compared to 67 percent of natives who believe in sovereignty. And whereas 85 percent of Americans consider themselves as US citizens rather than "citizens of the world," just 54 percent of naturalized citizens even appreciate this foundational sentiment.[48]

Americans have long welcomed immigrants who embrace our values and American exceptionalism. But as Bobby Jindal recently observed, "immigration without assimilation is an invasion."[49] Thus, what we have today is an invasion spawned by the political elites.

Our initial immigration laws, passed in 1790, made all naturalized citizens swear off prior allegiances and pledge allegiance to the Constitution. What has become of that ideal? Clearly, the sheer record number of immigrants, reinforced in wave after wave from the third world over such a short period of time, have served as an insuperable countervailing pressure against patriotic assimilation.

Yet, despite the increasing number of naturalized citizens, the immigration wave has been so deep and expansive that there are still about 8.8 million legal permanent residents who are eligible for naturalization but have not yet exercised their privilege. Thirty-one percent of them are from Mexico alone, a country steeped in antirepublican views.[50]

COUNTRY OF BIRTH OF LEGAL PERMANENT RESIDENT POPULATION: 2012

	LegaL Permanent Residents		Legal Permanent Residents Eligible to Naturalize	
COUNTRY OF BIRTH	NUMBER	PERCENT	NUMBER	PERCENT
Total	13,300,000	100.0	8,770,000	100.0
Mexico	3,330,000	25.1	2,690,000	30.6
China	640,000	4.8	280,000	3.2
Philippines	590,000	4.4	340,000	3.8
India	540,000	4.1	240,000	2.7
Dominican Republic	490,000	3.7	310,000	3.5
Cuba	420,000	3.2	300,000	3.4
Vietnam	340,000	2.5	200,000	2.3
El Salvador	330,000	2.5	260,000	2.9
Canada	320,000	2.4	260,000	3.0
United Kingdom	290,000	2.2	240,000	2.7
Korea, South	290,000	2.2	180,000	2.0
Haiti	260,000	1.9	160,000	1.8
Jamaica	240,000	1.8	160,000	1.8
Colombia	240,000	1.8	140,000	1.6
Guatemala	190,000	1.5	130,000	1.5
Germany	180,000	1.4	150,000	1.7
Poland	150,000	1.1	110,000	1.3
Peru	140,000	1.1	80,000	0.9
Pakistan	140,000	1.1	60,000	0.7
Japan	140,000	1.0	110,000	1.3
Other	4,030,000	30.3	2,370,000	20.7

Note: Detail may not sum to totals because of rounding. Source: U.S. Department of Homeland Security.

No wonder Democrats are pulling out all the stops to get them to become citizens. Keep in mind that if Democrats would successfully naturalize these 8.8 million citizens, they would have the ability to bring in millions more relatives through chain migration and further multiply the Democratic advantage.

In a country deeply polarized by the two-party system, millions of new voters from the third world can easily create a permanent Democratic majority. According to a 2012 survey conducted by YouGov, current immigrants favor Democrats over Republicans by almost four to one.[51]

For many Democrats, this is mission accomplished. And it dates back to their patient and dogged pursuit of this permanent transformation in 1965.

* * *

The source of our modern-day "immigration system" can be traced back to the Immigration and Nationality Act of 1965, also known as the Hart-Celler Act, most notoriously associated with the strong support of Ted Kennedy. Yet nothing in the bill should have led to mass waves of immigration. Had members of that Congress known how unelected bureaucrats and outside NGOs representing foreign interests would use the legislation to disenfranchise the citizenry, it likely would have failed to garner a single vote.

At the time, the Immigration and Nationality Act of 1965 was actually not a big deal.[52] It was sold as a minor tweak to the immigration system, and Phil Hart (D-MI), one of the sponsors, promised that it would only foster a slight increase in overall numbers. Given the past few decades of low immigration and the successful assimilation of the great wave, the bill did not garner much controversy relative to other civil rights–era legislation. The primary purpose of the bill, according to its sponsors, was family reunification and creating a skills-based category for employment-centered immigration. Not a bad proposition given the low foreign-born population of the time.

The "Kennedy" bill passed the House 320 to 69 and the Senate by a vote of 76 to 18.[53] Most of the small minority of opposition votes actually came from Democrats.[54] During a Senate Judiciary Committee hearing on the bill on Feb. 10, 1965, Kennedy himself upheld the longstanding principles expressed by all political leaders since our founding and promised the public that the bill would not do what in reality it wound up doing. "The bill will not flood our cities with immigrants. It will not upset the ethnic mix of our society. It will not relax the standards of admission. It will not cause American workers to lose their jobs," he bellowed.

Kennedy sounded like the best of the so-called restrictionists from the previous century:

First, our cities will not be flooded with a million immigrants annually. Under the proposed bill, the present level of immigration remains substantially the same . . . Secondly, the ethnic mix of this country will not be upset . . . Contrary to the charges in some quarters, S.500 will not inundate America with immigrants from any one country or area, or the most populated and economically deprived nations of Africa and Asia. In the final analysis, the ethnic pattern of immigration under the proposed measure is not expected to change as sharply as the critics seem to think. Thirdly, the bill will not permit the entry of subversive persons, criminals, illiterates, or those with contagious disease or serious mental illness. As I noted a moment ago, no immigrant visa will be issued to a person who is likely to become a public charge.[55]

In terms of changing the orientation of the country, Attorney General Nicholas Katzenbach predicted the bill would induce a net increase of only about sixty thousand immigrants per year.[56]

Despite abolishing the country-of-origin quotas, Secretary of State Dean Rusk promised that the bill would not spawn a wave of low-skilled immigration because the job opportunities, in his estimation, required more skill.[57]

In reality, the 1965 bill brought in 59 million immigrants, dwarfing the 14.3 million of the first wave, which began in the 1840s, and 18.2 million during the great wave from 1890-1919.[58] As for not creating public charges, just consider that in 1970, 18 percent of immigrants were living below the poverty line. At present, 28 percent of immigrants are living in poverty. The poverty rate among natives, on the other hand, has held steady between 13 and 15 percent.[59] Thus we see that immigrants before the post-1970 wave of immigration were only slightly more impoverished than the native population. This was all changed by the 1965 act, which led to a system that prioritized immigrants from third-world countries over Europe and Canada.

While there are individuals who are likely to be public charges from all regions of the world, origin matters when it comes to admitting mass numbers of immigrants.[60] In 1910, 89 percent of immigrants were from Europe; today that number is just 10 percent. As of 2013, the median family income for immigrant families from Europe was $66,600, roughly twice the income of those from Mexico ($31,100), the Caribbean ($31,100), Africa ($34,800), and central/South America ($37,400).[61] This, despite the fact that most of the recent job growth has gone to the immigrant population.[62]

As leading immigration historian Aristide Zolberg has observed, as early as the dawn of the Reagan era, people began to realize that the 1965 law engendered a transformation that dwarfed that of the great wave of the turn of the century. And it was that transformation, which pales in comparison to the wholesale makeover of America that has occurred since the '80s, that conflicted with the very essence of what the people's representative supported in 1965. "Whether hailed or deplored, there is no gainsaying that this development was contrary to the tacit agreement to maintain immigration as a minor feature of American existence that underlay the 1965 reform," wrote Zolberg in *A Nation by Design*.[63]

Fifty years later it is truly breathtaking to behold just how consequentially this bill has remade America—in direct contravention to every last promise of the bill's supporters.

In response to the growing concern over the influx of low-skilled immigrants during the late '80s, in conjunction with the absorption of the illegal aliens amnestied from the 1986 bill, Congress worked on immigration again in 1990. And once again, the bill was advertised as a means of shifting our immigration priorities to those with high skills and opening doors to western European immigrants who had been disadvantaged for decades.[64] Ultimately, it disenfranchised the citizenry once again by expanding the overall caps and increasing the number of family-based "chain migration" visas, which in turn, spawned a reinforcement and augmentation of the original wave created under the 1965 Act.[65]

In addition, the 1990 bill created fifty-five thousand more visas to be chosen from a lottery. As we will discuss in chapter 8, this was another program sold to the American people as a means of bringing in European immigrants but wound up serving as an additional tool for low-skilled, culturally divergent immigrants, largely from the third world.

When advocating passage of the '65 bill, Attorney General Katzenbach brazenly declared, "If I were to illustrate this point on a chart and compare sixty thousand with our internal growth of nearly three million each year, it would be nearly invisible."[66] Well, fifty years later, we can now look at our own charts and conclude that our internal growth is nearly invisible compared to the influx of immigrants.

THE PRICE WE HAVE PAID

Not only have the 1965 and 1990 laws, in conjunction with endless illegal immigration, completely transformed the character and values of this nation, but they have brought in low-skilled immigrants who have become a public charge and an endless wave of violent criminals.

Consider the following crime statistics:[67]

- Illegal aliens account for 13.6 percent of all offenders sentenced for crimes committed in the United States, even though they only represent 3.5 percent of the population.
- Illegals account for 12 percent of murder sentences, 20 percent of kidnapping sentences, and 16 percent of drug-trafficking sentences.
- There are 2.1 million illegal and legal immigrants convicted of crimes, but 1.2 million criminal aliens remain at large in the United States and have not been deported.

- Nine hundred thousand legal and illegal immigrants are arrested every year, and 700,000 are released from prison into the public without being deported.

- From 2008 to 2014, legal and illegal immigrants committed 611,234 crimes, including nearly 3,000 homicides, in the state of Texas.

What's worse, the numbers are likely much higher, because the federal government refuses to track and categorize crimes, convictions, and sentencing by nativity or legal status the way they do with other demographics.

This is a vivid illustration of how unelected judges, who have mandated release of criminal aliens, and bleeding-heart bureaucrats, who have brought in security risks, have granted ad hoc rights to the rest of the world at the expense of Americans' safety. The rampant flow of immigrants who have committed violent crimes against Americans has infringed on the fundamental rights of life, liberty, and property, as well as popular sovereignty for the American citizen.

Now let's examine the fiscal cost of our immigration regime:

- According to census data, 93.7 percent of immigrant families with four children are on welfare.[68] Overall, 87 percent of illegal immigrant families and 72 percent of legal immigrant families are on welfare.[69]

- More than 90 percent of recent refugees from the Middle East are on food stamps.[70]

- Roughly 28 percent of immigrant families from Guatemala and Honduras are in poverty.[71]

- In 2013, hospitals located in the Rio Grande Valley reported $131 million in uncollected medical bills due to the influx of illegal aliens flooding the hospitals to give birth to babies on American soil.[72] This is just one example of the crushing burden on hospitals in the Southwest.

- After working so hard as a country to eradicate infectious diseases, we are now suffering from intermittent recurrences of enterovirus, TB, and whooping cough due to illegal immigration and the lack of enforcement of health standards for immigrants.[73]

This is not the "infinitesimal price" we were told we would pay for the "advancement and advantage" of the 1965 immigration bill, as promised by Katzenbach.[74] This is an astronomical cost none of those members of Congress could have conceived of in their worst nightmares.

Examining the breathtaking numbers of impoverished and criminal immigrants we admit—and in the case of criminal aliens refuse to deport—one could only imagine the reaction of James Blaine, secretary of state for President Chester Arthur, were he alive today. Writing to a diplomat in Switzerland in December 1881, Blaine expressed the following commonsense principle on immigration held by every great American leader—from our Founders until fairly recently: "While, under the Constitution and the laws, this country is open to the honest and the industrious immigrant, it has no room outside of its prisons or almshouses for depraved and incorrigible criminals or hopelessly dependent paupers who may have become a pest or burden, or both, to their own country."[75]

Not only did the people's representatives never vote for mass immigration of low-skilled immigrants, but the laws on the books dictate the contrary. Section 212(a)(4) of the Immigration and Nationality Act (INA) states that any prospective immigrant that is "likely at any time to become a public charge is inadmissible." This section of the INA directs immigration officials to factor in an applicant's "age, health, family status, assets, resources, financial status, education and skills" when determining whether an immigrant would likely be a public charge.

Therefore, it's not the laws that have changed since the immigration laws of the 1880s and naturalization laws of the 1790s; it's the unelected bureaucrats who have refused to enforce those laws, thereby disenfranchising the people. According to Sen. Jeff Sessions (R-AL), just 9,700 applications out of more than 116 million—a mere .00008 percent of immigration applications—were disqualified "on the public charge basis between FY 2005 and FY 2011."[76] In fact, on the federal Welcome to USA website, there is an entire page dedicated to advertising a selection of welfare benefits to newly arrived immigrants.[77]

One particular program, the Cuban Adjustment Act, has been abused so much that thousands of Cuban immigrants can come to Florida without legal status and immediately apply for welfare. According to an exposé by the Florida *Sun-Sentinel*, a number of these welfare recipients collect their benefits only to return home to Cuba! They discovered that "het sense of entitlement is so ingrained that Cubans routinely complained to their local congressman about the challenge of accessing U.S. aid—from Cuba."[78]

Isn't it interesting how the political class is wont to say that a court decision is "the law of the land" even when it countermands long-standing law passed by the legislative branches of government, yet when unelected bureaucrats violate the most foundational public charge laws, nobody is there to remind them of the "law of the land"?

As we all know, the rest is history.

NO COMPARISON

Are we being too critical of the current immigration regime? Immigration advocates believe apprehension over immigration is reminiscent of the sentiments expressed about Irish immigrants in the 1840s and eastern and southern Europeans around the turn of the century. Yet, despite those concerns, didn't those immigrants enrich our society? How can we be so certain that this time is different?

In 2001, Michael Barone, then an advocate for more liberal immigration policies, expressed just such a sentiment. He predicted that Hispanics would become assimilated and economically successful like the Italians and eastern European immigrants of a century ago. However, in 2014, he recanted that prediction, noting that the rationale for most immigration from Mexico, coupled with the new policies of special privileged minority status, have worked against his previously held assumption. The welfare state, the ethnic grievance industry, affirmative action, and a change in attitude at the elite level regarding assimilation, has rendered any comparison to previous waves of immigration moot.[79]

Moreover, as noted earlier, that immigration wave was followed by a cooling-off period, which aided assimilation. They were also naturally closer in cultural habits to existing native Americans than the current wave of immigrants. After this greater wave of immigration, not only are we declining to support a slowdown, but the numbers are actually rising beyond 1 million new immigrants per year. According to census data, 5.2 million immigrants arrived from 2010 to July 2014 alone, more than any other period in American history.[80] Just from July 2014 to July 2015, the immigration population increased a whopping 1.7 million.[81]

According to the Pew Research Center, as of 2010, Mexicans were the largest immigrant group in thirty-three states, with immigrants from other Latin American countries winning first place in six other states. At the height of the first great wave in 1910, on the other hand, Germans held the distinction of the most represented immigrant group in just seventeen states.[82] Moreover, German culture was much closer to our native culture at the founding. In fact, they already represented 8 percent of the population during colonial times.[83] Anyone who tells you we've gone through such a transformation earlier in our history clearly is not schooled in history or is not in touch with existing reality.

THE FUNDAMENTAL TRANSFORMATION OF AMERICA

What is perhaps most alarming and disenfranchising is that the largest percentage increase in is from predominantly Muslim countries. At a time when Islam is going through tremendous upheaval and the Muslims living in western countries are being radicalized by the successful global cyber-Jihad effort from groups such as the Islamic State, the Muslim population in America has increased by over 680,000 in just five years.[84] There has been a 93 percent increase in immigration from Saudi Arabia. The next countries on the list of those with the sharpest increase in immigrants sent to this country are Bangladesh, Iraq, Egypt, and Pakistan.[85]

While a number of Muslim immigrants will undoubtedly live peacefully in America, how many truly love America and seek to join this common cause and embrace our founding republican values? I'm sure there are some, but consider some recent polling data from the Center for Security Policy. The survey found that 51 percent of Muslims in America believe "Muslims in America should have the choice of being governed according to sharia." Twenty-nine percent agree that violence against those who insult Muhammad is acceptable, and 25 percent agree that violence against America can be justified as part of global jihad. Among males under the age of forty-five, that number rises to 36 percent. Twenty-nine percent of males under forty-five also believe that violence against America is justified to make Sharia the law of the land.[86] With an estimated 3 million Muslims in this country (projected to triple by 2050), that could mean there are at least hundreds of thousands of radicalized ones.[87]

In addition to bringing in large numbers of Islamic immigrants, we have admitted millions of foreign students from the Middle East in recent years. It's no coincidence that college campuses have become replicas of Europe—a breeding ground for anti-Semitism and pro-Palestinian activism.[88] During the 2014–15 academic year we admitted roughly 158,000 foreign students from predominantly Muslim countries, nearly 975,000 in total from around the globe. The majority of them are male and all of them are young—the most volatile and potentially dangerous demographic in the Middle East.[89] Not only does this present us with an existential security threat; it further dilutes American culture with radical views from these countries.

Instead of our higher institutions of learning being oriented toward patriotism and appreciation for American culture and republicanism, as our Founders envisioned and Reagan longed for, they have become international classrooms hostile to our values. As Professor Wilfred McClay recently bemoaned, "Instead of teaching my students how to intelligently appropriate the knowledge and traditions and historical memories of America, I found it necessary to teach as if those traditions were to be regarded neutrally, a view from nowhere carrying no inherent weight."[90]

Shouldn't the citizens of this country have some sort of input into these transformational and likely suicidal policies?

According to a 2015 Ipsos poll, 58 percent of Americans identify with the following sentiment: "more and more I don't identify with what America has become." Even 45 percent of self-identified Democrats agreed with this disconsolately nostalgic sentiment.[91] Undoubtedly, this is a clear reflection of the damage incurred by a rapid societal transformation carried out without popular consent.

The fundamental transformation of America is particularly pronounced in small to midsize cities. While some of our large cities, such as New York, Los Angeles, and Chicago, have long been populated by large contingents of immigrants, this new great wave has significantly altered the character of smaller cities. Nashville, Tennessee, best embodies this new reality. A whopping 30 percent of the city's public school children do not speak English as their first language. Spanish is by far the most common language among the foreign-born school children, but Arabic and Somali are numbers two and four respectively, indicating that the rapidly growing Muslim immigration is creeping into many corners of the heartland.[92] This is a contrast to the most generous years of the great wave when we strove to keep out those who would represent a public charge, health concern, security risk, or harm the general character of the country?

Consider how, after five decades of unprecedented third-world immigration, our society has been fundamentally transformed in a radically different way from the first great wave of immigration. In 1921 there was unanimity of opinion among both the general public and politicians that there was an urgent need to curtail immigration in order to buy time needed to pass legislation to restructure our immigration system, as did happen in 1924, when the House unanimously passed a bill curtailing immigration across the board. There was no recorded vote! The bill passed the Senate 78-1.[93] Expressing the universal view at the time, the accompanying report from the House Committee on Immigration and Naturalization stated, "There is a limit to our power of assimilation."[94]

One could argue that by the early '90s we had already surpassed the size, scope, and cultural transformation of the equivalent period of the first great wave. At the time, even liberals like Harry Reid warned that we had never seen anything like this before and introduced a bill to "restore immigration to its traditional and more manageable level of about 300,000 annually."[95]

Fast-forward twenty-three years, and we've admitted roughly 23 million more legal immigrants, countless millions of illegal immigrants, and have established a trajectory through chain migration that will bring in even more immigrants, dwarfing the current unprecedented wave. Under current trajectory, by 2065, 88 percent of our population growth will be from immigrants.[96] Yet, instead of unanimous resolve to immediate slow down immigration, those of us who even question *increases* in current immigration are called nativists. There is almost not a single elected Republican who would vouch for the position of liberal Harry Reid from 1993, even though the rationale for his policy is even more compelling two decades later. Political correctness is killing this country, and the people have been disenfranchised from making the decisions about the future membership of their own society. If decisions over future immigration policy are not given back to the people, the societal, fiscal, and security harms to this country will be irrevocable and the unelected bureaucrats will continue to foster lawless policies that double down on existing failed policies rather than pursuing prudent immigration policies that help assimilate the current wave of immigrants.

We will now explore those specific immigration policies that are most harmful to our sovereignty and how we can re-empower the citizenry to make future decisions on immigration.

8

DILUTING AMERICAN CITIZENSHIP AND DISENFRANCHISING AMERICANS

In a republic the sovereignty resides essentially, and entirely in the people. Those only who compose the people, and partake of this sovereignty are citizens, they alone can elect, and are capable of being elected to public offices, and of course they alone can exercise authority within the community: they possess an unqualified right to the enjoyment of property and personal immunity, they are bound to adhere to it in peace, to defend it in war, and to postpone the interests of all other countries to the affection which they ought to bear for their own.

—WILLIAM RAWLE 1829

One can fill copious pages writing proposals to solve our illegal immigration problem and restore our immigration system to the intent of our Founders. Indeed, in my regular columns at *Conservative Review*, I've proposed a number of solutions to the problem.

However, in this chapter I'd like to focus on the most systemic and consequential examples of how our sovereignty has been stolen by the political elites and how the citizenry has been disenfranchised. Further, we will explore what can be done to re-empower the people so that the debate over the future of immigration is done through their elected representatives.

Sovereignty can be defined as "freedom from external control."[1] As we've explained, the foundational principle of a nation-state and the social compact of republican governance is that the citizens have the right to self-government and can only be governed by the consent of their membership. Yet, the most important decisions of our future society—namely, our elections, representation, the makeup of our communities, and population growth—are not free from "external control" at all; they are irrevocably influenced and even determined by external control, particularly by the federal courts' officious use of international laws and "universal values." Five practices related to immigration undermine our sovereignty and threaten to permanently dilute our culture and ability to self-govern: They are: chain migration, refugee resettlement, birthright citizenship, counting illegal aliens in the census and reapportionment, and non-citizens voting in our elections.

Unlike other aspects of immigration, if these policies are not overturned, we will no longer have any semblance of representative republicanism, sovereignty of a nation-state, or the ability to win elections as conservatives. Let's examine these practices individually.

CHAIN MIGRATION

There is probably no aspect of our immigration system that is more pernicious than chain migration. It tilts our immigration system toward family ties and empowers immigrants to bring in an unlimited number of relatives. It also disenfranchises the citizenry from deciding who will join the society and, instead, places the future decision making of immigration—the most consequential societal decision—in the hands of the immigrants.

As noted in the last chapter, backers of the 1965 immigration bill promised that annual immigration levels wouldn't rise above several hundred thousand and that we would not be flooded with a million immigrants a year. So how is it that we now have one million new immigrants per year, with recent census data suggesting an even larger increase?

In one of the more consequential, yet surreptitious acts of disenfranchisement, the 1965 act established family-based ties as a new category of immigration, which over time has completely undermined the ideal of an immigration model based on skill. Under our policies of chain migration, a single immigrant could potentially be responsible for an automatic chain of 273 immigrants, irrespective of their qualifications—or worse—their likelihood to be criminals or security risks.[2]

Under our existing system, only about 15 percent of green cards issued per year are awarded to individuals based on some measure of skills. The lion's share of the remaining green cards—roughly 65 percent are granted to those with family ties to existing immigrants, with the remainder going to refugees, asylees, and the absurd diversity visa lottery.[3] Put another way, 85 percent of the 10.8 million green cards issued over the past 10 years were allocated toward admission categories that have nothing to do with skills, not that all is well with our employment-based visas.[4]

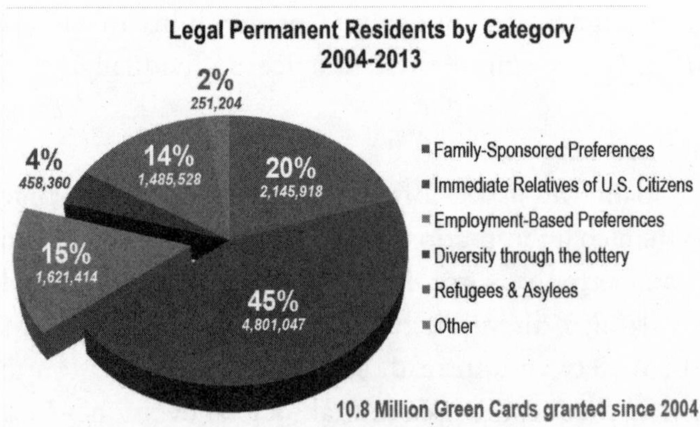

Source: Department of Homeland Security Yearbook of Immigration Statistics

By prioritizing family members of existing immigrants, many of whom are low skilled, we have departed from our long-standing tradition of only admitting those who will be a net fiscal benefit to the country. In 2013, 471,041 of the 990,000 green cards issued went to those who were categorized as "no occupation" or "not working outside the home."[5]

Chain migration essentially says, "if you like your broken immigration system, you can keep it." Everything that is undesirable about the existing system—the plethora of low-skilled, impoverished, criminal elements, and Sharia-law adherents—is on autopilot and is compounded by chain migration. The people have no ability to evaluate future immigrants based on merit because 85 percent of the record-high immigration is predetermined by the existing and new immigrants themselves. Given that this past wave of immigration has resulted in the growth of the indigent and criminal and even terrorist elements, chain migration will merely produce more of the same result and compound the problem.

Chain migration also sits at the nexus of the birthright citizenship and refugee problems we will discuss momentarily. If an illegal alien has a baby on American soil, that child, erroneously recognized as an American citizen, can bring in an unlimited number of family members when he grows up. In the case of refugees, picture all of the problems we are having from the Somali community in Minneapolis.[6] Many of those individuals can now bring in more family members from Somalia.

Over the next fifty years, the United States is projected to admit an unprecedented 100 million immigrants.[7] Chain migration will likely bring in mainly impoverished immigrants from the Third World as well as criminal elements. And worse, we will continue to import millions of immigrants from the Middle East whose fervent adherence to Sharia Law will prevent them from Americanizing, placing our nation at grave risk.

From 2000 to 2009, almost all of the extended family categories of immigrants, accounting for roughly two million green cards, originated from Latin America, Asia, and Africa.[8] Looking ahead, almost all of the 4.2 million prospective immigrants already in the "visa queue" for family-preference green cards are from these same countries, with 31 percent slated for Mexican nationals alone. The Muslim countries of Bangladesh and Pakistan rank among the top countries in the pipeline.[9]

* * *

America must end chain migration. That is the single most effective systemic policy change our government can make. Everyone agrees we should keep nuclear families intact, but by winding down the extended family categories of immigration, we will reduce immigration by about two hundred thousand admissions each year. Over time, this will have a reverse chain effect, allowing us to prioritize those who will truly benefit this country's existing citizenry across the board.

In 2015, Rep. Jody Hice (R-GA) introduced a bill to abolish the chain migration category, yet Republicans have refused to allow it through the committee process.[10] The next GOP president must champion similar legislation. In one fell swoop, this single policy change would mend the current broken immigration system and serve as the first step toward realigning our immigration policy with the priorities of the citizenry.

In addition to abolishing extended family preferences, we must also end automatic preferences for foreign parents of adult US citizens, which is a standing subcategory within the "immediate relatives" category. This is one of the fastest-growing categories, increasing from 67,000 in 2000 to 120,000 in 2013.[11]

Even open-borders fanatic Jeb Bush, at least while running for president in the GOP primary, voiced his support for this idea, saying "We need to narrow the number of people coming here through family petitioning…I would cut it down to spouse and minor children."[12]

Finally, Congress must abolish the Diversity Immigrant Visa Lottery. Nothing is more antithetical to our principle of immigration by consent than the practice of awarding fifty thousand visas per year based on nothing more than a random lottery. The lottery was instituted as part of the 1990 immigration bill and was designed to foster more immigration from countries that don't typically send large numbers of immigrants to this country.[13]

But far from fostering more diversity, the lottery, like every other facet of our immigration system, has been shifted toward third world countries. During the early years of the lottery, European countries were the predominant beneficiaries of the lottery system, especially given the fact that we take so few immigrants from most of Europe.[14] In fact, like every other immigration proposal, this one was sold as a way of attracting more immigrants from Europe.[15] But in recent years, the primary recipients of diversity visas are from Africa and the Middle East, including Islamic countries, such as Iran, Egypt, Bangladesh, Uzbekistan, and Turkey. Over 77 percent of the diversity visas over the past decade have come from Africa and Asia.[16] It is estimated that more than half of visa lottery recipients are from countries with a predominant Muslim population.[17]

When combined with chain migration, the diversity visa lottery seeds America with many more immigrants who are likely to become a public charge and who are unlikely to assimilate, while creating an automatic chain for multiplying their numbers in the future. The nation's best interests are left out of the equation. This bill would never have passed had its true consequences been communicated to Congress.

Taken as a whole, by abolishing primarily low-skilled extended family preferences, the parent category, and the diversity visa lottery, Congress can eliminate approximately four hundred thousand green cards per year. This will decrease the rate of immigration by 40 percent in the first year of enactment and have a multiplying effect in the future with the elimination of chain migration. While there are many other reform ideas, taking this first step will re-empower the citizens. The time has long passed for citizens through their elected representatives to keep immigration on a short leash under sharp scrutiny to ensure that it works for the benefit of the citizenry as a whole and is not controlled by the special interests and the immigrants themselves.

REFUGEE RESETTLEMENT

America has long served as a beacon of freedom for millions of people who have come as refugees since World War II to escape tyranny and seek the American dream. In the past, refugees from Europe, the former Soviet Union, and Southeast Asia—just to name a few—have contributed to our culture and economy. But in recent years, the refugee resettlement program has ostensibly become a Muslim resettlement program that has engendered a massive transformation of society in terms of culture, public charge, and security risks. Once again, this represents one of the most profound manifestations of social transformation without representation. Thanks to statutes that were written broadly enough to cede power away from the elected branch—the United Nations, State Department bureaucrats, and nine private contracting organizations have the keys to our civil society in their hands. They have the power to colonize parts of this country with poor, predominantly fervent Muslims from Africa and the Middle East. Nowhere in this process do the local jurisdictions that are forced to resettle the refugees have any say in the process.

Consider the following:

- Since FY 2004, we've admitted roughly 728,900 refugees, approximately 472,000 since FY 2009 alone.[18] And that doesn't include a number of other categories of immigration that are similar to refugees.

- The United States admitted 73 percent of the world's refugees in 2014.[19]

- America has admitted 128,000 refugees from Iraq alone since FY 2007. We've taken in over 130,000 refugees from Somalia since 1993.[20]

- *74.2 percent of all refugees in 2013 were receiving food stamps*—up from 50 percent in 2008. Fifty-six percent received some sort of medical assistance. Among refugees from the Middle East, 91.3 percent received food stamps and 73.1 percent received Medicaid.[21]

- According to the State Department, Arabic is the most common language spoken by refugees, and that has been the case for over a decade. Somali, spoken almost exclusively by Muslim refugees, is the third most widely spoken language of all refugees. *Since FY 2008, 105,000 refugees have been native Arabic speakers and 44,000 have been native Somali speakers.*[22]

- In recent years, most of the refugees have come from Somalia, Iraq, Burma, and Bhutan. We are likely to see a flood of refugees from Syria.[23] And in the ultimate violation of sovereignty, those refugees are being selected by the UN.[24]

- Twenty to forty thousand immigrants come in each year on asylum status. Additionally, Cuba and Haiti have their own special status, but all of them have the same benefits as refugees.[25]

- Small, homogenous states are being transformed by refugee resettlement. North Dakota was forced to resettle the most refugees per capita of any state in 2014. Most of them are from Bhutan, Iraq, Somalia, and Congo—countries with radically divergent cultures from local residents.[26]

- The number of refugees deported for committing violent crimes has increased from just 9 individuals in 2003 to 185 in 2013. This, despite a recalcitrant administration that wants to leave no refugee behind. In total, 1,033 refugees have been deported over the past decade, for crimes including murder, rape, and assaults.[27]

By now you might be asking the same question we've posed throughout this book: who the hell voted for this? Who voted for this societal transformation? The answer is nobody voted for it. Congress abdicated its power long ago and has empowered the unelected branches of government, as well as international and private organizations, to change our destiny.

In 1980, Congress passed the Refugee Act, which established the modern refugee system. The caps were raised from 17,400 annually to

50,000, but other legal immigration caps were reduced by 20,000.[28] At the time, the public was promised that this act would not flood the country with impoverished immigrants and that the newly created Office of Refugee Resettlement (ORR) within the Department of Health and Human Services (HHS) would be tasked with resettling them to ensure they can stand on their own two feet.[29] The program was sold as a way to reign in the president's abuse of parole, streamline our patchwork system and encourage self-sufficiency.[30] It passed the Senate unanimously on September 6, 1979 and the House by 328-47 on December 20 of that year. Jimmy Carter signed it into law on March 17, 1980.[31]

Nobody envisioned that this would become a tool to transform America and bring in indigent immigrants from the third world, an endless flow of Muslim immigration, and a torrent of security risks. Most of the refugee needs at the time were directed towards the Vietnamese and the Soviet Jews. Refugees used to come from a few select countries from which it made sense to take refugees and from which we already had many family members living here, such as Cuba and the former Soviet Union. In recent years the State Department has worked with the UN, pressured and guided by private refugee activist groups, to focus on resettlement of people from the third world nations that are predominantly Muslim.[32] With this political mission in mind, the executive agencies have used the broad authority irresponsibly granted to them by Congress to disenfranchise the voters from fulfilling the original intent of the program.

Ted Kennedy explained how the final version of the bill really gave the president the authority to raise the caps without congressional input even as it was sold as being in the hands of Congress. "The conferees agreed on a normal flow of 50,000 a year until 1983; thereafter, the limitation would be decided by Congress," wrote Kennedy in a law review article. "The limit can be increased by the President after consultations with Congress, prior to the beginning of the fiscal year. In an emergency situation, the President may admit additional refugees after appropriate consultations with Congress."[33] Notice the sleight of hand? Congress has the power to merely consult with the president, but ultimately the president can do what he wants. Initially, Congress took the annual consultations, usually occurring each September before the next fiscal year, very seriously. They conducted hearings and spelled out the refugee needs and concerns. Now it has become nothing more than State Department officials briefing the House and Senate Judiciary Committees on how many refugees they will take in—with no recourse from Congress to say no. That is how we've gotten more than seventy thousand refugees a year, often from parts of the world the American people would never agree to admit. There is no accountability whatsoever.

In some respect, refugee resettlement is a more destructive form of social transformation for local communities than any other form of immigration. Unlike other categories of immigration, refugees by definition do not go through the organic process of becoming immigrants. They are brought over and resettled, often in large numbers concentrated in specific localities, with no acclimation to American culture or the ability to support themselves. Despite the plethora of resettlement assistance programs run by the State Department, HHS's Office of Refugee Resettlement, and taxpayer-funded NGOs, most refugees wind up on the full array of welfare programs. Most important, they strain the public services and public education of the local jurisdictions that are forced to accept them. Whereas much of the social transformation has been triggered by unelected courts and bureaucrats, refugee resettlement represents coerced transformation at the hands of private government contractors. As far back as 2000, David M. Robinson, a former acting director of the refugee bureau in the State Department, described the insidious power of the contractors as follows:

> The agencies form a single body [that] wields enormous influence over the Administration's refugee admissions policy. It lobbies the hill effectively to increase the number of refugees admitted for permanent resettlement each year and at the same time provides overseas processing for admissions under contract to the State Department. In

> fact, the federal government provides about ninety percent of its collective budget. If there is a conflict of interest, it is never mentioned.
>
> [Its] solution to every refugee crisis is simplistic and the same: increase the number of admissions to the United States without regard to budgets or competing foreign policy considerations.[34]

The private resettlement agencies are the reason our refugee policies seem to be either random or at odds with our national interests. Why do we bring in so many Muslim refugees who are not persecuted religious minorities but are simply caught in the crossfire of Islamic civil wars? Why have we admitted so many individuals from Burma and Bhutan when there is no national outcry or even an awareness of why these countries should be our top priority? Why would we allow so many individuals from countries with such dramatically different social, cultural, and political values and burden our states with the socioeconomic costs?

These questions are especially salient given that it costs twelve times more to resettle refugees in America than in areas closer to their country of origin.[35] Isn't it more humanitarian to save fifteen times as many individuals while keeping them in countries closer to, say, Burma, Bhutan, and Somalia, until the problems subside? If the goal was to protect Americans and America's national interests, and, engage in true humanitarian work, then the answer would be clear. However, given that the policies are all set by the private refugee resettlement agencies, which see their taxpayer-subsidized salaries and revenue grow commensurate to the number of refugees admitted to the United States their goals will always be to bring in as many refugees as possible—no matter the cost, security risk, the underlying need, or the prudence of settling them here rather than in their regions.

Federal and international bureaucrats, along with private contractors looking to self-perpetuate their business venture, can forcibly alter the culture, language, fiscal solvency, education, crime, and security concerns of a local society without the locals having any say in the matter. The state of Texas has been inundated with more refugees than any other state over the past few years.[36] When did the people of Texas ever vote for this?

Remember, the power over immigration was transferred from the states to the federal government precisely to prevent a state from transforming other states through endless immigration, not to allow the federal government to punitively saddle a state with public charges, culture changes, and security risks. The states would have never adopted the Constitution had they been subjected to this treatment.

A number of small to midsize cities, located in predominantly rural and Christian counties, are being colonized with large numbers of refugees from radically divergent backgrounds. According to recent census data, while the larger states, such as California, New York, Florida, and Texas, absorb the most immigrants in raw numbers, the sharpest increase in percentage since 2010 have come from smaller, more homogenous states: North Dakota, Wyoming, Montana, Kentucky, and New Hampshire. North Dakota's immigrant population has increased by 45 percent, more than any other state.[37] Minnesota's foreign-born population has risen from 2.6 percent in 1990 to 7.4 percent in 2013 thanks, in large part, to the influx of forty thousand Somalis.[38] There are eighty-four thousand immigrants from Central America residing in Minnesota, and one in every six children is now born to immigrant parents.[39] When did the people of Minnesota ever vote for such an acerbic alteration over such a short period of time?

Not only have the people never voted for this; in fact, the 1980 Refugee Act explicitly requires the Office of Refugee Resettlement to "insure that a refugee is not initially placed or resettled in an area highly impacted by the presence of refugees or comparable populations unless the refugee has a spouse, parent, sibling, son, or daughter residing in that area." They are supposed to take into account the population, job, education, and housing opportunities, the likelihood of the refugee becoming a public charge, and "the secondary migration of refugees to and from the area that is likely to occur."[40]

Immigration laws are always written in accordance with popular sentiment, but they are immediately countermanded by unelected bureaucrats refusing to uphold the letter and spirit of the law. The policies governing refugee resettlement have deviated so far from the original intent of Congress that in 2014 Obama even relaxed regulations to allow admission of those who gave "limited" material support to terrorists.[41] Forget about public charge and health concerns; we are now letting in terrorists through our front door.

THREE STEPS TO RE-EMPOWERMENT

Three immediate actions can be taken to re-empower the people, local communities, and Congress to rein in the dangerous and costly refugee program.

First, Congress must immediately suspend the program while they play catch-up from the years of complacency and engage in proper oversight to study the details and effects of refugee resettlement. They should pass a bill placing a moratorium on all new admission of refugees until the Government Accountability Office (GAO) conducts a full audit of the fiscal, social, and national security effects of the program. Rep. Brian Babin (R-TX) has proposed a similar bill in the 114th Congress, and that would be a great place to start.[42]

Next, once Congress reinstates the refugee program, the authority for that law should expire at the end of every fiscal year or every other fiscal year. This will force Congress to start from scratch every year and reevaluate which refugees are truly persecuted and which ones we want to exclude. It will contribute to the fabric of this country by stripping the power from the executive branch to dictate the terms of refugee policy set without Congressional input. The default position under this proposal—in the event Congress fails to act—is that no refugees are resettled that year. Every decision to admit major categories of refugees would be placed under the strict scrutiny of the public, with a dramatic vote in Congress before signing off on something as important as importing more refugees from the Middle East.

Finally, it's time to give local communities a say in the orientation of their civil society. As part of any refugee reform legislation, the county governments must be granted authority by Congress to approve or disapprove of resettlement of more than ten refugees in their jurisdiction at a given time. Congress should require the federal government to conduct a public hearing in the county tagged with resettlement and be represented by an official from the Office of Refugee Resettlement and the Department of Homeland Security, along with a representative of the relevant private contracting agency. The government officials would be required to brief the public on the background of the refugees, their likelihood to become a burden on the local education system and community services, and their geopolitical situation.

Most important, this legislation would then require that the county government approve the resettlement in a formal vote. If the county government declines to approve the resettlement, the federal government would be prohibited from continuing the process and would be forced to look elsewhere.[43]

This plan will restore the essence of the social compact and representative government. Allowing local citizens to weigh in through a majority vote in their closely represented county council will place the keys to the community in the hands of the existing residents. Americans are a very giving and accepting people. If a majority of the citizens view the refugees as an asset, they will embrace them. If they have concerns about their security or fiscal charge, they will have recourse to reject them.

I'm not proposing this idea for every sphere of immigration, but as noted, refugee resettlement is unique in that it is an unnatural and momentous shift in the demographics of a community. As such, it must be decided *by* the community.

Unquestionably, the city of Boston would have never agreed to resettle the Tsarnaev family and their two sons, who bombed the Boston Marathon, had they known of their volatile background. The residents of Franklin County, Ohio, were probably never told they'd be saddled with almost two thousand predominantly Hindu Bhutanese who are straining their mental health services with an astronomical suicide rate.[44] The fine citizens of Minneapolis and its suburbs were never consulted before thousands of Somalis were seeded in their communities, with dozens of them becoming terrorists or security risks.

Under existing law, to qualify for refugee status an applicant must demonstrate a "credible fear" of persecution in their home country. Isn't it time the politicians listen to the credible fear of Americans who have become strangers in their *own* country and victims of terror and a great fiscal strain?

BIRTHRIGHT CITIZENSHIP

As noted in chapter 4, the courts didn't mandate birthright citizenship, but they will likely get in our way if we seek to overturn current policy. The reason 350,000 to 400,000 children of foreign infiltrators are granted automatic citizenship is the result of the other prong of stolen sovereignty—the executive bureaucrats—acting lawlessly because of lax congressional oversight.[45]

The federal government has never deliberately decided to grant children born to illegal aliens automatic citizenship. No national discussion occurred to apply the *Wong* case to illegal aliens, as indicated in the footnote of the *Plyler* case. And as we proved conclusively, nobody ever thought to actively grant such a right because it would have contradicted our immigration laws.

It likely evolved from sheer laziness and practicality. Given that all children born to legal immigrants were granted birthright citizenship before the influx of illegal aliens—either as a matter of practice or resulting from the 1898 court decision—the relevant agencies never bothered to enforce verification and give the hospitals forms that required one parent to show their Social Security card. It was easier to grant anyone born in an American hospital citizenship, especially because illegal immigration en masse did not occur until the mid-twentieth century.

It was only after the problem became so pervasive and conservatives began calling attention to it in the early '90s that liberals retroactively created a convoluted legal rationale based on the Brennan footnote and the obscure *Wong* case to defeat popular and commonsense efforts to end the practice.

The negligence is so bad that they are automatically granting citizenship even to children born to foreign diplomats. Even the champions of the birthright citizenship cause concede that, under English Common Law, "subject to the jurisdiction thereof" necessarily excludes this category. In extensive research, Jon Feere of the Center for Immigration Studies found that the lack of enforcement on the part of the Social Security Administration, the US Citizenship and Immigration Services, the State Department, and several other agencies has allowed all children of foreign diplomats to become *de facto* citizens, with birth certificates and Social Security cards.[46]

While the issuance of a birth certificate and Social Security card doesn't necessarily make someone a citizen, it has the effect of granting him *de facto* citizenship until the agencies clamp down on this practice. This is an especially perverse outcome since foreign diplomats and their families are granted diplomatic immunity from prosecution of many laws. By illegally granting them citizenship, they are not only becoming equal with the rest of the civil society, against the consent of the citizenry; they are becoming super-citizens—enjoying the rights of American citizens but maintaining the extra protection reserved for diplomats.

Fixing the birthright citizenship scam does not require a constitutional amendment; it doesn't even require a change in statute. There is no statute granting citizenship to children born to illegal aliens, tourists, or foreign diplomats. Section 301 of the Immigration and Nationality Act merely copies the language of the Fourteenth Amendments' citizenship clause. Once we (correctly) assert that the citizenship clause extends—at most—to children born to at least one legal permanent resident—this change can be implemented administratively.

Obviously, for a variety of political, legal, and practical reasons, it is better for Congress to write a statue defining citizenship and establishing a process mandating the relevant agencies to require parents of children born here to show proof of permanent legal residence in the country before they are issued a birth certificate and Social Security card. Numerous bills have been written since the early '90s to correct this issue, not the least of which was crafted by Harry Reid in 1993.[47] During this past session, Rep. Steve King introduced a bill in the House, and Sen. David Vitter has a similar bill in the Senate, fixing the scam once and for all.[48]

Eight percent of all children born in 2013 had at least one illegal-alien parent. Either we remain a sovereign nation or our destiny will be controlled by foreign countries.[49] America is still the envy of the world; therefore an unlimited number of people would love to come here. According to Pew, 35 percent of Mexicans—or 39 million people—want to emigrate to the United States.[50] Gallup found that 138 million people worldwide would like to emigrate to the United States.[51] If we continue to grant citizenship to those who come here illegally, allowing them to secure welfare and de facto permanent resident status on behalf of their American-born children, no amount of border security will overcome the enticement to come here and overstay a temporary visa. At that point we will no longer function as a sovereign nation.

DUAL CITIZEN AND DOUBLE VOTING

There is another complex and deleterious angle to the birthright debate: dual citizenship. Most illegal aliens are from Mexico and Central America. These countries grant citizenship to children born to their nationals abroad, with liberal residency requirements. So these anchor babies are also citizens of their countries of origin. To a certain extent, this is a problem with legal immigration as well. There is no way of knowing how many dual citizens are in this country, but there are well over a million, and with the growing explosion of immigration from countries that encourage dual citizenship, we are likely to see this number grow.[52]

While there has been a long-standing debate over the prudence and legality of dual citizenship, there is one aspect to this dynamic that must be addressed: dual citizens who vote in foreign elections. This is both illegal and contrary to our founding values. Under current law, all immigrants who become naturalized citizens must take an oath to "absolutely and entirely renounce and abjure all allegiance and fidelity to any" foreign power.[53] That has been our tradition since our founding immigration law in 1790. Even if one can justify the practice of dual citizenship, to actively vote in a foreign election is an incontrovertible violation of this solemn oath.

Most dual citizens (those who are naturalized and not natural-born citizens) are probably unaware of this restriction because our government has failed to preserve our sovereignty and enforce the oath. But it's time to clamp down on this odious practice. In 1967, the Supreme Court struck down a law that stripped citizenship of those naturalized citizens who voted in foreign elections.[54] However, there is nothing stopping Congress from criminalizing the behavior and enforcing it with a stiff fine, while actively discouraging and warning against "double voting."

Those who extol the virtues of mass migration often lecture us about the need to reach out to those who yearn to become Americans. Well, this is a simple test. Anyone who truly wants to become an American and abide by the oath of citizenship should have no problem surrendering their right to vote in foreign elections.

There is nothing of greater importance to the American people than the preservation of American citizenship. If the people don't reclaim control over citizenship and instead allow the courts and the political elites to concoct a birthright for anyone in the world to claim for their children at will, the sovereignty of the American people and the birthright of American citizens will be forever lost.

ILLEGAL ALIENS COUNTED IN CENSUS

Not only do illegal aliens disenfranchise the citizenry by giving birth to American-born children and erroneously obtaining citizenship; their very presence in the country allows them to be counted in the census, thereby artificially inflating the representation of certain states and congressional districts.

Counting illegal aliens in the census is a double-whammy. Not only has the default position of counting illegals in the census been decided without citizens' consent; it further disenfranchises the people by diluting their representation—all without consent through representation.

On net, most illegal immigrants cluster in states and districts that heavily tilt Democratic electorally. By counting them in the census, Democratic districts are able to inflate their numbers, and liberal states are afforded a larger share of the reapportionment pie that is divided into 435 congressional districts. According to an analysis conducted by American University scholar Leonard Steinhorn, counting illegals in the census gives California an extra five seats in the House, with New York and Washington cashing in on one extra seat apiece.[55] While solid-Republican Texas gains an extra two seats and GOP-leaning Florida picks up one extra seat, it's very likely that, due to the geographical distribution of the illegal-immigrant population in those states, Democrats benefit from those seats as well. This theoretically gives Democrats a seven-seat advantage.

Even more disconcerting, the artificially inflated number of House seats on net in blue states could tilt the presidential election to Democrats as well. Republicans are already at a disadvantage and are facing an increasingly narrow path to victory, thanks in large part to the broader immigration problems discussed in the past few chapters. According to an analysis by *Politico* in 2015, illegals could very plausibly deny Republicans the 270-vote majority they need in the Electoral College to win the presidency by giving Democrats a net gain of four extra electors.[56] Four electoral votes might not sound like a lot, but it will very likely require Republicans to win an entire additional state in order to win back the White House—at a time when the demographic time bomb forces them to walk a tightrope in achieving the magic number of 270.

Imagine the thought of losing an entire election and the future of our country because of the mere presence of illegal immigrants, in addition to their children who will begin voting in large numbers in the coming years? Our Founders would not have countenanced this violation of the social compact, emphasized in the preamble of the Declaration of Independence which made consent at the heart of governance an inalienable right.

As noted in chapter 6, the Founders wanted the federal government to control naturalization instead of the states. They wanted to ensure that individual states wouldn't give themselves an extra advantage through importing innumerable migrants in order to inflate their numbers and saddle the rest of the union with "an influx of foreigners, hostile to its institutions, ignorant of its powers, and incapable of a due estimate of its privileges."

Now, thanks to the refusal of the federal government to protect the citizenry from the distorted representation engendered by illegals counted in the census, individual states like California are incentivized to pursue sanctuary-city policies and thwart federal immigration law to bolster their numbers and inflate their share of congressional representation and the Electoral College. It is no surprise that roughly half of all illegal immigrants reside in five metropolitan areas—all of which are sanctuary cities: New York City–Newark, Los Angeles, Chicago, Miami, and San Francisco–Oakland.[57]

Could anyone possibly conjure up a governing model more antithetical to the vision of our Founders? Federal lawlessness in refusing to take illegals out of the census encourages states to thwart federal immigration law, thereby disenfranchising the residents of other states—undermining the very reason immigration decisions were placed in the hands of the federal government in the first place. Hence, the sovereignty of the individual citizen, the state, and the nation-state is undermined.

So how *did* we get here?

Once again, much like the development of automatic citizenship for illegal aliens, counting illegals in the census evolved from bureaucratic laziness and was possibly politically motivated. And once again, liberals are trying to maintain the status quo. But instead of vouching for and defending their views through the political process, they have retroactively enshrined this act of disenfranchisement as a constitutional right, pursuant to—you guessed it—the Fourteenth Amendment.

Proponents of counting illegal aliens in the census point to the fact that many agree, based on the context and debate of section 2 of the

Fourteenth Amendment, that immigrants were intended to be included in the census.[58] Continuing with the logic they use to justify birthright citizenship, they contend that because there were no illegal aliens at the time, by default, the Fourteenth Amendment covered anyone present in the country.

It is specious to compare illegal aliens to legal immigrants. We have already thoroughly debunked the notion that once Congress exercised its broad power to regulate immigration, people can be considered present in the country when violating the consent of the people. They are not considered to be present in the country, and as such, are certainly not entitled to be counted in the census for purposes of congressional representation.

But what is particularly jarring about this argument is that it flies in the face of the entire intent of section 2. This part of the Fourteenth Amendment was designed to incentivize southern states to treat freed slaves as full *citizens* and allow them to vote. The reason they chose the term "whole persons" was to repeal the original apportionment clause, which only counted blacks as three-fifths of a person.[59] Northern politicians feared that granting blacks full representation in the census would empower the southern states with stronger representation in Congress so they could further disempower black voters. To prevent these states from pocketing the benefits of civil rights—namely, counting blacks as part of their population while denying them the right to vote—section 2 conditioned their inclusion in the census to the Southern states allowing blacks to vote.[60]

Accordingly, the entire purpose of the Fourteenth Amendment was to prevent southern states from disenfranchising newly minted black *citizens*. The Framers certainly never envisioned this being used as a tool to disenfranchise the entire citizenry—black and white—at the hands of illegal invaders.

Moreover, although it is clear the Framers intended to include noncitizen immigrants in the census, the scope of section 2 was not designed to be *more* expansive than the citizenship clause of section 1, which applied only to those present "and subject to the jurisdiction thereof." Once again, even proponents of the status quo must agree that the counting of all persons was not intended to apply unconditionally to *anyone* present no matter the circumstances. Judge Timothy Farrar, a New Hampshire judge and law partner of Sen. Daniel Webster in the mid-nineteenth century, in perhaps the earliest treatise written on the definition of the Fourteenth Amendment, described the scope of those to be counted as follows: "The whole number of persons in each State cannot mean everybody on the soil at the particular time, nor exclude everybody who may happen not to be on it at the same time."[61]

Obviously section 2 was never intended to include those in the country, even American citizens who resided in another state, who happened to be temporarily passing through a state during the time of the census. Conversely, it wasn't intended to exclude those permanent residents or citizens temporarily sojourning or vacationing in another country or state. Much like the citizenship clause, the apportionment clause was not designed as an Amelia Bedelia–literal phrase without qualification. It was meant to include domiciled permanent residents who had complete allegiance to the United States and lived here indefinitely with the intention and legal ability to seek citizenship.

As with birthright citizenship, there will always be some ambiguity as to which immigrants would meet the criteria, but as Farrar wrote in his treatise on the Constitution, those parameters were given to Congress to define with more specificity. Farrar wrote with certitude, "and of course [the scope of persons counted in the census] should be authoritatively construed by the law-making power."[62]

No rational person can intellectually honestly assert that millions of illegal aliens, almost all of whom are citizens of foreign countries with allegiance to foreign powers, in this country in violation of our laws and the consent of the people are included in the Fourteenth Amendment. In 1867, the very year the Amendment was sent to the states, Farrar wrote that "certainly persons who are at the time actual citizens of other states in the union cannot be included [in the census]; and, for *much stronger reasons*, persons who are citizens of *foreign* states cannot."[63]

For executive officials to count them in the census and count towards representation is a dereliction of one of the most sacred duties of the federal government—to secure governance by the consent of the governed.

In reality, it is proponents of counting illegal aliens in the census who are violating the Fourteenth and Fifteenth Amendments' broader guarantee of equal protection and fair representation. In *Gray v. Sanders* (1963) the Supreme Court established the concept of "one person, one vote," requiring states to weigh each vote equally and not dilute the impact of some voters with unfair representation in weighting elections.[64] A year later, in *Reynolds v. Sims*, the Court defined the objective of the one person, one vote mandate as requiring "substantial equality of population among the various districts, so that the vote of any citizen is approximately equal in weight to that of any other citizen in the State."[65]

There is no greater example of diluting and disenfranchising American voters than by granting large urban areas, which tend to have more illegal aliens, greater representation in Congress, and states with more illegal aliens greater representation in presidential elections.

There is also another perverse effect of this policy. Areas with higher numbers of nonvoting residents empower the citizen-voters of that district with more representation because their vote is more potent and impactful than their citizen-counterparts in more rural districts that have fewer noncitizens, and therefore, more voters. For example, although California's congressional districts all comprise the same number of "residents," the First District in the rural north has approximately 521,000 eligible voters while the LA County–based Fortieth District has only 261,000 eligible voters, the fewest in the entire nation. This means that votes cast in the Fortieth are twice as impactful as those in the First—all because the LA area has so many immigrants that only 42.9 percent of the district is eligible to vote. All this flies in the face of what the Founders envisioned.

In fact, the entire reason why the Founders vested the naturalization power (which confers voting rights upon an immigrant) in the hands of the federal government, in the words of Justice Story, was so that the Union would not be "endangered by an influx of foreigners, hostile to its institutions, ignorant of its powers, and incapable of a due estimate of its privileges." Now, states such as California, Nevada, Texas, and Florida have become magnets for boundless immigration that not only disenfranchises the rural voters in these states; it debases the representation of other states entirely in the Electoral College and with representation in the House of Representatives.

This is yet another example of how the Left uses an extreme interpretation of the Fourteenth Amendment to violate the very preamble of our Declaration of Independence, which bases our system of governance on popular sovereignty. It is also another example of the bell curve of rights we spoke of in chapter 1—how granting noncitizens extra privileges or additional status necessarily infringes on the inalienable rights of the citizenry, in this case, the right to governance by the consent of the governed.

Recently, there was a case before the Supreme Court in which two Texans from rural counties sued the state for debasing their franchise by empowering citizen voters in large immigrant districts. A majority of justices signed onto an opinion indicating that states not only had the right to include illegal aliens in drawing the maps, they had a constitutional mandate to do so.

Any new Republican administration must make it a priority to push legislation removing the inclusion of illegal aliens in the next decennial census. Congress must pass a bill requiring the census to ask questions regarding citizenship and legal status when counting populations of each jurisdiction. They must also prohibit states, at least for federal elections, from drawing new districts based on noncitizen populations.

Back in 1989, when the problem of illegal immigration and the distortion of our representation was a fraction of the problem it poses today, the Senate passed an immigration bill that contained a provision excluding illegals from being counted in the census.[66] Even Harry Reid voted for it. The bill was later hijacked in conference and transformed into an immigration expansionist bill that was signed into law in 1990.

Coupled with birthright citizenship for illegal aliens, counting them in reapportionment poses a more foundational threat to our democratic republic than almost any other misinterpretation of the Constitution, and it demands an immediate remedy. If illegal aliens can permanently distort our representation, debase our franchise, and dilute our political power, there is no sovereignty, republican form of government, or self-respect as a nation state. There is no issue of greater importance that restoring the franchise to where it rightly belongs—with the citizens of these United States.

NON-CITIZENS VOTING

Lawlessness tends to beget more lawlessness. That is why the large presence of illegal aliens in this country often engenders the abrogation of other laws. For example, illegal aliens are not supposed to receive welfare, but millions of them benefit from it. In fact, a recent effort to prohibit Section 8 housing grants to illegal aliens was opposed by Democrats and liberal Republicans, even though they are barred from welfare under current law.[67]

Tragically, the same dynamic applies to voting. The franchise is the hallmark of citizenship in a democratic republic, and the practice of noncitizens voting represents one of the greatest and most deleterious forms of disenfranchisement. Not only are American-born children of illegals granted citizenship and voting rights; a number of other illegal immigrants and legal noncitizens have been found to vote in elections, and it appears to be a growing phenomenon.

So much of this problem stems from the Motor Voter laws that require states to automatically offer voter registration to those signing up for drivers' licenses. Many noncitizens don't even realize it is illegal for them to vote. Worse, given all the liberal states that offer drivers' licenses to illegals, and even the conservative states that are forced to do so as a result of the courts, many illegal aliens are registered to vote as well. In 2015, 605,000 drivers' licenses were handed out to illegal aliens in California, accounting for half of all licenses issued in the state that year![68]

According to an analysis conducted by two political science professors in 2014, more than 14 percent of all noncitizens in the country are illegally registered to vote.[69] With approximately 22.5 million noncitizens in this country according to the Census Bureau, that would mean over 3 million noncitizens are registered to vote.[70] They also estimated that 6.4 percent of noncitizens voted in 2008, accounting for roughly 1.4 million illegal ballots. They further project that 80 percent of these voters are registered Democrats.

Consider the following agonizing thought for conservatives. Obamacare is the seminal issue and the most consequential legislative victory of the Left this past decade. The bill passed the House 220-210 and garnered sixty votes in the Senate, the bare minimum needed to overcome a filibuster. During the 2008 elections, Democrats won two Senate seats by less than 2 percent. In 2006, they won three Senate seats by 2 percent or less. Some of these elections were decided by a few thousand votes. It is hard to imagine that there were not more than enough noncitizens to account for the entirety of the margin of victory in at least one of these races, thereby rendering Obamacare null and void.

Moreover, as we already noted, Democrats hold at least seven House seats due to the illegal practice of counting illegal aliens in the census. That is more than enough to cover the margin of victory that was needed to pass Obamacare in the House.

If we desire to remain a sovereign nation, this must be stopped now. And it must be shut down at the federal level. States have no right to disenfranchise the rest of the union on federal elections. It's time for Republicans to reform the Motor-Voter laws and use a carrot-and-stick approach to the states. They should explicitly empower the states to require proof of citizenship by allowing them to use state registration forms to verify such information.

At the same time they should punish states that fail to comply with federal guidelines and treat states that offer drivers' licenses to illegal aliens like sanctuary cities. Although states have full control over drivers' licenses, there is no reason Congress cannot cut highway funding to states that thwart federal law and steal the sovereignty of the voters throughout the country. A quarter of the states already offer licenses to illegal aliens, charting them on a collision course with the franchise of the American citizen.[71]

CUTTING THE HEAD OFF THE SNAKE

Taken as a whole, the policies of refugee resettlement, mass and chain migration from the Third World, illegal aliens counted in the census, and birthright citizenship for illegal alien children, are not merely examples of odious public policy. They are not legitimate policies at all because they never garnered a constitutional mandate from the citizenry.

In the case of self-immolating legal immigration policies, they never enjoyed popular support or a valid legislative mandate. In the case of illegal immigrants voting, asserting jurisdiction and citizenship for their children, and affecting our representation, they are completely disenfranchising the American citizen. These policies are fundamentally transforming America without the consent of the people, and if they are not addressed expeditiously, the citizens will be powerless to control the destiny of their society. All other issues will be moot.

Perhaps the most consequentially destructive social transformation that is going to transpire under the existing trajectory is the admission of well over 1 million new immigrants from predominantly Muslim countries over the next decade, in addition to at least as many foreign students from the same region. These countries are known for their ubiquitous hatred of Jews, subjugation of women, and antidemocratic ideals.

Undoubtedly, some people emigrating from the Middle East are seeking to flee those values, but as we've learned from ominously observing the destruction of Europe and the growing Islamic radicalization in America, many of them bring with them views that are incompatible with American republicanism. Even with the existing Islamic population, America is now facing an endless threat of homegrown terror. Who in this country thinks it's a good idea to double down on these policies and bring in millions more in the coming years?

One poll conducted in November 2015, following the terror attack on a Paris theater, showed 84 percent of Americans feel immigration from the Middle East is "very or somewhat dangerous." These views cut across every demographic and are shared by 75 percent of Democrats, 80 percent of blacks, and 90 percent of Hispanics.[72] Indubitably, Americans, even the diverse and transformed America of today, still share Theodore Sedgwick's hope that "Congress might use their discretion, and admit none but reputable and worthy characters; such only were fit for the society into which they were blended."[73] The existing government has no mandate from the people to fundamentally transform their society without their consent.

The next president has an immediate responsibility to fix these systemic flaws, addressing both illegal and legal immigration. However, as we've seen from the growing tyranny in the court system, if nothing is done to strip the courts of their illegitimately acquired power over immigration policy, the unelected branch of government will likely veto the will and sovereignty of the people—even if we are lucky enough to elect political leaders willing to address these problems.

The courts will use their contorted version of the Fourteenth Amendment to invalidate any of the fixes prescribed above. They will create an affirmative right to immigrate. They have already and will continue to bestow rights on illegal aliens and throw sand in the gears of any administration that wants to enforce our laws. There is an insatiable army of immigration lawyers who will encumber any enforcement act or law in endless litigation.[74]

For this reason, we must turn our attention to the courts and cut the head off the snake that has stolen our individual sovereignty, lest our sovereignty as a nation be lost forever. As Alexander Hamilton asked over two hundred years ago, "Where is the virtuous pride that once distinguished Americans?"[75]

9

RECLAIMING THE KEYS TO SOCIETY AND SOVEREIGNTY FROM THE COURTS

The germ of dissolution of our federal government is in the constitution of the federal judiciary; an irresponsible body, (for impeachment is scarcely a scarecrow,) working like gravity by night and by day, gaining a little today and a little tomorrow, and advancing its noiseless step like a thief, over the field of jurisdiction, until all shall be usurped from the States, and the government of all be consolidated into one.

—THOMAS JEFFERSON

In 2004, conservative talk radio host Mark Levin spawned a national discussion in his book *Men in Black*, when he warned that the Supreme Court "has broken through the firewalls constructed by the framers to limit federal, and especially, judicial power."[1] After recent calamitous court opinions, and with the growing number of Obama-era judges adjudicating major cases affecting our sovereignty, it is clear that the judicial tyrants have dismantled the firewall altogether, creating their own firewall to permanently inoculate their political decisions from popular recourse. That can and must change if we plan to function as a democratic republic.

We cannot afford to continue retreating. We are at the edge of the cliff. Federal judges are now throwing people in jail for peacefully declining to act contrary to their religious beliefs. Who hasn't heard about Kim Davis, the Kentucky county clerk who was jailed for refusing to issue marriage licenses to gay couples? Or Vermont pastor Paul Horner, who was sentenced to a year in a federal prison for refusing to marry gay couples?[2] At the same time, the courts of Sodom and Gomorrah[3] are releasing criminal aliens from jail. There is nowhere to run or hide. We must stand our ground and fight this judicial tyranny once and for all.

Those of us who adhere to the constitutional republicanism of our founding have been flummoxed and paralyzed by the paradox of constitutional constraints over the past half century. On the one hand, the forces of tyranny have instigated a surreptitious yet relentless coup against our constitutional system of government, turning it on its head in every way imaginable. On the other hand, we are constrained by that very constitutional system that was rightfully designed to lock in the status quo. Unfortunately, at this point, that status quo is the antithesis of our constitutional system.

At some point we must stop limiting ourselves in the fight to restore our Constitution. If the courts declare the Constitution and Declaration "unconstitutional," we must delegitimize their decisions every which way, including fighting back in the states and by civil disobedience. Or we could just lose our religious liberty and sovereignty. The choice is ours.

Either way, there is one very important remedy that will restore the proper balance of power. So many of us have been brainwashed into thinking the courts are the last word on all issues we often forget that there is a subtle, yet all-encompassing and fully solvent solution written in the Constitution itself. Congress has the full authority to strip the courts of their jurisdiction to adjudicate cases that would strike down any specific bill passed by Congress and state legislatures or entire categories of legislation. As always, Congress has the final say. It's time to use the tool of jurisdiction stripping once and for all—the only viable solution separating us from absolute despotism.

That Congress has full power to regulate the district and appellate courts is indisputable. As part of the enumerated powers of Congress in Article I, Section 8 and the Judicial Vesting Clause of Article III, Section 1, the legislative branch has full authority over the creation of the "inferior courts and tribunals."[4] In fact some argued at the constitutional convention that state courts should oversee federal issues, with appeal available directly to the Supreme Court.[5]

Implicit in the power to create these courts is the power to break these courts. As Roger Sherman, one of the most respected Founders and drafters of the Declaration wrote, "the constitution does not make it necessary that any inferior tribunals should be instituted, but it may be done if found necessary."[6]

In 1812, the Supreme Court ruled that the lower courts "possess no jurisdiction but what is given them by the power that creates them, and can be vested with none but what the power ceded to the general government will authorize them to confer."[7] In *Sheldon v. Sill* (1850), the Supreme Court ruled that "Congress, having the power to establish the courts, must define their respective jurisdictions." Justice Robert Grier, writing for a unanimous Court, left no ambiguity that "courts created by statute can have no jurisdiction but such as the statute confers."[8]

Congress can regulate the jurisdiction of federal courts and make it clear that these courts have no authority to overturn, say, immigration enforcement laws or abortion restrictions, or to redefine marriage and strike down public prayer. Congress could bar the courts from fining or imprisoning someone for peacefully declining to violate their religious conscious.

As for the Supreme Court, the Constitution grants it three spheres of original jurisdiction that cannot be removed without a constitutional amendment: cases dealing with ambassadors and government ministers, cases of admiralty and maritime jurisdiction, and disputes between multiple states or residents of multiple states. The rest of the Supreme Court's purview is "appellate jurisdiction" from cases they receive on appeals from the lower courts.[9] Article III, Section 2, Clause 2 of the Constitution explicitly grants Congress the authority to regulate and limit the appellate jurisdiction of the Supreme Court.

Here are the operative words: "In all the other Cases before mentioned, the Supreme Court shall have appellate Jurisdiction, both as to Law and Fact, *with such Exceptions, and under such Regulations as the Congress shall make.*"[10]

Alexander Hamilton particularly emphasized the "exceptions and regulations" clause when he debated Robert Yates in the *Federalist Papers* over the power of the newly proposed judiciary. He mentioned the exceptions and regulations power of Congress over the court on three separate occasions in Federalist No. 81, highlighting the importance of this clause in keeping the courts within arm's length of Congress:

> To avoid all inconveniencies, it will be safest to declare generally, that the Supreme Court shall possess appellate jurisdiction, both as to law and *fact,* and that this jurisdiction shall be subject to such *exceptions* and regulations as the national legislature may prescribe. This will enable the government to modify it in such a manner as will best answer the ends of public justice and security.[11]

While Hamilton rigorously denied the charge that the courts would be the final say on all important issues, as he felt they had "neither force nor will," he observed that minor inconveniences born from judicial review could be rectified by Congress's authority to strip the courts of their jurisdiction over some matters:

> If some partial inconveniencies should appear to be connected with the incorporation of any of them into the plan, it ought to be recollected that the national legislature will have ample authority to make such *exceptions* and to prescribe such regulations as will be calculated to obviate or remove these inconveniencies.[12]

While there have been scholarly debates over the extent of Congress's power to regulate and make exceptions, there is zero doubt that such power can and must extend to the most fundamental societal issues, such as marriage, abortion, and issues concerning sovereignty. After all, the courts were never intended to have force or will over political questions and sovereignty *in the first place*.

Who can have more credibility on the power of Congress over the Supreme Court than John Marshall, the fourth Chief Justice of the Supreme Court, the man who legitimized judicial review? When speaking before the Virginia ratifying convention in 1788, he rebutted claims lodged by George Mason that the federal courts would usurp their power and that the "exceptions and regulations" power of Congress was too weak. The grandfather of judicial activism himself left no uncertainty about the very real limits of judicial power: "What is the meaning of the term exception? Does it not mean an alteration and diminution? Congress is empowered to make exceptions to the appellate jurisdiction, as to law and fact, of the Supreme Court. These exceptions certainly *go as far as the Legislature may think proper*, for the interest and liberty of the people."[13] If the definition of marriage, religious liberty, and sovereignty are not "for the interest and liberty of the people" to have that power vested in the elected branch of government, it is difficult to conceive what exactly would qualify as legitimately within the power of Congress. Edmund Randolph is perhaps the most incisive authority for revealing the extent to which Congress has full control over the court's jurisdiction and how instrumental it was in quelling concerns about judicial tyranny. Randolph was one of five members of the Committee of Detail at the Constitutional Convention, which was tasked with drafting the Constitution. However, he left the convention without signing the compromise document over his concerns that the federal judiciary would pose a grave threat to the states.[14] Nonetheless, Randolph endorsed the Constitution at the Virginian ratification convention because he believed the compromise allowing Congress to except and regulate the court's appellate jurisdiction was a sufficiently strong remedy.

Randolph defended the powers vested in the court from skeptical delegates at the convention in Richmond by noting that the power to strip the courts of jurisdiction allayed his personal fears. "My objection would be unanswerable, were I not satisfied that it contains its own cure, in the following words: 'with such exceptions and under such regulations as Congress shall make,'" said Randolph. He concluded that he felt confident that the cure of jurisdiction stripping would obviate any dangers posed by judicial tyranny. "Congress can regulate it [appellate jurisdiction] properly, and I have no doubt they will."[15]

Randolph went on to serve as the first Attorney General of the United States under President Washington and was asked by Congress to draft recommendations for reforming the judiciary following passage of the Judiciary Act of 1789.[16] In his memorandum, the first chief law enforcement officer in our nation's history made it abundantly clear that the courts rely on Congress for their jurisdiction over issues, not the other way around. "The Supreme Court, though inherent in the Constitution, was to receive the first motion from Congress; the inferior courts must have slept forever without the pleasure of Congress. Can the sphere of authority over value be more enlarged?"[17]

Clearly, Randolph believed that Congress need not have created the lower courts and could regulate most of the Supreme Court's power. Randolph's only mistake was not his interpretation of the Constitution but his underestimation of Congress's cowardice in asserting their own authority over the unelected branch in future generations. Randolph likely never imagined a Congress that would be unwilling to strip courts of jurisdiction to protect our sovereignty and public safety after such courts granted baseless rights and protections to illegal aliens.

Even Justice Joseph Story, who disliked congressional limitations on court jurisdiction, admitted that Congress indeed has this authority. "The jurisdiction of the courts of the United States is almost wholly under the control of the regulating power of Congress," wrote the respected justice and constitutional historian.[18] In 1816, while sitting on the Supreme Court, Story asserted that "the exception was intended as a limitation upon the preceding words to enable congress to regulate and restrain the appellate power, as the public interests, might, from time to time, require."[19]

That public interest is clear now. The courts seek to be judge, jury, and executioner of our constitutional republic by deciding every societal and political question of consequence according to their insular and often radically liberal and secular bias. Why then should they be insulated from the people, serving lifetime appointments *and* being beyond the reach of congressional checks and balances? Why not invoke the plain language of Article III, Section 2 and strip the courts of their power to adjudicate the most potent political issues of our time, forcing them to focus on their job—interpreting the law as written?

Stripping the courts of their role over these issues will restore popular sovereignty, and will restore legitimacy to the work of the courts on the issues Congress leaves within their jurisdiction. On cases and controversies they have the power to adjudicate, they will still have the opportunity to engage in judicial review. But there will be a safety valve protecting the public interest and liberty of society. Undoubtedly, the courts will try to strike down the power of Congress to strip them of jurisdiction over some issues. The same convoluted arguments from the legal community that believes the commerce clause means infinite power to regulate, that Congress no longer has plenary power over immigration, that there is a constitutional right to homosexual marriage but not to religious liberty, that illegal aliens have the rights of Americans—also believes that Article III, Section 2 doesn't really mean what it says.[20] But why should Congress cede them authority?

If judges serve life tenures, can decide political issues, and are inoculated from congressional checks on their authority, then what was the purpose of the revolution? Even King George lacked the authority to violate his nation's sovereignty the way the courts are now doing.[21]

If court stripping is successful, at least its opponents have recourse. They can always defeat those members of Congress in an election and repeal the laws, thereby returning jurisdiction to the courts. But if *they* get their way and deny us any recourse to fight back, we will never have a chance to preserve our society and sovereignty from the tyranny of a highly patrician and unelected oligarchy. How could anyone of any political persuasion believe this is what the Founders envisioned? The reason Hamilton mentioned the jurisdiction stripping clause so often is because it was intended to be a plenary power of Congress; not merely an independent power of Congress to be reconciled ambiguously with the independent plenary power of the Supreme Court to adjudicate appeals. There is no such independent power granted to the court. The entire appellate jurisdiction of the court is anchored, conditioned, and restricted—in the clearest and most absolute terms—to "such Exceptions, and under such Regulations as the Congress shall make." If Congress lacks the authority to strip them of the ability to redefine marriage and create rights for those who violate our sovereignty . . . how could Hamilton have expressed his confidence that jurisdiction stripping would be broad enough to protect "public justice and security?"[22]

A number of "legal scholars" contend that the Court can always strike down a jurisdiction stripping law if they feel it violates the Constitution, aka, their version of the Fourteenth Amendment.[23] But that is absurd, because entrusting and abiding by a court opinion on jurisdiction stripping would necessarily render an entire clause of the Constitution, which was considered vital to the preservation of sovereignty, meaningless. Congress must not be deterred from exercising its clear and undeniable authority to strip federal courts of their jurisdiction. And if a federal court asserts that such a law is "unconstitutional," that decision must be disregarded in order to ensure proper obedience to popular sovereignty. If the citizens feel Congress has overstepped its boundaries they have the ability to punish those members. Moreover, as mentioned in chapter 1, section 5 of the Fourteenth Amendment granted Congress the power to enforce the other provisions of that amendment. In 1879, in the first Court ruling explaining the meaning of section 5, Justice William Strong wrote unambiguously that the Court lacked the authority to overturn state laws under the Fourteenth

Amendment in the first place. "It is not said the *judicial power* of the general government shall extend to enforcing the prohibitions and to protecting the rights and immunities guaranteed. It is not said that branch of the government shall be authorized to declare void any action of a State in violation of the prohibitions. It is the power of Congress, which has been enlarged. Congress is authorized to *enforce* the prohibitions by appropriate legislation. Some legislation is contemplated to make the amendments fully effective."[24]

Thus, were Congress to strip the courts of their "power" over immigration, marriage, abortion, protected status for homosexuals, affirmative action, and state crime laws, the courts cannot assert a Fourteenth Amendment violation because Congress, not the courts, get to define the scope of the Fourteenth Amendment, which, as noted before, was never designed to create a single new right. Certainly Congress can use the full force of jurisdiction stripping to combat ill-gotten judicial powers and phantom constitutional interpretations. The radical courts of the twentieth century have never explained or acknowledged this clear directive from the authoritative courts of the civil rights era that explicitly made Congress supreme in enforcing the Fourteenth Amendment. How can legal "scholars" deny Congress's authority to strip the courts of their power to strike down laws under the Fourteenth Amendment when the courts never had that authority in the first place, and certainly don't have that authority after Congress exercises its Article III powers?

Are we to believe in the superiority of the courts and the subservience of Congress—completely backwards from the Founders' vision– to such an extent that we will deny Congress, its constitutional authority to strip the courts because of Fourteenth Amendment challenges that are, in themselves, within the scope of Congress to enforce?

The legal community always conveniently adopts the broadest views on the courts' role in creating new constitutional rights, yet they always embrace the most stringent view against Congress's recourse to rein in that power. Their living and breathing legal doctrines of the power of Congress shrink commensurately to the growth of their doctrines, granting the courts more power, in contravention to the history of our founding.

There is no better way to ascertain the original intent of the congressional power to regulate the jurisdiction of the federal courts than by examining the Judiciary Act of 1789, which basically established the entire judiciary process.[25] The inferior and Supreme Courts, in their respective realms, were not even granted original or appellate jurisdiction over critical issues in the first place under the initial act of Congress.[26] The act did not grant the inferior courts original jurisdiction over federal constitutional questions, and it wasn't until 1875, in the twilight of the Reconstruction era, that Congress transferred that authority from state courts to federal courts,[27] and it wasn't until 1914 that Congress granted the Supreme Court appellate jurisdiction over all cases heard by state supreme courts.[28] The 1789 act limited their jurisdiction to state cases that ruled against a federal right. But as it related to individual cases not involving interstate litigation, the state courts had the final say in upholding a state or federal statute.[29]

In fact, the 1789 law severely limited the appellate jurisdiction of the Supreme Court even over some cases heard by federal appeals courts, such as federal criminal cases.[30]

Even as it relates to the Supreme Court, it required the original act of Congress in 1789 to vest it with appellate jurisdiction. As James Kent observed in his highly foundational and respected commentaries on the Constitution, "if congress had not provided any rule to regulate the proceedings on appeal, the court could not exercise an appellate jurisdiction; and if a rule be provided, the court could not depart from it." Kent asserted that the early case law recognized the principle "that though the appellate powers of the court were given by the constitution, they were limited entirely by the judiciary statutes, which are to be understood as making exceptions to the appellate jurisdiction of the court, and to imply a negative on the exercise of such a power in every case, but those in which it is affirmatively given and described by statute."[31]

Consequently, the Framers of Article III, as evidenced by the 1789 Act of Congress, intended the appellate jurisdiction of the Supreme

Court to rest upon the authority granted to it by Congress through statute. The great "father of the national judiciary," Oliver Ellsworth, served as Chief Justice of the Supreme Court after serving as the first Chairman of the House Judiciary Committee.[32] There can be no greater authority on the original intent of the power of Congress over the judiciary. Writing an opinion in a 1796 case, Ellsworth authoritatively asserted that "If Congress has provided no rule to regulate our proceedings, we cannot exercise an appellate jurisdiction; and if the rule is provided, we cannot depart from it."[33]

Roger Sherman, who was among the greatest of all the Founders, was very clear about the limited scope of the federal judiciary and how it was restricted to congressional regulations. Here is what Sherman, the only man to have signed all four founding documents—the Declaration of Independence, Continental Association, Articles of Confederation, and the Constitution—had to say about the power of the federal judiciary: "The judiciary department is perhaps the most difficult to be precisely limited by the constitution, but congress have full power to regulate it by law, and it may be found necessary to vary the regulations at different times as circumstances may differ.[34] A few weeks later, he was even more emphatic: "It was thought necessary in order to carry into effect the laws of the union, and to preserve justice and harmony among the States, to extend the judicial powers of the confederacy, they cannot be extended beyond the enumerated cases, but may be limited by Congress, and doubtless will be restricted to Such cases of importance & magnitude as cannot Safely be trusted to the final decision of the courts of the particular States."[35] Thus, Sherman took congressional limitations on the jurisdiction of the judiciary as a given, and predicted that Congress would use common sense in limiting its authority.

The notion that Congress lacks the power to strip the courts of jurisdiction over certain issues contradicts the historical record. Congress created much of the Supreme Court's appellate jurisdiction; it can certainly revoke it as it relates to the most political issues, which should be the exclusive domain of Congress anyway. While some legal scholars believe that the language of the Constitution mandating that the Supreme Court "shall" have appellate jurisdiction, requires that Congress leave them some scope of jurisdiction over appeals, that is an abstract debate of no consequence to our discussion. Nobody is arguing that Congress should strip the court of every single issue aside from its original jurisdiction. We just seek to take from them the few social issues they illegally grabbed from the people's representatives in Congress and state legislatures.

Furthermore, we must apply the same principle we established with the legal debate over birthright citizenship. Whenever there is a supposed ambiguity in certain constitutional concepts, it makes no sense to narrowly read the Constitution so as to void other sections of the Constitution in their entirety. And when that ambiguity presents a conflict between the Congress and the Judiciary, in a republic, the legislative branch must always have the upper hand.

Consequently, it makes no sense to read "subject to the jurisdiction thereof" in strictest manner—granting automatic citizenship even to illegal aliens—thereby voiding an entire enumerated power of Congress in Article I, Section 8 and their ability to enforce the Fourteenth Amendment itself in section 5. Likewise, it is unconscionable to read the Fourteenth Amendment's due process and equal protection clauses to nullify Congress's authority to make exceptions to the Court's jurisdiction.

Especially as it relates to jurisdiction over immigration, the courts (until recently) have already shown that the judiciary ostensibly has no significant jurisdiction over this sphere of policy, even without a jurisdiction-stripping bill. As late as 1976, even the Warren court observed in a case concerning immigration that "Any rule of constitutional law that would inhibit the flexibility of the political branches of government to respond to changing world conditions should be adopted only with the greatest caution."[36] Could there possibly be any changing world conditions more consequential to the political survival of a nation than endless waves of illegal immigration?

Ironically, in 1982, even as Justice William Brennan was setting the stage for judicial tyranny on immigration, he recognized that Congress had the power to exercise control over the judiciary. He wrote "Of course, virtually all matters that might be heard in Art. III courts could also be left by Congress to state courts . . . [and] the principle of separation of powers is not threatened by leaving the adjudication of federal disputes to such judges."[37]

Once again, it's important to reiterate that if our side wins, our opponents can always countermand an act of Congress with a subsequent act of Congress. On the other hand, if their side wins, our side has no ability to override the rewriting of our Constitution. Unless we pursue this remedy, we will have no lawful and peaceful remedy to restoring our system of governance.

STRIPPING THE COURTS

While jurisdiction stripping was rarely implemented successfully, one seminal court case demonstrates its legitimacy. As part of the Reconstruction-era clampdown on those in the South who voiced opposition to the Radical Republican agenda of the time, William McCardle, a newspaper publisher, was arrested under the Military Reconstruction Act of 1867. McCardle took his case to the courts and appealed all the way to the Supreme Court. To prevent the Supreme Court from letting McCardle out of prison, Congress repealed the section of the 1867 act granting the Supreme Court appellate jurisdiction.

This case is illustrative because Congress stripped the Court's jurisdiction even after oral arguments were heard in the case (but before the decision was announced) and even as it related to denying the fundamental right to habeas corpus.

Yet, Chief Justice Samuel Chase wrote a unanimous opinion stating that the court had no jurisdiction to decide this case now that Congress cut the legs out from under them. In language similar to the many court cases we cited in chapter 4 concerning Congress's plenary power over immigration, Chase said, "We are not at liberty to inquire into the motives of the legislature. We can only examine into its power under the Constitution, and the power to make exceptions to the appellate jurisdiction of this court is given by express words."[38] From the plain language of the ruling, it's clear that Chase was not trying to split hairs over the unique circumstances of McCardle. The power of Congress to strip jurisdiction, even after the case was argued before the court, spoke for itself.

In 1893, the Court observed that "[I]t has been held in an uninterrupted series of decisions that this court exercises appellate jurisdiction only in accordance with the acts of Congress upon that subject."[39]

Individual members of Congress have attempted to pass legislation stripping the courts of jurisdiction over particular subject matter, but almost all of them never made serious headway.[40] However, on occasion these efforts have gained traction. In 2004, the House passed the Marriage Protection Act of 2004, stating that, "no court created by Act of Congress shall have any jurisdiction, and the Supreme Court shall have no appellate jurisdiction, to hear or decide any question pertaining to the interpretation of, or the validity under the Constitution of" defining marriage.[41] The bill passed the House 233-194.[42] Later that year, the House passed the Pledge Protection Act, which stripped the courts of their jurisdiction over hearing cases prohibiting the recitation of the Pledge of Allegiance with God's name.[43]

One modern success story was the passage of the Prison Litigation Reform Act of 1996. Following decades of federal intrusion in criminal justice in which the courts would grant all sorts of rights to prisoners and invalidate different forms of incarceration, Congress passed a law regulating the court's ability to strike down such arrangements and tailored its scope of jurisdiction with a great degree of specificity.[44] The bill was signed into law by Bill Clinton and upheld by the Supreme Court.[45] It's high time for Congress to relentlessly focus on stripping courts over political questions under the banner of no societal transformation" without representation. "This is of far greater urgency than having the next president deal with legislation concerning tax or entitlement reform. Nobody is suggesting that courts lose all of their jurisdiction or that Congress pass laws denying judicial review over issues dealing with long-held constitutional rights. But it is clear the Founders never envisioned the courts granting new super rights to protected classes, granting constitutional rights to illegal aliens, or having the courts eradicate God's name from our society. Why not start by stripping them of jurisdiction over issues for which the courts have said for one hundred years they lack the power?

Sen. Ted Cruz (R-TX) has already introduced legislation in response to the marriage decision, which would freeze any action implementing the court's decision by stripping the federal courts of any jurisdiction over marriage. His bill also invokes Congress's power to make exceptions to the appellate jurisdiction of the Supreme Court by making it clear that the judgment only applies to the parties in the existing case and cannot be applied to other cases.[46] This will return the power over marriage to the state, as it has been since the founding of this country.

If we are to remain a sovereign nation-state, we must also strip the courts of their ability to overturn state or federal immigration enforcement laws. As we've shown in chapter 5, the courts are striving to undo one hundred years of congressional plenary power over immigration and are on the cusp of granting full citizenship to all illegal aliens. They must be stopped.

They must also be stripped of the power to apply international law. Justice Stephen Breyer has recently published a book defending the use of international law. What is particularly concerning about his book is his advocacy of applying international law in the realm of detaining foreign fighters.[47] According to the Congressional Research Service, "In recent years, foreign or international legal sources have increasingly been cited by the Supreme Court when considering matters of U.S. law."[48]

We have already seen courts apply international law to override the political branches and our sovereignty on immigration issues. There is currently a bill in the House of Representatives that would prevent the courts from applying international law.[49] This must be a priority for any new GOP administration.

Most important, the courts must be prevented from pursuing the most odious and consequential form of social transformation without representation—violating our sovereignty as a nation and overturning efforts of the political branches to protect us from illegal immigration.

To be clear, state courts would still have authority to adjudicate cases within the sphere of policy that Congress chooses to strip from the federal courts. Many scholars believe that Congress must leave the state courts as an avenue to redress those grievances in order to fully strip the federal courts of power over those issues. But the majority of states have some sort of election process for trial, appellate, or high court judges within the states.[50] If judges will have the ability to decide political and societal questions, such as abortion, marriage, immigration, and public prayer, let it be the state judges who must face the voters in some capacity. This process worked in Iowa when three of the judges who vitiated the state's marriage law were defeated in an election.[51] Furthermore, the citizenry of the states who don't have popular elections or retention ballots for judges can work through their political processes to amend their state constitutions to restore the power to the people. A number of naysayers, even within the conservative legal community, will howl about the side effects of jurisdiction stripping. They will complain about the disjointed patchwork of jurisprudence and legal opinions that will ensue as a result of transforming power from the federal court system to the fifty systems of the individual states. But have we not reached the nightmare scenario already when courts are creating a constitutional right to gay marriage and releasing dangerous criminal aliens in violation of our sovereignty as a nation-state? There is no ideal solution to the violence the Left has foisted upon our constitutional system of governance over the past half century, but it's better to live under a patchwork of tyranny that can be redressed at the ballot box than under one federal oligarchy that can immutably transform society without any recourse by the citizenry.

A half century of complacency has allowed this anti-constitutional cancer to spread throughout our nation's body. Sure, the political chemotherapy will have its side effects. But to continue on the current path will ensure that this disease becomes terminal.

WHY JURISDICTION STRIPPING?

Mark Levin has proposed a constitutional amendment using the Article V convention of the states process, which would subject judges to term limits, elections, a three-fifths congressional override of Supreme Court decisions, and the ability for three-fifths of state legislatures to override the decision as well.[52] While this is a worthy idea, Levin refers to it as a "hundred year plan." It is nearly insurmountable to muster the support of three-fourths of the states to enact a constitutional amendment. This must be part of a relentless long-term plan to rein in the courts, but we need immediate relief. Jurisdiction stripping is the only immediate relief that can be brought to the people by the next Congress and president without a constitutional amendment.

The only other check on the judiciary is the congressional power of impeachment. Clearly, the Founders considered impeachment to be a strong deterrent against lawlessness. Hamilton said that impeachment "is alone a complete security" against usurpation of congressional power. "There never can be danger that the judges, by a series of deliberate usurpations on the authority of the legislature, would hazard the united resentment of the body entrusted with it, while this body was possessed of the means of punishing their presumption, by degrading them from their stations."[53]

However, as we are all painfully aware, impeachment has been neutered by the political party system. As is the case with impeachment of a president, the two-party system is so inveterate in the body politic of America, that congressional members of the president's party or those who share the values of the judicial tyrants will always vote to retain the impeached individual on a Senate vote. Absent sixty-seven senators from one party, the check of impeachment has been completely neutralized.

What else is there to do? Have the next president appoint only solid originalist judges?

First, it will take decades to undo the damage from the Obama-appointed judges who have often replaced Reagan-era judges. At present, there are solid post-constitutional majorities on nine of the thirteen circuit courts as well as a majority of district courts. Obama has filled 55 of the 179 appellate judgeships in the federal circuits and over 252 of the 673 on a district level.

Although the next president could potentially appoint many new judges to counteract Obama's judges, it will unlikely be enough to even return to pre-Obama days—a time that was not exactly an era of widespread constitutional jurisprudence. As liberal legal pundit Linda Hirshman notes, the Democrat control of the lower courts is so complete that even if the next president gets to fill the current vacancies, "filling them wouldn't make an immediate difference."[54] That is because most of the oldest judges are Reagan appointees and most of the upcoming vacancies will not fundamentally alter the balance of any circuit. Democratic appointees now have a 7–4 majority on the D.C. circuit court of appeals, the second most important court as it relates to constitutional issues.

Moreover, Republicans have rarely batted more than .500 in nominating originalists, especially on the lower courts. Our sovereignty as a nation-state will be dead by the time we reclaim majorities on the federal benches, unless we immediately take the ball of tyranny out of their political game. Plus, a recent analysis shows how almost all justices, even the more conservative ones, invariably drift left throughout their tenure while the liberal justices become even more radical.[55]

Further, the prospect of nominating "originalist" judges is even worse than electing more Republican politicians. Even many Republican appointees have become judicial tyrants. As we noted in chapters 2 and 3, a number of Republican-appointed judges sided with the far left even in the most egregious cases of redefining marriage, jailing Kim Davis for being a Christian, and upholding the constitutionality of Obamacare. Even to the extent conservatives can clamp down on Supreme Court nominees and force the next president to nominate someone in the mold of Thomas or the late Antonin Scalia, that degree of scrutiny has never worked for the lower courts. We simply have a poor track record in nominating reliable originalists. And only 1 percent of cases ever make it to the Supreme Court.

Finally, even those who have displayed a consistent originalist bent throughout their legal career are as reliable once they get on the bench as political conservatives are once they enter Congress. In other words, not very reliable at all. There is so much peer pressure to join with the half century of ratcheted post-constitutional jurisprudence that few originalist judges have the guts to do what it takes to serve as an equal and opposing force to the judicial tyrants. A sitting judge thumbing his nose at the one-directional *stare decisis* or belief in "substantive due process" requires more courage than Ted Cruz calling Mitch McConnell a liar on the Senate floor.

The Fourteenth Amendment alone has been contorted so much that the anti-constitutional jurisprudence is already baked into the cake of the legal profession, and isolated conservative judges don't have much recourse to roll it back on their own. It is virtually impossible for lower court originalists to not be bound by fifty years of post-constitutional precedent from the Supreme Court. And with an impervious block of four liberals on the Supreme Court, together with Kennedy and Roberts, who join them in expanding the post-constitutional ratchet, coupled with the judicial time bomb of super radicals Obama appointed to the lower courts, the judiciary is irreparably broken.

Let's hark back to the despair felt by Robert Bork, the father of the modern conservative legal movement, as far back as twenty years ago—long before some of the most egregious decisions were made:

> Republican Presidents have used the nomination process in an effort to change the direction of the Court with almost zero results on the major issues. After twelve years of Presidents Reagan and Bush, each of whom made a determined effort to appoint Justices who would abide by the Constitution as originally understood, we seem farther than ever from a restrained Court. Between them, Reagan and Bush

> had five appointments. Only two try to relate their decisions to the Constitution as the men who wrote, proposed, and ratified it understood it. A majority of the Justices has become more arrogantly authoritarian than ever.[56]

Since Bork's declaration of failure on the part of conservatives to constrain the court, we have had another term of President Clinton, plus the most radical packing of the benches ever during the Obama era. Sandwiched in between those two presidencies was George W. Bush, who, once again, appointed one good Supreme Court justice while whiffing on John Roberts as chief justice of the court. As many good judges as he appointed to the lower courts, he appointed a number of liberal judges as well.

Recently, the late Justice Scalia revealed in a speech that the Supreme Court has always been liberal since he'd sat on the bench. He further noted that the court is a fundamental threat to democracy and that he could not "imagine the system can continue with more and more of the basic rules made by the Supreme Court."[57] Scalia was at the front lines and was telling us the courts are irrevocably broken. Can anyone say with a straight face that there is a way to fix this without directly limiting the power of the courts?

Additionally, there is a permanent bifurcation between the approach of Democrats to conservative judicial nominees and the approach of many Republicans to anti-constitutionalist nominees. Democrats aggressively fight originalist nominations, while Republicans generally defer to Democratic nominations as long as the nominee has no glaring ethical problems.

In 2009 Pat Toomey, regarded as a more conservative Republican, noted that had he been serving in the Senate at the time, he would have confirmed Sonia Sotomayor. "If I were a U.S. senator, I would vote for her confirmation, because objective qualifications should matter more than ideology in the judicial confirmation process," wrote Toomey in an op-ed.[58] Justice Sotomayor has since voted with the liberals on every egregious decision that has upended our Constitution and Declaration of Independence, including cases on Obamacare, marriage, religious liberty, immigration, and affirmative action.

It is precisely this mentality that, among other factors, has contributed to the permanent liberal supermajority throughout all levels of the judiciary. This problem is terminal and it will not go away on its own. Therefore the courts must be changed from the outside.

OTHER JUDICIAL REFORMS

Congress can use its powers to regulate the court's jurisdiction and proceedings in other ways as well. A more limited, but possibly more politically viable solution would be to require the courts to garner a supermajority in support of any opinion that exercises judicial review in striking down state or federal laws as unconstitutional.

For example, if Congress passes a law to remove illegal aliens from the census or deny their American-born children citizenship under the authentic interpretation of the Fourteenth Amendment, they can attach a provision defining the quorum needed by the court to invalidate the law. If Congress has the power to strip the courts of jurisdiction over immigration, they certainly have the authority to allow the courts to exercise judicial review, albeit requiring that a supermajority or unanimous opinion be issued in order to have the effect of nullifying the laws passed by the duly elected representatives of the people.

The requirement for supermajority opinion on the court is not only within Congress's power to regulate the courts, it is also in line with the spirit of judicial review countenanced by the Framers of our Constitution.

Defenders of judicial review like to say that, although the legislature is the most important branch of government, the courts are needed to protect minority rights. As noted in chapters 1 and 3, judicial review was only designed to strike down laws passed by legislatures when they are flagrantly in violation of the Constitution as it was originally adopted. As Justice Samuel Chase said, "if I ever exercise the jurisdiction [of judicial review], I will not decide any law to be void but in a very clear case."[59]

Consequently, the entire rationale for judicial review has been obviated by the modern assault on the Constitution. Judicial review is only valid and is only a tool for protecting fundamental rights against majoritarian rule if the courts use as their blueprint the Constitution, not a modern-day social agenda.

There is a glaring contradiction in their rationale for judicial review. Assuming Congress violates constitutional rights, who is vested with the power to define those rights and defend them from elective despotism of the majority or legislative tyranny? A *majority* opinion of unelected judges, who are even more unaccountable and prone to abuses? As Justice Iredell, one of the first Supreme Court justices and a strong early proponent of judicial review, conceded, courts should only overturn legislative statutes that violate "marked and settled boundaries," and even in those instances their ad hoc veto power should only be exercised "in a clear and urgent case."[60] With regards to any other act that the courts (even rightfully) perceive as a violation against "natural justice," albeit not incontrovertibly spelled out in the Constitution, Iredell believed they lacked the power to overturn the law.[61]

Ultimately, our Founders—even those who advocated judicial review—envisioned that only the people themselves could effectively police their legislators through elections, protests, and peaceful uprisings.[62] James Wilson, one of the key architects of the Constitution,[63] especially as it relates to the judiciary, best embodied this view that the people, not the courts must ultimately guard against the abuses of majoritarian rule via the legislature. Although a strong supporter of a minimal power of judicial review, like Justice Iredell, Wilson famously said "Laws may be unjust, may be unwise, may be dangerous, may be destructive; and yet not be so unconstitutional as to justify the judges in refusing to give them effect."[64] Hence, as bad as majoritarian rule can be, judicial oligarchy is even worse.

The problem with granting the courts the final say over every issue, especially when they use politics instead of the Constitution to police the boundaries of legislative authority, is that we are merely replacing the inherently imperfect majoritarian process of an elected branch of government with a majoritarian process of an *unelected* branch of government.

Look at all these major societal decisions that have been decided by a 5-4 vote of the court, with very sharply worded dissents from the minority. In what way can anyone assert, with any degree of intellectual honesty, that a 5-4 decision of unelected judges is any better that an acrimonious 51-49 vote to approve the law in the Senate? At least congressmen and senators can be thrown out of office.

It would be one thing if the court would speak with one unified voice in striking down a statute. That way, as a society, we could take comfort in knowing that laws are passed by the people's representatives but are subject to review by the court to protect minority rights. If the court speaks with one voice that will most assuredly give the public confidence that the law passed by the legislature is indeed flagrantly unconstitutional and that their decision is rooted in law, not politics.

My proposition is for Congress, at least on a limited basis and with regard to important issues, to pass legislation requiring the appeals courts to rule unanimously to strike down a law in order for it to be binding against the legislature. If upon appeal to the Supreme Court, the high court also agrees to strike down the law, they must garner at least seven votes in support of their decision.

Any decision to invalidate a state law should require at least as high a threshold because states would never have joined the union had they been told an unelected federal tribunal could strike down their most commonsense laws governing their sovereignty, security, public safety, and society. Ideally, those decisions should be unanimous.

Congress could easily defend a bill requiring the courts to rule unanimously when invalidating state laws designed to protect people from illegal immigration. Simple majorities would suffice for cases interpreting statutes or striking down acts of the Executive Branch. But to strike down the laws passed by the people's representatives, it makes sense to require that they move beyond the majoritarian rule they seek to overturn in the first place.

This plan would have the effect of harmonizing the popular sovereignty of majoritarian rule with the check of judicial review and protect the people against elective majoritarian rule when it truly violates the Constitution, at least in the estimation of the overwhelming majority of the judicial branch.

You may be asking, "But is this proposal constitutional? As a separate branch of government, can Congress dictate voting majority requirements to the judiciary?" Of course they can. The people can and must always have the final say. And as we've noted, if Congress can strip the courts of their ability to overturn a law altogether, they can certainly maintain the court's power of judicial review, prescribing limits and regulations on how they go about doing it.

Congress itself established the rules for quorums and proceedings of the courts in the first place, as part of the Judiciary Act of 1789.[65] As Justice Story observed, "it is for congress alone to furnish the rules of proceeding, to direct the process, to declare the nature and effect of the process, and the mode, in which the judgments, consequent thereon, shall be executed."[66] There is no reason Congress can't modify those proceedings and tinker with the quorum requirements. Moreover, Congress has the power to set the number of justices that sit on the Supreme Court. Indeed, as part of the original act of Congress, they set the number of justices on the court at six.[67] Consequently, at our founding, any case overturning a statute automatically had to garner a two-thirds majority of 4-2 to have effect. Evan Caminker, a professor of law at the University of Michigan Law School, has identified over sixty congressional proposals from 1823 to 1981 that have sought to impose some sort of supermajority or unanimous consent requirement on the courts when seeking to invalidate a law.[68] Caminker also notes that North Dakota and Nebraska have already imposed supermajority requirements on their respective state supreme courts as a prerequisite for striking down state laws.[69] If the Washington cartel wants to compromise on jurisdiction stripping, this would represent an authentic middle ground.

Other modest reforms include stripping or regulating the jurisdiction and quorums of the lower courts. Congress can start by punishing the ninth circuit, the worst offender, and shrinking their jurisdiction to a small geographical area in California, thereby freeing Arizona and some of the other western states from its clutches.[70] The point is that Congress was given a lot of tools by the Constitution to rein in judicial power. It's time they start using them or at least educating the public that there is such recourse. Merely threatening to exercise them a few times would work wonders in humbling the judicial bullies.

I've often wondered if the anti-federalists were correct in their critique of the Constitution, especially as it relates to their concern about judicial tyranny. The words of Robert Yates, writing as Brutus in the *Anti-Federalist Papers,* seem prophetic as he predicted every aspect of judicial tyranny with which we are now confronted. In *Anti-Federalist* No. 15, Yates wrote:

> There is no power above them, to controul [*sic*] any of their decisions. There is no authority that can remove them, and they cannot be controuled [*sic*] by the laws of the legislature. In short, they are independent of the people, of the legislature, and of every power under heaven.[71]

Yates concluded that the power of the judiciary would supersede that of the legislature. "If, therefore, the legislature pass any laws, inconsistent with the sense the judges put upon the constitution, they will declare it void."

Undoubtedly, Yates was prophetic in predicting the judicial time bomb. But in defense of Hamilton, Madison, and some of the other federalists, they never conceived of a scenario in which the legislature would allow the courts—who lack the force and will of execution and the power of the purse—to encroach upon their power, even to a fraction of the degree it has.

The bottom line is that the Founders never envisioned that members of Congress would not defend their power from the encroachment of the weaker judiciary. In dismissing concerns over judicial encroachment, Hamilton observed that "from the general nature of the judicial power, from the objects to which it relates, from the manner in which it is exercised, from its comparative weakness, and from its total incapacity to support its usurpations by force."[72]

Hamilton is speaking to our very predicament. Why in the world would Congress not exercise its power over the purse and lawmaking to either strip the courts of their jurisdiction over societal issues or defund implementation of particularly pernicious court cases? The excuses must end now if we are to remain a democracy.

Madison never even entertained the possibility of judicial tyranny, being primarily concerned with legislative tyranny because it held lawmaking powers and the power of the purse. He believed the legislature could use the power of the purse to make the other branches dependent upon its will.[73] The system of governance established and the powers vested in the House of Representatives in particular—the branch most directly accountable to the people—satisfied Madison's overarching principle of republicanism that "the people are the only legitimate fountain of power."[74] "This power over the purse may, in fact, be regarded as the most complete and effectual weapon with which any constitution can arm the immediate representatives of the people, for obtaining a redress of every grievance, and for carrying into effect every just and salutary measure."[75]

Madison never countenanced a complacent congress that would refuse to redress a single grievance with the power of the purse or their lawmaking powers over the weakest branch of government. He never thought for one minute that the champion boxer would be mugged by the preadolescent boy. This is why Madison said he was "at a loss to comprehend" George Mason's warning of a dangerous judiciary.[76]

Fortunately, the radicalism of the past few years from President Obama and his allies has awakened millions of Americans to the appalling degree of disenfranchisement that has taken place. Conservatives must begin to make a relentless case for judicial reform as the top priority—even over other policies. The next Republican president and Congress must restore the political power to the political branches of government by stripping the courts of their power over political issues—one by one with every piece of legislation. As we've explored in these chapters, there is no greater threat to our national and state sovereignty than our failed immigration policies, but the only way we can even get our foot in the door to enact vital reforms is if we first reclaim our stolen sovereignty and system of governance from the clutches of the courts.

Already in 2003 Justice Scalia proclaimed, "I've been predicting this for twenty years that ultimately this theory of the living Constitution will destroy us, it will destroy the federal courts."[77] Robert Bork warned in 1996 that we were slouching towards Gomorrah.[78] Well, we are no longer slouching toward Gomorrah; we are *in* Gomorrah. The federal courts have been destroyed from the inside, and the only constitutional and practical remedy is for the elected branch of government to reclaim the territory stolen by the unelected branch of government.

Thomas Jefferson warned us that "our peculiar security is in possession of a written Constitution. Let us not make it a blank paper by construction."[79] This is our document. This is our birthright. It's time to tell the judicial bullies they can't erase its last vestige.

10

CONCLUSION: OUR LAST CHANCE TO RESTORE THE REPUBLIC

Freedom is the right to question, and change the established way of doing things. It is the continuing revolution of the marketplace. It is the understanding that allows us to recognize shortcomings and seek solutions. It is the right to put forth an idea, scoffed at by the experts, and watch it catch fire among the people. It is the right to stick—to dream—to follow your dream, or stick to your conscience, even if you're the only one in a sea of doubters.

—RONALD REAGAN

The potential for Republicans to win back the White House in 2017, with control of Congress, might very well present us with the final opportunity to re-empower the people against societal transformation and the assault on our sovereignty.

The radicalism and destruction on display in the waning months of the Obama presidency has shown signs of engendering a political rubber band effect. There is a great awakening in this country and people are starving for leaders who will steer the country in the opposite direction.

It's time to harness this opportunity and make this election meaningful by building the momentum for long-term systemic reforms that will ensure we are never one court decision or one executive order away from losing our society, sovereignty, and government.

Republicans will be tempted to continue to focus on the typical policy issues—taxes, regulations, health care, energy, and foreign policy—all critical to our nation's future. But if they fail to harness this last opportunity to fix the *systemic* flaws in our post-constitutional government—the disenfranchising of the people and social transformation carried out by the courts and the bureaucracy—none of those other issues will matter anymore.

If Republicans fail to stop the assault on religious liberty, we will be left without the most foundational of rights in this country. If they fail to address the disenfranchising of the people on immigration policy, they will never win another federal election and will lack the ability to implement some of their favorite fiscal reforms. If they decline to strip the courts of their power over society and sovereignty, and reclaim congressional power from the bureaucrats over immigration, elections will no longer mean anything. And if the mass migration from the Middle East is not immediately stopped, our security and Western values will be immutably jeopardized as badly as the European nations'.

As a nation, we can and have survived a financial collapse. We cannot survive a collapse of the civil society or the eradication of our sovereignty at the behest of a judicial oligarch.

For far too long, conservatives have shrugged their shoulders over the illegal usurpation of power by the unelected branches of government. They have tolerated illegal immigrants voting in elections, being counted in the census, obtaining citizenship for their children, and controlling the future of our society. They have reluctantly retreated and tolerated the courts having the final say in all social issues, while promising to appoint better judges when they are in power.

That time has come to an end.

We are now at the precipice of the ultimate time for choosing. There is nowhere to retreat; we are teetering at the edge of a cliff. The transformation that has occurred over the past half century—without the representation or input from We the People—has brought our society and sovereignty to the brink.

Democrats have become so radical they couldn't field a presidential candidate in 2016 possessing a modicum of common sense, or who could appeal to anyone beyond the fringe Left. According to Gallup, the number of self-identified Democrats in this country has dropped to its lowest point in a generation.[1] Yet, even after eight years of a failed and unpopular Obama presidency, the Democrats have such a high floor of automatic electoral support, as a result of the great transformation, that Republicans have to struggle to win Ohio, Virginia, and Colorado, even in this auspicious political climate.

It is incontrovertibly clear that if Republicans fail to utilize this last opportunity, in which they will likely squeak through the closing gates of electoral viability, they will never win another national election again. And as we've painfully learned from the past seven years of executive and judicial decisions governing the most essential aspects of our culture, we cannot survive another era like this and remain a sovereign nation and an intact civil society.

The endless waves of illegal and legal immigration, illegal aliens voting in elections and distorting our representation in Congress and the Electoral College, will make it impossible to win by the time the next decennial reapportionment comes due. A number of key states have seen a doubling or tripling of immigration over the past few decades, and the current trajectory portends a growing tsunami of voters who will unmovably favor the Democratic Party. President Obama is naturalizing immigrants at a record pace and is doing everything he can to create the final movement toward the tipping point of a permanent electoral majority.[2]

Furthermore, what good is the passage of new conservative legislation in a Republican administration if the courts are not first stripped of their power to decide these issues for themselves? With President

Obama remaking a third of the federal bench, the creation of anti-constitutional legal precedent in a tightening Marxist societal ratchet, and a number of Republican-appointed judges following their lead on key issues, there is no limit to the degree of rights the courts will bestow on illegal immigrants or special super rights they will grant to favored classes of Americans. It's time for Republicans to treat the issue of judicial disenfranchisement with the urgency it deserves.

Inaction or complacency is not an option as it relates to immigration policy or the courts. As a movement, we can bat .1000 in stopping every single bill granting amnesty to illegals or increasing legal immigration—no easy task in itself—yet it won't make a difference if we fail to immediately re-empower the people and Congress to bring our immigration policy more in line with our historical priorities. Under the current trajectory Texas will invariably turn blue and serve as the knockout punch to our electoral prospects.[3]

These critical changes must be made before that narrow window of electoral opportunity and viability rapidly slams shut, a time that, if nothing is done to preempt it, will likely transpire during the following administration. The new massive wave of immigration we spoke of in chapters 7 and 8 impels an even greater urgency to prioritize these issues *immediately* during the next administration.

In this book we have found an urgent need to take the following actions:

- pass federal civil rights legislation protecting religious liberty
- abolish birthright citizenship for illegal aliens
- end chain migration
- impose a number of reforms on refugee resettlement
- stop counting illegal aliens in the census
- reform the motor voter law that has resulted in noncitizens voting *en masse*; and

- pass an array of judicial reforms, most prominently, one stripping the federal courts of jurisdiction over these critical issues and other vital policies dealing with society and sovereignty in a way that disenfranchises the people

The beauty of this plan is that every one of these changes has a systemic and multiplying effect in re-empowering the people through their elected representatives. Most important, every one of these ideas can be enacted through the traditional legislative process, and as we've studied in great detail, does not require a constitutional amendment. Mark Levin has proposed a comprehensive, one-hundred-year plan via constitutional amendments to restore our republic. Those ideas are vital to eventually rebuilding a healthy republic. But the ideas proposed in this book are essential *short-term* acts of triage to preempt the imminent collapse of our existence as a democracy and as a sovereign nation-state. As it relates to this issue, time is one resource we surely lack.

You might ask, "How we can ever secure enough Democratic support to pass these initiatives through the Senate, where, even in the best-case scenario, Republicans will lack the votes to overcome a filibuster? Further, won't we face a truculent and unrelenting opposition from the deep-pocketed legal community, academics, and ethnic power lobbies who will smear us with every pejorative imaginable?"

We must remember that this is the degree of opposition we will face in pursuit of every conservative reform idea, even those universally accepted by all Republican insiders. Any push for entitlement reform, changes to the tax and welfare structure, and free-market health care will run into the ferocious opposition of inveterate constituencies that are even more powerful and relevant in the electoral scheme than the forces of mass migration and judicial tyranny. Not a single Democrat will willingly support a single conservative fiscal policy initiative.

Accordingly, either way conservatives will have to think long and hard about the future of the filibuster if they hope to enact a single significant conservative policy initiative on any issue. The truth is the Democrats will almost certainly abolish the filibuster anyway the next time they hold the keys to all three branches, even if they feel stymied by a GOP-filibuster in the Senate. The filibuster has been an indispensable tool in preserving our republic and serving as a bulwark against tyranny for many years. But with Democrats undermining our sovereignty and transforming society before our eyes, without ever having to use the legislative process, and with the likelihood that they will abolish the filibuster on their next watch anyway, we might very well have no choice but to limit its use.

Some conservatives will scoff at resorting to such "drastic" tactics, repeating the mantra that conservatives are not revolutionaries and should not upend the stability of some procedures and protocols. Again, they would be correct had we not suffered from this century-long bloodless coup against the Constitution. In that case, we would merely pursue the status quo and seek to guard against radical changes, for which we would absolutely need critical tools like the filibuster to prevent transformation. But that ship has sailed. And it sailed a long time ago. The transformation is well under way and almost complete. We can no longer sit back idly; we must be revolutionaries to merely restore our republic.

Additionally, all of the systemic reforms we've proposed, while violently opposed by the political elites, will be a much easier sell with the general public than some of the fiscal ideas championed by conservatives. They even have broad bipartisan appeal. Immigration is the ultimate silent majority issue, and the particular ideas we've proposed—ending the disenfranchising of all citizens—Republicans and Democrats—at the hands of illegal aliens would have an enormous appeal. Poll after poll has shown the country wants less immigration. Numerous surveys have shown the country is growing concerned over refugee resettlement and increased immigration from the Middle East.

A November 2011 Rasmussen poll showed that 83 percent of all conservative voters opposed automatic citizenship for illegals and 71 percent of moderates agreed. Overall, 73 percent of all mainstream voters opposed the loophole, while a plurality of only "political insiders" supported it.[4] Common sense dictates that stopping illegals from entering, voting, debasing our representation, and stealing our citizenship are much easier sells with the public than, say, reforming Medicare and Social Security—as critical as those issues are.

Even with the growing success of the homosexual (super) rights movement, most Americans still believe in religious liberty for those who want to peacefully uphold their religious beliefs. A recent poll showed 82 percent of voters believe that individuals should not be coerced to service gay weddings in contravention to their religious beliefs.[5] A bill protecting religious liberty and stripping the courts of judicial review on the entire subject matter is very easy to message relative to many other conservative agenda items.

Finally, although the effort to strip the courts of power would be feverishly denounced by liberal and conservative legal academics alike, there is something intuitive and prudential in the eyes of commonsense voters about the rallying cry of "No social transformation without representation." Even many ordinary Democrat voters can be convinced that although we disagree on some of the political ramifications of these critical issues, the decisions governing those issues can and must be made by our elected representatives, not the judicial oligarchy.

As much as we all hate Congress, the reality is that the legislative process works much better for society than the unelected judiciary and the bureaucrats. This is especially true in our modern era of mass and instant communications. It's not just that legislators are up for election, in part, every two years. The public scrutiny of the legislative process with dramatic and public votes held on each critical issue holds a greater degree of accountability than even elections. With the Internet and social media, members of the public on all sides of the political divide can instantly weigh in and flood Congress with calls demanding their members vote a certain way. In some sense, the advent of modern communications, which has shed a great degree of sunlight through the dark corridors of Congress—something that has not happened in the case of the executive agencies and certainly the judiciary—has improved the democratic process from the time of our Founders.

Consider this for a moment: when was the last time Congress passed a bad immigration bill? It's been about thirty years. Every time they try to pass an open borders bill through both houses of Congress, the public weighs in swiftly and decisively against it. This is why liberals resort to using the administrative offices and the judiciary to enact their transformative agenda. Were we to successfully restore authority over the major societal questions to the body of government that conducts public votes, we would go a long way in re-empowering the people and at least affording conservatives a fighting chance to right this ship.

This is exactly what our Founders had in mind. Far from the judiciary having the final say over political questions or over the legislature, "[a] dependence on the people is, no doubt, the primary control on the government," in the words of Madison.[6] Ultimately, Madison felt that "the circulation of newspapers through the entire body of people," "representatives going from, and returning among every part of them," and "sound argument & conciliatory expostulations addressed both to Congress & to their Constituents" would win the day.[7]

As the traditional liberal media continues to decline and conservatives successfully exert their influence over legislative endeavors through sound arguments, we are making tremendous progress in restoring our republic. But unless the gravity of power is returned to the legislature from the clutches of the courts, we will never have a fighting chance to even affect our destiny through "sound argument & conciliatory expostulations."

A FINAL WARNING

Our republic was founded upon a successful revolution, which was spawned by a unifying rallying cry against "taxation without representation." What we have today—social and societal transformation without representation—makes the very impetus for our revolution seem trivial. Our economy, society, culture, political system, safety, and security—and most prominently—our destiny, have been irrevocably compromised by this transformation. Our most sacred inalienable right of religious conscience is under imminent threat of extinction. This has all been wrought by decisions made by a judicial oligarchy and bureaucratic politburo without the people's consent.

Moreover, during the times of the revolution and the grievances against King George, there was no republican form of government to hold up as a standard. The revolution created the very first successful model. Our modern-day "long train of abuses and usurpations," on the other hand, come on the heels of two centuries' worth of successful republican governance. In that sense, both the consequences and the degree of illegality behind the current usurpations dwarf the magnitude of the grievances expressed during the time of our founding.[8]

Yet, for the cause of taxation without representation and establishing for the first time a government built upon popular sovereignty, our Founders were willing to "mutually pledge to each other" their Lives, Fortunes, and sacred Honor.[9] Even before establishing a government built upon natural law, inalienable rights, popular sovereignty, and republicanism, our Founders strongly believed that "whenever any Form of Government becomes destructive of these ends, it is the Right of the People to alter or to abolish it, and to institute new Government, laying its foundation on such principles and organizing its powers in such form, as to them shall seem most likely to effect their Safety and Happiness."[10]

As we've explored in detail, our property rights are violated even to the point of regulating inaction; our most sacred property right and liberty—religious freedom—is under assault; our right to self-governance and sovereignty has been debased and contorted in every immoral, illogical, and self-conflicting way imaginable. These are the antithesis of "light and transient causes" for which our Founders advised against pursuing a wholesale rebellion to remedy. Is it too much to demand that we at least use the existing political process and constitutional remedies—without abolishing the government—to restore our nation and sovereignty to what it was rightfully and legally founded upon?

Ignoring this challenge, the consummate challenge of our time, is not an option. For if we squander our final chance to restore our republic through the existing political process; if we so choose to "to suffer while evils are sufferable," our only remaining recourse will be a path far more painful and insurmountable.

NOTES

INTRODUCTION

1. Obergefell v. Hodges, 576 U.S. ___ (2015); "Gay Marriage Goes Dutch," CBS News, April 1, 2001, http://www.cbsnews.com/news/gay-marriage-goes-dutch/.
2. *Obergefell, Id.* (Scalia, J., dissenting) (slip. op., at 6)
3. Jennifer Duffy, "25 Interesting Facts about the 2012 Elections," Cook Political Report, December 20, 2012, http://cookpolitical.com/story/5219
4. "Simple Definition of Sovereignty," Merriam-Webster Dictionary, http://www.merriam-webster.com/dictionary/sovereignty
5. Lolita C. Baldor, "Pentagon Announces Plan Aimed at Lifting Transgender Ban," Associated Press, July 13, 2015, http://bigstory.ap.org/article/67db24e3b2604c39b20c4b7f7e5bcbf7/apnewsbreak-pentagon-readying-plan-lift-transgender-ban
6. Erica Getto and Kavish Harjai, "8 times that a 10 Commandments monument had its day in court," MSNBC, July 8, 2015, http://www.msnbc.com/msnbc/8-times-10-commandments-monument-had-its-day-court
7. Peyton M. Craighill and Scott Clement, "Liberals have won a series of victories on social issues. Most Americans aren't thrilled about it," *Washington Post*, July 22, 2015, https://www.washingtonpost.com/news/the-fix/wp/2015/07/22/liberals-have-won-a-series-of-victories-on-social-issues-most-americans-arent-thrilled-about-it/
8. Robert H. Bork. *Coercing Virtue: The Worldwide Rule of Judges*. (Washington D.C.:The AEI Press, 2003); Mark R. Levin. *Men in Black: How the Supreme Court is Destroying America* (Washington D.C.:Regnery Publishing, 2006).
9. *Obergefell, Id.* (Alito, J., dissenting) (slip. op., at 8)
10. "How many cases are appealed to the Court each year and how many cases does the Court hear?," as posted on the Frequently Asked Questions (FAQ) Page of the U.S. Supreme Court's website, http://www.supremecourt.gov/faq.aspx#faqgi9.

CHAPTER 1: THE COURTS: NEITHER FORCE NOR WILL

1. Avendano-Hernandez v. Lynch, 800 F.3d 1072, No. 13-73744 (9th Cir. Sept. 3, 2015).

2. Although the Supreme Court did strike down state laws completely banning handguns (McDonald v. Chicago, 561 US 742 (2010)), the high court has declined to overturn lower court decisions upholding sweeping gun control laws that stopped short of categorical bans. Numerous states have imposed bans on magazine clips and certain rifles and handguns. San Francisco required that all handguns be locked up in one's home. On two occasions, the Supreme Court refused to hear an appeal after lower courts upheld these state and local laws. Justices Thomas and Scalia vigorously dissented from the decision not to grant cert to those petitioners, noting that the courts were "relegating the Second Amendment to a second-class right." See more from Josh Blackman, "Justice Thomas: Second Amendment Is Not a 'Second-Class Right,'" *National Review*, December 8, 2015, http://www.nationalreview.com/article/428173/second-amendment-supreme-court. Also, courts have upheld full restrictions on concealed carry of firearms, despite the unambiguous language of the Second Amendment: "the right of the people to keep and *bear* Arms, shall not be infringed." Woollard v. Gallagher, 712 F.3d 865, 874 (4th Cir.), *cert. denied*, 134 S. Ct. 422 (2013). Thomas Jefferson was clear that the natural right to self-defense applied to carrying weapons at all times. "That it is their right and duty to be *at all times armed*." Letter to John Cartwright, June 5, 1824 (On unalienable rights and their immutability), Founding.com: a Project of the Claremont Institute, http://www.founding.com/founders_library/pageID.2195/default.asp; emphasis added. "A strong body makes the mind strong. As to the species of exercise, I advise the gun. While this gives a moderate exercise to the body, it gives boldness, enterprise, and independence to the mind. Games played with the ball and others of that nature, are too violent for the body and stamp no character on the mind. *Let your gun therefore be the constant companion of your walks*." Letter to Peter Carr, August 19, 1785 (On the mind and exercise and education), Founding.com, http://www.founding.com/founders_library/pageID.2180/default.asp; emphasis added.
3. On August 20, 2015, the Seventh Circuit Court of Appeals opined that illegal aliens have gun rights. United States v. Meza-Rodriguez, No. 14-3271 (7th Cir. 2015). Just a few months earlier, the same circuit court upheld Illinois's draconian restrictions on gun ownership for American citizens. Friedman v. City of Highland Park, 784 F. 3d 406, 412 (7th Cir. 2015).
4. "The Big List of Christian Coercion," WND, April 6, 2015, http://www.wnd.com/2015/04/courts-conclude-faith-loses-to-gay-demands/. This article chronicles stories of private Christian business owners who were fined for declining to service same-sex weddings. During the same year, the U.S. District Court for the Central District of Illinois fined Star Transport $240,000 for firing two Muslim workers who refused to transport truckloads of beer, a core part of their job, citing violations of religious liberty. Andy Kravetz, "Two Men Awarded $240K in Suit Alleging Religious Discrimination by Trucking Company," *Journal Star* (Peoria, IL), October 22, 2015, http://www.pjstar.com/article/20151022/NEWS/151029737.
5. Brian Ross et al., "Secret US Policy Blocks Agents from Looking at Social Media of Visa Applicants, Former Official Says," ABC News, December 14, 2015, http://abcnews.go.com/US/secret-us-policy-blocks-agents-social-media-visa/story?id=35749325.
6. Caroline May, "Obama Admin Unilaterally Changes Law to Allow Immigrants with 'Limited' Terror Contact into US," *Daily Caller*, February 5, 2014, http://dailycaller.com/2014/02/05/obama-admin-changes-immigration-law-allows-immigrants-who-supported-terrorists-into-us/.
7. "Presidential Thanksgiving Proclamations 1789–1815: George Washington, John Adams, James Madison," as reprinted on the Pilgrim Hall Museum Website, accessed February 3, 2016, http://www.pilgrimhallmuseum.org/pdf/TG_Presidential_Thanksgiving_Proclamations_1789_1815.pdf. George Washington, October 3, 1789: ". . . to protect and guide all sovereigns and nations (especially such as have shown kindness to us), and to bless them with good governments, peace,

and concord; to promote the knowledge and practice of true religion and virtue . . ."; John Adams, March 6, 1799: ". . . be observed throughout the United States of America as a day of solemn humiliation, fasting, and prayer; that the citizens on that day abstain as far as may be from their secular occupations, devote the time to the sacred duties of religion in public and in private; that they call to mind our numerous offenses against the Most High God, confess them before Him with the sincerest penitence . . ."

8. The Declaration of Independence, par. 2 (U.S. 1776).
9. From the notes of Dr. James McHenry, a Maryland delegate at the Constitutional Convention, as cited in J. Franklin Jameson, et al., eds., *The American Historical Review*, vol. 11 (London: MacMillan, 1906), 618.
10. In the case of the Senate, they were originally elected by the state legislatures, but elected nonetheless.
11. James Madison, *Federalist* No. 51.
12. Alexander Hamilton, *Federalist* No. 78.
13. Ibid.
14. U.S. Const. art. III, § 2, cl. 2 only grants the Supreme Court original jurisdiction over "all Cases affecting Ambassadors, other public Ministers and Consuls, and those in which a State shall be Party."
15. Louis de Secondat, Baron de Montesquieu, *The Complete Works of M. de Montesquieu* (London: T. Evans, 1777), 4 vols., as reprinted on the Online Library of Liberty website; emphasis added, http://oll.libertyfund.org/titles/837#Montesquieu_0171-01_910.
16. Max Farrand, *The Framing of the Constitution of the United States (1913)* (New Haven, CT, and London: Yale University Press, 2013), Kindle edition, location 1497.
17. Alexander Hamilton, *Federalist* No.78, emphasis added.
18. Mark R. Levin. *Men in Black: How the Supreme Court Is Destroying America* (Washington, D.C.: Regnery, 2006), 12.
19. U.S. Const. art. III, § 2, cl. 1.
20. Oliver Ellsworth, "Letters of a Landholder," V, in *Essays on the United States Constitution*, ed. Paul Leicester Ford (New York: Historical Printing Club, 1892), 159.
21. Joseph Story, *Commentaries on the Constitution of the United States*, 3 vols. (Boston: 1833), § 1577.
22. Farrand, *The Framing of the Constitution of the United States (1913)*, location 1513.
23. John Jay, *The Correspondence and Public Papers of John Jay*, ed. Henry P. Johnston, vol. 4 (1794–1826) (New York: G. P. Putnam's Sons, 1890–93), as republished on the Online Library of Liberty website, http://oll.libertyfund.org/titles/2330#lf1530-04_head_144.
24. "Throughout most of our history the form of the Supreme Court's contributions to public policy was negative." Archibald Cox, "The New Dimensions of Constitutional Adjudication," *Washington Law Review* 51, no. 2 (March 1976): 813
25. Marbury v. Madison, 5 US 137 (1803).
26. Thomas Jefferson letter to William Jarvis, September 28, 1820, in *The Writings of Thomas Jefferson*, ed. H. A. Washington, vol. 7 (New York: Derby & Jackson, 1859), 178.
27. *Marbury*, 5 US at 179, emphasis added. Further, Marshall promised the 1788 Virginia Ratifying Convention the Judiciary would not be vested with the power to overturn state laws. However, Marshall clearly deviated from that promise while serving on the bench.

28. Judiciary Act of 1789, § 13, granted the Supreme Court original jurisdiction to issue "writs of mandamus, in cases warranted by the principles and usages of law, to any courts appointed, or persons holding office, under the authority of the United States." Marshall struck that down because the Constitution does not include writs of mandamus in the court's original jurisdiction.
29. Alexander Hamilton, *Federalist* No. 78.
30. Calder v. Bull, 3 US (3 Dall.) 386, 399 (1798). While debating the Constitution in 1787, Iredell emphatically declared that a law "should be unconstitutional beyond dispute before it is pronounced such." Letter from James Iredell to Richard Spaight (Aug. 26, 1787), *The Papers of James Iredell*, 3:310.
31. Speech before the Chamber of Commerce, Elmira, New York, May 3, 1907, published in *Addresses and Papers of Charles Evans Hughes: Governor of New York 1906–1908* (New York and London: Knickerbocker Press, 1908), 139.
32. William J. Quirk and R. Randall Bridwell, *Judicial Dictatorship* (Piscataway, NJ: Transaction, 1996), 38.
33. Coleman v. Alabama, 399 US 1, 15 (1970).
34. Josh Blackman, "Judge Posner on Judging, Birthright Citizenship, and Precedent," *Josh Blackman's Blog* (blog), November 6, 2015, reporting on a speech delivered by Judge Richard Posner at the Loyola Constitutional Law Colloquium, http://joshblackman.com/blog/2015/11/06/judge-posner-on-judging-birthright-citizenship-and-precedent/.
35. Obergefell v. Hodges, 576 US ___ (2015), slip. op., at 8 (Alito, J., dissenting).
36. Thurgood Marshall in a speech made at the annual seminar of the San Francisco Patent and Trademark Law Association in Maui, Hawaii, May 6, 1987, http://thurgoodmarshall.com/the-bicentennial-speech/.
37. U.S. Const. amend. XIV, § 5.
38. Katzenbach v. Morgan, 384 US 641, 651n10 (1966).
39. Plyler v. Doe, 457 US 202, 211n10 (1982). Brennan used the Fourteenth Amendment to invalidate a Texas law that prohibited public education funds from being used for children of illegal aliens. He also said that children born to illegal aliens are entitled to automatic citizenship. We will discuss this case and its ramifications in greater detail in chapters 4 and 5.
40. Margaret Thatcher, *The Downing Street Years* (London: Harper Collins, 1993) 6–7.
41. *Marbury*, 5 US at 177.
42. Reynolds v. Sims, 377 US 533, 624–25 (1964) (Harlan, J., dissenting).
43. Letter to Justice William Johnson, June 12, 1823, as posted on the Teaching American History website, accessed February 3, 2016, http://teachingamericanhistory.org/library/document/letter-to-justice-william-johnson/.
44. Vanhorne's Lessee v. Dorrance 2 US 304, 308 (1795).
45. James Madison, letter to Henry Lee, June 25, 1824, *Writings of James Madison*, ed. Jack Rakove (New York: Library of America, 1999), 803.
46. Edward J. Erler, *The American Founding and the Social Compact*, ed. Robert J. Pestritto and Thomas G. West (Lanham, MD: Lexington Books, 2003), at 6, as posted on the Claremont Institute website, http://www.claremont.org/js/ckeditor/ckfinder/userfiles/files/citizen7.pdf.
47. Calvin Coolidge, "Address at the Celebration of the 150th Anniversary of the Declaration of Independence, Philadelphia, Pa.," July 4, 1926, as posted on the American Presidency Project website, http://www.presidency.ucsb.edu/ws/index.php?pid=408.
48. John Quincy Adams, letter to Moritz Von Fuerstenwaerther, Department of State, Washington, June 4, 1819, printed in *Niles' Weekly Register*, vol. 18, on April 29, 1820, https://archive.org/stream/nilesweeklyregis18balt#page/157/mode/1up.

49. Ronald Reagan, Farewell Address to the Nation, January 11, 1989, printed on the website of the American Presidency Project, http://www.presidency.ucsb.edu/ws/?pid=29650.
50. Joseph Story. *Commentaries on the Constitution of the United States of America*, 3 vols. (Boston: Hillard, Gray, 1833), § 1901.

CHAPTER 2: COURTS AND OBAMACARE: LIMITLESS FEDERAL POWER

1. Josh Blackman, "Judge Posner on Judging, Birthright Citizenship, and Precedent," *Josh Blackman's Blog* (blog), November 6, 2015, http://joshblackman.com/blog/2015/11/06/judge-posner-on-judging-birthright-citizenship-and-precedent/; emphasis added.
2. National Federation of Independent Business v. Sebelius, 567 US ___ (2012), 132 S.Ct 2566.
3. Drew Gonshorowski, "How Will You Fare in the Obamacare Exchanges?," Heritage Foundation, October 16, 2013, http://www.heritage.org/research/reports/2013/10/enrollment-in-obamacare-exchanges-how-will-your-health-insurance-fare.
4. See Michael D. Shear, "GOP Turns to the Courts to Aid Agenda," *New York Times*, January 3, 2015, http://mobile.nytimes.com/2015/01/04/us/politics/gop-turns-to-the-courts-to-aid-agenda.html?referrer=&_r=3.
5. Alexander Hamilton, *Federalist* No. 78.
6. *National Federation of Independent Business*, 567 US ___ (2012), 132 S.Ct 2566 (slip. op. at 44): "The Affordable Care Act's requirement that certain individuals pay a financial penalty for not obtaining health insurance may reasonably be characterized as a tax."
7. James Madison, letter to Joseph C. Cabell, February 13, 1829, as posted on the Founders' Constitution website, http://press-pubs.uchicago.edu/founders/documents/a1_8_3_commerces19.html; emphasis added.
8. James Madison, *Federalist* No. 45.
9. United States v. Lopez, 514 US 549, 585 (1995) (Thomas, J., concurring)
10. *Lopez*, 514 US at 601.
11. U.S. Const. art. I, § 8, cl. 18. ("The Congress shall have Power to . . . make all Laws which shall be necessary and proper for carrying into Execution the foregoing Powers, and all other Powers vested by this Constitution in the Government of the United States, or in any Department or Officer thereof.")
12. Justice John Marshall clearly expressed this view of the "elastic clause" in *McCulloch v. Maryland*, 17 US (4 Wheat.) 316, 421 (1819). He upheld the constitutionality of the National Bank only on the premise that it was a means to the legitimate ends of executing the taxing and spending powers. ("We admit, as all must admit, that the powers of the Government are limited, and that its limits are not to be transcended. But we think the sound construction of the Constitution must allow to the national legislature that discretion with respect to the means by which the powers it confers are to be carried into execution which will enable that body to perform the high duties assigned to it in the manner most beneficial to the people. Let the end be legitimate, let it be within the scope of the Constitution, and all means which are appropriate, which are plainly adapted to that end, which are not prohibited, but consistent with the letter and spirit of the Constitution, are constitutional.")
13. Judge Frank Hull of the Eleventh Circuit Court of Appeals was the only Democrat to strike down the individual mandate. He joined in the majority opinion of the Eleventh Circuit in *Florida ex rel. Attorney General v. US Dept. of Health and Human Services*, 648 F. 3d 1235 (11th Cir. 2011).

14. They include Judge Jeffrey Sutton in *Thomas More Law Center v. Obama*, 651 F. 3d 529 (6th Cir. 2011) (Sutton, J., concurring in part); Judge Laurence Silberman in *Seven-Sky v. Holder*, 661 F. 3d 1 (D.C. Cir. 2011); and Judge Stanley Marcus (*Thomas More*, 651 F. 3d 529) (Marcus, J., dissenting), who was originally appointed to a district judgeship by Ronald Reagan and elevated to the Sixth Circuit by Bill Clinton.
15. King v. Burwell, 576 US ___ (2015).
16. 42 U.S.C. §18031(b)(1).
17. Judge Roger Gregory was appointed to the Fourth Circuit by George W. Bush and wrote the decision to uphold the unconstitutional subsidies in *King v. Burwell*, 759 F. 3d 358 (4th Cir. 2014). In addition, Chief Justice Roberts and Associate Justice Kennedy, two GOP appointees, ruled with the Obama administration.
18. *King* 576 US, slip op. at 20.
19. Ibid. at 21.
20. Ibid. at 20 (Scalia, J., dissenting).
21. Religious Freedom Restoration Act of 1993, Pub. L. No. 103-141, 107 Stat. 1488 42 U.S.C. § 2000bb-1. The government may only "substantially burden a person's exercise of religion" if it demonstrates that application of the burden to the person— (1) is in furtherance of a compelling governmental interest; and (2) is the "least restrictive means of furthering that compelling governmental interest."
22. The Eighth Circuit was the only court to side with the religious institutions. Sharpe Holdings, Inc. v. United States Department of Health and Human Services, 801 F. 3d 927 (8th Cir. 2015). As of the writing of this book, the Supreme Court has agreed to rule on a number of similar cases, and the litigation is still pending.
23. The list of GOP judges who sided with the administration against religious freedom include: Judge Richard Posner (Reagan) in *Wheaton College v. Burwell*, 791 F. 3d 792 (7th Cir. 2015) (petition for preliminary injunction denied); Judge Jerry Smith (Reagan) in *East Texas Baptist University v. Burwell*, 793 F. 3d 449 (5th Cir. 2015); Judge Ilana Rovner (George H. W. Bush) in *Grace Schools v. Burwell*, 801 F. 3d 788 (7th Cir. 2015); Judge Robert Dow (George W. Bush) in *Wheaton College v. Burwell*, 50 F. Supp. 3d 939 (N.D. Ill. 2014) (petition for preliminary injunction denied).

CHAPTER 3: THE COURTS REMAKE CIVILIZATION AND THREATEN RELIGIOUS LIBERTY

1. John Witherspoon, "The Dominion of Providence over the Passions of Men," sermon preached on May 17, 1776, at Princeton, in Political Sermons of the American Founding Era: 1730–1805, ed. Ellis Sandoz, 2nd ed., vol, 1 (Indianapolis: Liberty Fund, 1998).
2. Obergefell v. Hodges, 576 US ___ (2015), slip op. at 11, emphasis added.
3. See United States v. Carlton, 512 US 26 (1994) (Scalia, J., dissenting): "If I thought that 'substantive due process' were a constitutional right rather than an oxymoron . . ."
4. *The Papers of Alexander Hamilton*, ed. Harold C. Syrett et al., 26 vols. (New York and London: Columbia University Press, 1961–79), as posted on the Founders' Constitution website, http://press-pubs.uchicago.edu/founders/documents/amendV_due_processs13.html, emphasis added. Justice Story made it clear that a due process violation was the denial of a proper judicial proceeding in a criminal trial. "Without due presentment or indictment, and being brought in to answer thereto by due process of the common law. So that this clause in effect affirms the right of trial according

to the *process* and *proceedings* of the common law." *Commentaries on the Constitution* § 1783; emphasis added.

5. Washington v. Glucksberg 521 US 702 (1997).
6. *Washington*, 521 US at 703.
7. Ibid. at 715.
8. *Obergefell*, slip op. at 4. (Scalia, J., dissenting)
9. *Obergefell*, slip op. at 15 (Thomas, J., dissenting).
10. Ibid. at 15.
11. *Obergefell* at 2 (Scalia, J., dissenting).
12. Peter Sprigg, "How many states have banned gay 'marriage'?," LifeSite, May 24, 2012, https://www.lifesitenews.com/news/how-many-states-have-banned-gay-marriage.
13. Michael Martinez, "Who Is Kim Davis, Kentucky Clerk Jailed over Same-Sex Marriage Licenses?" CNN, September 8, 2015, http://www.cnn.com/2015/09/04/us/kim-davis-things-to-know/.
14. *Obergefell* at 1 (Thomas, J., dissenting).
15. Ogden v. Saunders, 25 US (12 Wheat.) 213, 332 (1827) (Marshall, C. J., dissenting). This was the only opinion of his career in which he found himself on the losing side of a constitutional question. In *Ogden*, Marshall chastised the majority for upholding the constitutionality of New York's bankruptcy law, noting that it was in clear violation of the plain meaning of the Obligation of Contract Clause, Art. I, § 10, cl. 1, which prohibited states from passing laws "impairing the Obligation of Contracts." Marshall couldn't imagine an innovative reading of state contract authority in contravention to the plain reading of the Constitution; could he possibly have ever envisioned the redefinition of marriage itself read into the plain language of *any* portion of the Constitution?
16. James Madison, letter to Henry Lee, June 25, 1824, *Writings of James Madison*, ed. Jack Rakove (New York: Library of America, 1999), 803.
17. Bob Egelko, "At Santa Clara, Scalia says he's a dissident on a liberal court," *San Francisco Chronicle*, October 29, 2015, http://www.sfgate.com/news/article/At-Santa-Clara-Scalia-says-he-s-a-dissident-on-6597321.php.
18. 28 USC 455 says: "Any justice, judge or magistrate of the United States shall disqualify himself in any proceeding in which his impartiality might reasonably be questioned."
19. Justice Ginsburg performed several gay marriages inside the Supreme Court: Kirsten Anderson, "Justices O'Connor, Ginsburg Perform Same-Sex 'Marriage' Ceremonies Inside Supreme Court," LifeSiteNews, October 31, 2015, https://www.lifesitenews.com/news/justices-oconnor-ginsburg-perform-same-sex-marriage-ceremonies-inside-supre. Ginsberg reportedly said, "I think it will be one more statement that people who love each other and want to live together should be able to enjoy the blessings and the strife in the marriage relationship." Robert Barnes, "Ginsburg to Officiate Same-Sex Wedding," *Washington Post*, August 30, 2013, https://www.washingtonpost.com/politics/ginsburg-to-officiate-same-sex-wedding/2013/08/30/4bc09d86-0ff4-11e3-8cdd-bcdc09410972_story.html. Justice Kagan performed her first gay marriage service for a former law clerk in 2014; "Supreme Court Justice Performs her First Same-Sex Wedding," CBS News, September 22, 2014, http://www.cbsnews.com/news/supreme-court-justice-elena-kagan-performs-her-first-same-sex-wedding/.
20. *Obergefell* 576 US at 1–2: "The Constitution promises liberty to all within its reach, a liberty that includes certain specific rights that allow persons, within a lawful realm, to *define and express their identity*" (emphasis added); at 3: "The lifelong union of a man and a woman always has promised *nobility and dignity* to all persons, without regard to their station in life" (emphasis added); at 7:

"Even when a greater awareness of the humanity and integrity of homosexual persons came in the period after World War II, the argument that gays and lesbians had *a just claim to dignity* was in conflict with both law and widespread social conventions" (emphasis added); at 10: "In addition these liberties extend to certain personal choices central to individual *dignity and autonomy*, including intimate choices that define personal identity and beliefs" (emphasis added); at 28: "They ask for *equal dignity* in the eyes of the law. The Constitution grants them that right" (emphasis added); at 15: "Without the recognition, stability, and predictability marriage offers, their children suffer the *stigma* of knowing their families are somehow lesser" (emphasis added); at 19: "But when that sincere, personal opposition becomes enacted law and public policy, the necessary consequence is to put the imprimatur of the State itself on an exclusion that soon demeans or *stigmatizes* those whose own liberty is then denied" (emphasis added).

21. United States v. Windsor 570 U.S. ___ (2013).
22. Ibid. at 16 (slip opinion).
23. Ibid. at 17.
24. Arizona State Legislature v. Arizona Independent Redistricting 576 U.S. ___ (2015).
25. *Arizona State Legislature*, 576 US at 35: "Invoking the Elections Clause, the Arizona Legislature instituted this lawsuit to disempower the State's voters from serving as the legislative power for redistricting purposes."
26. Ibid. (Thomas, J., dissenting) at 1: "Just last week, in the antithesis of deference to state lawmaking through direct democracy, the Court cast aside state laws across the country—many of which were enacted through ballot initiative—that reflected the traditional definition of marriage"; at 3, Thomas notes how this ballot initiative actually disenfranchised the people of Arizona, rather than empowering them: "And how striking that it changed here. The ballot initiative in this case, unlike those that the Court has previously treated so dismissively, was unusually democracy-reducing. It did not ask the people to approve a particular redistricting plan through direct democracy, but instead to take districting away from the people's representatives and give it to an unelected committee, thereby reducing democratic control over the process in the future."
27. *Obergefell*, No. 14556. Oral argument of Mary L. Bonauto. Transcript p. 18–19 ["JUSTICE ALITO: Well, what if there's no—these are 4 people, 2 men and 2 women, it's not—it's not the sort of polygamous relationship, polygamous marriages that existed in other societies and still exist in some societies today. And let's say they're all consenting adults, highly educated. They're all lawyers."]
28. *Obergefell*, majority opinion, at 15.
29. *Obergefell* at 28.
30. Ibid. at 13 (emphasis added).
31. Ibid. (Roberts, C. J., dissenting) at 20: "Although the majority randomly inserts the adjective 'two' in various places, it offers no reason at all why the two-person element of the core definition of marriage may be preserved while the man-woman element may not. Indeed, from the standpoint of history and tradition, a leap from opposite-sex marriage to same-sex marriage is much greater than one from a two-person union to plural unions, which have deep roots in some cultures around the world. If the majority is willing to take the big leap, it is hard to see how it can say no to the shorter one."
32. Adrian A. Mojica, "Tennessee Judge Rules Against Couple's Divorce, Cites SCOTUS Gay Marriage

Decision," Fox 17 News Nashville, September 2, 2015, http://www.fox17.com/news/features/top-stories/stories/Tennessee-Judge-Rules-Against-Couple-39-s-Divorce-Cites-SCOTUS-Gay-Marriage-Decision-199334.shtml.

33. Richard A. Posner, "Eighteen Years On: A Re-Review," *Yale Law Journal* 125, no. 2 (November 2015): 326–559, http://www.yalelawjournal.org/article/eighteen-years-on.
34. Josh Blackman, "Judge Posner on Judging, Birthright Citizenship, and Precedent," *Josh Blackman's Blog* (blog), November 6, 2015, http://joshblackman.com/blog/2015/11/06/judge-posner-on-judging-birthright-citizenship-and-precedent/.
35. Timothy Farrar, *Manual of the Constitution of the United States of America* (Boston: Little, Brown,1867) 408–9.
36. Cong. Globe, 39th Cong., at 2539 (May 10, 1866).
37. *The Works of James Wilson*, ed. Robert Green McCloskey, 2 vols. (Cambridge: Belknap Press of Harvard University Press, 1967).
38. Joseph Story, *Commentaries on the Constitution of the United States of America*, 3 vols. (Boston: Hillard, Gray, 1833), § 1901.
39. Callie Granade (George W. Bush) in *Searcy v. Strange*, 81 F. Supp. 3d 1285 (S.D. Ala. 2015); John Jones III (George W. Bush) in *Whitewood v. Wolf*, 992 F. Supp. 2d 410 (M.D. Penn. 2014); Bernard Friedman (Reagan) in *DeBoer v. Snyder*, 973 F. Supp. 2d 757 (E.D. Mich. 2014); Roger Gregory (George W. Bush) in Bostic v. Schaefer, 760 F. 3d 352 (4th Cir. 2014); Richard Posner (Reagan) in *Baskin v. Bogan*, 766 F. 3d 648 (7th Cir. 2014); Jerome Holmes (George W. Bush) in *Kitchen v. Herbert*, 755 F. 3d 1193 (10th Cir. 2014); Robert Shelby (although appointed by Obama, he is a Republican and was supported by Sen. Mike Lee) in *Kitchen v. Herbert*, 961 F. Supp. 2d 1181 (D. Utah, 2013).
40. See Scott Ott, "Federal Judge Says He's Above Natural Law as He Tosses Clerk Kim Davis in Jail," PJ Media, September 3, 2015, http://pjmedia.com/tatler/2015/09/03/federal-judge-says-hes-above-natural-law-as-he-tosses-clerk-kim-davis-in-jail/.
41. Burgess Everett, "McConnell: GOP out of Legislative Options to Fight Gay Marriage," Politico, July 1, 2015, http://www.politico.com/story/2015/07/mitch-mcconnell-gay-marriage-ruling-congress-legislation-119630.
42. See Todd Starnes, "Costly Beliefs: State Squeezes Last Penny from Bakers Who Defied Lesbian-Wedding Cake Order," Fox News, December 29, 2015, http://www.foxnews.com/opinion/2015/12/29/bakers-forced-to-pay-more-than-135g-in-lesbian-cake-battle.html; Chelsea Scism, "Christian Farmers Fined $13,000 for Refusing to Host Same-Sex Wedding Fight Back," *Daily Signal*, June 25, 2015, http://dailysignal.com/2015/06/25/christian-farmers-fined-13000-for-refusing-to-host-same-sex-wedding-fights-back/.
43. Robert H. Bork, "The End of Democracy? Our Judicial Oligarchy," *First Things*, November 1996, http://www.firstthings.com/article/1996/11/003-the-end-of-democracy-our-judicial-oligarchy.
44. Samuel Adams, speech delivered at the State House in Philadelphia on August 1, 1776, as republished by the National Center for Public Policy Research, http://www.nationalcenter.org/SamuelAdams1776.html.

CHAPTER 4: VIOLATING SOVEREIGNTY: THE ULTIMATE DISENFRANCHISING OF A NATION-STATE

1. Bob Egelko, "At Santa Clara Scalia Says He's a Dissident on a Liberal Court," *San Francisco Chronicle*, October 29, 2015, http://www.sfgate.com/news/article/At-Santa-Clara-Scalia-says-he-s-a-dissident-on-6597321.php.

2. Lana Shadwick, "Mexican and Central American Illegal Immigrants Sue Texas for Birth Certificates," Breitbart News, July 24, 2015, http://www.breitbart.com/texas/2015/07/24/mexican-and-central-american-immigrants-sue-texas-for-birth-certificates/.
3. "Mexico Warns Texas Not to Refuse Its Immigrants' Babies U.S. Birth Certificates," Fox News Latino, August 27, 2015, http://latino.foxnews.com/latino/news/2015/08/27/mexico-warns-texas-not-to-refuse-its-babies-usbirth-certificates/.
4. U.S. Const. amend. XIV, § 1.
5. Holmes v. Jennison, 39 US (14 Peters) 540, 570–71(1840): "In expounding the Constitution of the United States, every word must have its due force, and appropriate meaning; for it is evident from the whole instrument, that no word was unnecessarily used, or needlessly added. . . . Every word appears to have been weighed with the utmost deliberation, and its force and effect to have been fully understood. No word in the instrument, therefore, can be rejected as superfluous or unmeaning."
6. Afroyim v. Rusk, 387 US 262 (1967): "It is true that the chief interest of the people in giving permanence and security to citizenship in the Fourteenth Amendment was the desire to protect Negroes."
7. Civil Rights Act of 1866, S. 61, 39th Cong. (1866).
8. James Wilson, March 1, 1866. Cong. Globe, 39th Cong., 2d Sess. 39 (1866) 1117.
9. Lyman Trumbull, Cong. Globe, 39th Cong., 1st Sess. 2890.
10. Howard Jacobs, Ibid., 2890, 2895.
11. Indian Citizenship Act of 1924, 8 U.S.C. ch. 12, subch. III § 1401b (1924).
12. Slaughterhouse cases 83 US 36 (1872).
13. *Slaughterhouse*, at 74.
14. Ibid. at 73.
15. Elk v. Wilkins, 112 US 94 (1884).
16. Ibid. at 102.
17 .Attorney General George Henry Williams 14 Op. Atty-Gen. 300 (1873).
18. James Wilson, March 1, 1866. Cong. Globe, 39th Cong., 1st Sess. 39 (1866) 1117.
19. United States v. Wong Kim Ark 169 US 649 (1898).
20. *Wong* (Fuller, C. J., dissenting) at 713 ("In the opinion of the Attorney General, the United States, in recognizing the right of expatriation, declined from the beginning to accept the view that rested the obligation of the citizen on feudal principles, and proceeded on the law of nations, which was in direct conflict therewith").
21. Edward J. Erler, in *The Founders on Citizenship and Immigration: Principles and Challenges in America*, by Edmund J. Erler, Thomas J. West, and John Marini (Lanham, MD: Rowman & Littlefield, 2007), 19.
22. Thomas Jefferson, *Notes on the State of Virginia*, in *The Writings of Thomas Jefferson*, ed. H. A. Washington, vol. 7 (New York: Derby & Jackson, 1859), Query VIII, 211.
23. Erler, in Erler, West, and Marini, *The Founders on Citizenship and Immigration*, 50.
24. Cong. Globe, 40th Cong., 2d Sess. 868 (1868).
25. *Wong* (Fuller, C. J., dissenting) at 713. ("If the conclusion of the majority opinion is correct, then the children of citizens of the United States, who have been born abroad since July 8, 1868, when the amendment was declared ratified, were, and are, aliens, unless they have, or shall on attaining majority, become citizens by naturalization in the United States, and no statutory provision to the contrary is of any force or effect.")
26. Ibid. at 726.

27. U.S. Const. art. I, § 8, cl. 4 ("To establish a uniform Rule of Naturalization, and uniform Laws on the subject of Bankruptcies throughout the United States").
28. *Wong* (Fuller, C. J., dissenting), citing Fong Yue Ting v. United States 149 US 707 (1893).
29. U.S. Const. amend. XIV, § 5 ("The Congress shall have power to enforce, by appropriate legislation, the provisions of this article").
30. Plyler v. Doe, 457 U.S. 202, 211 n.10 (1982).
31. John C. Eastman, "We Can Apply the 14th Amendment While Also Reforming Birthright Citizenship," *National Review,* August 24, 2015, http://www.nationalreview.com/article/422960/birthright-citizenship-reform-it-without-repealing-14th-amendment.
32. John C. Eastman, "From Feudalism to Consent: Rethinking Birthright Citizenship," Heritage Foundation, March 30, 2006, http://www.heritage.org/research/reports/2006/03/from-feudalism-to-consent-rethinking-birthright-citizenship, in which he cites Erler, *Immigration and Citizenship,* at 77.
33. The Page Act of 1875, Chap. 141, 18 Stat. 477 (1875). The 1875 bill barred the entry of all prostitutes and shut down the importation of indentured servants from Asia, known as "coolies." It also barred all convicted felons from entering the country and ordered port officials to inspect all vessels and prohibit the entry of individuals until it could be certified that no such "obnoxious persons" were on board. The law also instructed the port inspectors to apprehend and deny the right to land to any individual suspected of being inadmissible pending the investigation into their status. Hence, anyone inadmissible after 1875 was deemed an illegal alien the same way we think of the term in the modern era.

    Chinese Exclusion Act, Pub. L. No. 47-126, 22 Stat. 58 (1882). On May 6, 1882, President Chester Arthur signed the Chinese Exclusion Act, which expanded upon the 1875 bill and fully banned most immigration from China for ten years. It allowed those already here to remain in the country but barred them from ever becoming naturalized. It also directed the executive branch to deport all Chinese present in the country without lawful status. Those already legally present in the country before passage of the bill had to obtain a certificate if they desired to travel abroad and could not be readmitted without producing the certification. However, in 1888, Congress passed another bill invalidating the certificates of any Chinese immigrant who had temporarily left the country, essentially making all Chinese immigrants, even those who had already obtained lawful status before the 1882 bill, inadmissible.

    Later that year, on August 3, Congress enacted the Immigration Act of 1882 (Chap. 376; 22 Stat. 214), which placed a head tax on all foreign passengers coming into US ports in order to fund the growing federal immigration bureaucracy. Until that point, states and local governments regulated immigration and passenger travel. This bill also codified into law a broad national immigration goal that had already been practiced by individual states and colonies dating back to the colonial era—that no immigrant be admitted who is likely to constitute a public charge. The bill directed customs inspectors to examine the passengers and prospective immigrants and "if on such examination there shall be found among such passengers any convict, lunatic, idiot, or any person unable to take care of him or herself without becoming a public charge, they shall report the same in writing to the collector of such port, and such person shall not be permitted to land" (Section 2, Immigration Act of 1882).

    In 1891, Congress increased the classes of those inadmissible and created the first robust system for screening and processing immigrants: the Immigration Act of 1891 (Chap. 551 26 Stat. 1084). The bill established the Bureau of Immigration under the auspices of the Treasury Department and directed it to inspect and enforce all immigration laws at land and sea ports. The bill added to the existing categories of inadmissibility those convicted of a "misdemeanor involving moral turpitude" (in addition to felonies), polygamists, paupers, and those suffering from contagious diseases. In addition to requiring a full interview with an immigration official, all immigrants had to undergo a medical exam, and anyone found to have a contagious disease was immediately quarantined and then deported. To prevent mass migration in general, and impoverished immigrants in particular, travel companies were barred from encouraging immigration through advertisements, and any immigrant suspected of coming as a result of such encouragement or any immigrant who had his passenger ticket paid for by others was deemed inadmissible. The bill ordered immigration officials to immediately deport any inadmissible immigrant, with the owner of the vessel that transported those aliens liable to pay the cost of the immigrant's return. Also, all immigrants who were found to be a public charge up to a year after being legally admitted into the country could be deported under this bill.

Finally, in 1892, Congress passed the Geary Act, Pub. L. No. 52-60, 27 Stat. 25 (1892), which, in addition to extending the ban on Chinese immigrants for another ten years, went a step further and required all existing Chinese residents to carry identification at all times, even if they did not plan to travel abroad. Failure to do so resulted in their deportation. The Scott Act of 1902 (Chap. 64132 Stat. 176) extended the ban indefinitely until it was repealed in 1943 (Magnuson Act of 1943, Pub. L. 78-199, 57 Stat. 600).

34. The Chinese Exclusion Case, 130 U.S. 581 (1889).
35. Ibid. at 603.
36. Ibid. at 606: "If, therefore, the government of the United States, through its legislative department, considers the presence of foreigners of a different race in this country, who will not assimilate with us, to be dangerous to its peace and security, their exclusion is not to be stayed"]; at 609" "The power of exclusion of foreigners being an incident of sovereignty belonging to the government of the United States as a part of those sovereign powers delegated by the Constitution, the right to its exercise at any time when, in the judgment of the government, the interests of the country require it, cannot be granted away or restrained on behalf of anyone."
37. Ibid. at 607–9.
38. Nishimura Ekiu v. United States, 142 US 651 (1892)
39. Lem Moon Sing v. United States, 158 US 538 (1895).
40. *Nishimura Ekiu* at 659.
41. Ibid. at 661.
42. Fong Yue Ting v. United States, 149 US 698 (1893).
43. Geary Act Pub. L. No. 52-60, 27 Stat. 25 (1892).
44. *Fong* at 705.
45. Ibid. at 707.
46. Ibid at 724.
47. The word *peace* is mentioned nine times, and the word *friendly* is mentioned on six occasions throughout the dissenting opinions of Justices Brewer, Field, and Fuller, in *Fong* at 733–63.
48. Vatt. Law Nat. lib. 1, c. 19, §§ 230, 231.
49. United States v. Ju Toy, 198 US 253 (1905).
50. Ibid. at 263, emphasis added. Justice Brewer and two others strongly dissented, but only because a claim of citizenship deserves, in their view, at least judicial review and procedural due process because on the chance that he is indeed a citizen, this action would have denied him fundamental rights. And in this case, they seemed to think it had been proven that indeed the petitioner was a citizen, which would have made this act of deportation appallingly unconstitutional (Brewer, J.,

dissenting, at 269). They also disagreed about whether the statute as written at the time did in fact grant immigration officials the authority to dismiss a claim of citizenship. The general principle, however, that all immigrants lack the fundamental right to enter the country or even due process was considered settled law.

51. Ibid.
52. Low Wah Suey v. Backus, 225 US 460 (1912).
53. Immigration Act of 1907, 34 Stat. 898 (1907); Mann Act, 36 Stat. 825 (1910).
54. *Low Wah Suey* at 476. It should be noted that the petition for habeas corpus filed in the *Low Wah Suey* case made a point of describing her family situation as follows: "The petitioner, Low Wah Suey, who instituted the proceedings in behalf of his wife, Li A. Sim, alleged that he was a resident of the City and County of San Francisco, California, *born in the United States of parents regularly domiciled therein*; that *consequently he is a citizen* of the United States and of the State of California" (emphasis added). This is yet another indication that to obtain automatic birthright citizenship, the child's immigrant parents must have been "regularly domiciled" in the country at the time of the birth, not illegal aliens.
55. Shaughnessy v. Mezei, 345 US 206 (1953).
56. Ibid. at 215.
57. Ibid. (Jackson, J., dissenting) at 227 ("Exclusion of an alien without judicial hearing, of course, does not deny due process when it can be accomplished merely by turning him back on land or returning him by sea. But when indefinite confinement becomes the means of enforcing exclusion, it seems to me that due process requires that the alien be informed of its grounds and have a fair chance to overcome them.")
58. Ibid. at 222–23, emphasis added. In a similar case in 1952, the court upheld the deportation of three former Communist Party members who had lived in the country for over thirty years and had US citizen spouses and children. Justice Frankfurter observed that although he might disagree with the policies, "the underlying policies of what classes of aliens shall be allowed to enter and what classes of aliens shall be allowed to stay are for Congress exclusively to determine." Harisiades v. Shaughnessy, 342 US 580 (1952), Frankfurter, J., Concurring, at 597.
59. In *Ng Fung Ho v. White,* 259 US 276 (1922), the court ruled that a petitioner claiming to be a citizen has a right to a judicial hearing to confirm that he is indeed not an alien. In *Fong Haw Tan v. Phelan*, 333 US 6, 8 (1948), the court stayed a deportation because they held that the immigration officials did not properly apply the statute in question, not on constitutional grounds. In *Kwong Hai Chew v. Colding*, 344 US 590 (1953), the court struck down an exclusion of a reentrant who was a longtime permanent resident but denied entry for national security reasons. However, the court was clear that this case was different because the alien was not even apprised of the charges and afforded an opportunity to be heard before an administrative tribunal. The alien was also a veteran of the Merchant Marines, in the process of applying for naturalization, and originally left the country not just with the permission of the government but to perform work for the Coast Guard. It is for this reason that the court felt this case should be judged as a deportation instead of an exclusion. But even in this case, the court was not invalidating the right to deport or requiring judicial review; they merely required the affording of some forum for procedural due process. However, by poking open a hole for judicial intervention with this legal fiction based on a humanitarian concern that earlier courts refused to consider, they created enough of an opening for contemporary courts to grant full judicial review even to illegal aliens.
60. Zadvydas v. Davis 533 US 678 (2001).
61. Ibid. at 692–93.

62. Ibid at 703 (Scalia, J., dissenting).
63. Kaplan v. Tod, 267 US 228 (1925).
64. Ibid. at 230; emphasis added.
65. Ibid.
66. "Full Definition of Sovereignty," *Merriam-Webster Dictionary*, s.v. "sovereignty," accessed February 4, 2016, http://www.merriam-webster.com/dictionary/sovereignty
67. Fiallo v. Bell 430 US 792 (1977); Oceanic Navigation Co. v. Stranahan, 214 US 339 (1909).
68. Galvan v. Press 347 US 531–32 (1954). This case involved the deportation of a Mexican immigrant who had lived in America for more than thirty years, but was expelled for being a member of the Communist Party.
69. They also reflected the political agenda of the labor unions concerned about the labor market.

CHAPTER 5: THE JUDICIAL COUP

1. Plyler v Doe, 457 US 202 (1982).
2. Ibid. at 210.
3. Ibid. (citing Shaughnessv v. Mezei, 345 US 206, 345 US 212 [1953]; Wong Wing v. United States, 163 US 228, 163 US 238 [1896]; Yick Wo v. Hopkins, 118 US 356, 118 US 369 [1886]).
4. Zadvydas v. Davis 533 US 678 (2001) (Scalia, J., dissenting) at 704.
5. *Plyler*, 457 US at 211 n.10. ("As one early commentator noted, given the historical emphasis on geographic territoriality, bounded only, if at all, by principles of sovereignty and allegiance, no plausible distinction with respect to Fourteenth Amendment "jurisdiction" can be drawn between resident aliens whose entry into the United States was lawful, and resident aliens whose entry was unlawful.")
6. U.S. Const. art. IV, § 4.
7. James Madison, *Federalist* No. 46.
8. The Declaration of Independence, par. 4 (U.S. 1776).
9. Illegal Immigration Reform and Immigrant Responsibility Act of 1996, 8 USC § 1357(g) (1996).
10. *Plyler*, 457 US at 226, citations omitted.
11. Federation for American Immigration Reform, "The Fiscal Burden of Illegal Immigration on United States Taxpayers: How Much Is Illegal Immigration Costing the Grand Canyon State?," 2013, http://www.fairus.org/DocServer/state_infographics/Arizona2013.pdf.
12. The United States Census Bureau, "Estimated Population of American Colonies: 1610 to 1780," from *Colonial and Pre-Federal Statistics*, http://www2.census.gov/prod2/statcomp/documents/CT1970p2-13.pdf, 1152.
13. Jeffrey S. Passel and D'Vera Cohn, "A Portrait of Unauthorized Immigrants in the United States," Pew Hispanic Center, April 14, 2009, http://www.pewhispanic.org/2009/04/14/a-portrait-of-unauthorized-immigrants-in-the-united-states/, 9.
14. Federation for American Immigration Reform, "The Fiscal Burden of Illegal Immigration on United States Taxpayers.
15. Federation for American Immigration Reform, "Immigration in Arizona: Fact Sheet (2012)," http://www.fairus.org/DocServer/Arizona_Fact_Sheet_%202012.pdf.
16. Bailey Netsch, "Heroin and Meth Seized in Arizona Sets Record in Busy Smuggling Corridor," Arizona PBS: Cronkite News, October 28, 2015, https://cronkitenews.azpbs.org/2015/10/28/heroin-and-meth-seized-in-arizona-sets-record-in-busy-smuggling-corridor/.
17. United States Border Patrol, "Sector Profile—Fiscal Year 2014," https://www.cbp.gov/sites/default/files/documents/USBP%20Stats%20FY2014%20sector%20profile.pdf.

18. See Sara Carter, "Arizona Ranchers Say Mexican Drug Lords Rule in U.S. Border Regions: 'We're Living by the Law of the Cartels'," Yahoo! News, September 12, 2013, http://news.yahoo.com/arizona-ranchers-mexican-drug-lords-rule-u-border-140214266.html; Liz Goodwin, "Fighting Drugs and Border Violence at Arizona's Organ Pipe Cactus National Monument: What about the Ranger's M14 Rifle, Yogi?," *The Ticket* (Yahoo! blog), February 28, 2012, http://news.yahoo.com/arizona-ranchers-mexican-drug-lords-rule-u-border-140214266.html.
19. SB 1070, 2010 Ariz. Sess. Laws 0113, amended by 2010 Ariz. Sess. Laws 0211 (H.B. 2162, 49th Leg., 2d Sess. (Ariz.2010)).
20. Arizona v. United States, 567 US ___, 132 S. Ct. 2492 (2012) (slip op. at 24). ("This opinion does not foreclose other preemption and constitutional challenges to the law as interpreted and applied after it goes into effect.")
21. Ibid. (syllabus, slip op., at 2) striking down Sections 3, 5(C), and 6 respectively of S. B. 1070.
22. Ibid. (Scalia, J., dissenting) at 3.
23. Joseph Story, *Commentaries on the Constitution of the United States*, 3 vols. (Boston: Hillard, Gray, 1833), §1098.
24. For more on the extent of state regulation of immigration, see Benjamin J. Klebaner, "State and Local Immigration Regulation in the United States before 1882," *International Review of Social History* 3, no. 2 (August 1958): 269–95, doi:10.1017/S0020859000001127; Anna O. Law, "An Assessment of Immigration Federalism in the Nineteenth Century" on the website of the University of Texas, accessed February 5, 2016, https://law.utexas.edu/calendar/uploads/UT_Law_Visit.pdf; and Edward Prince Hutchinson, *Legislative History of American Immigration Policy: 1798–1965* (Philadelphia: University of Pennsylvania Press, 1981).
25. Cal. Gov't code §§ 7282–7282.5 (2014); Conn. gen. stat.§ 54-192h (2014).
26. Jessica Vaughan, "Update on Sanctuary Cities," Center for Immigration Studies, January 7, 2016, http://cis.org/vaughan/update-sanctuary-jurisdictions.
27. *Arizona*, 567 US, slip op., at 3: "It is fundamental that foreign countries concerned about the status, safety, and security of their nationals in the United States must be able to confer and communicate on this subject with one national sovereign, not the 50 separate States."
28. *Arizona*, 567 US (Scalia, J., dissenting) at 21.
29. "From Thomas Jefferson to William Johnson, 12 June 1823," Founders Online, National Archives, http://founders.archives.gov/documents/Jefferson/98-01-02-3562, updated December 30, 2015). Jefferson was criticizing a Supreme Court decision, *Cohens v Virginia* (1821), in which the court struck down Virginia's law prohibiting the sale of out-of-state lottery tickets.
30. Immigration and Naturalization Act §1225(b)(2)(A).
31. Nigel Duara, "Arizona Defends Denying Driver's Licenses to 'Dreamers,' Faces Skeptical Judge," *Los Angeles Times*, July 16, 2015, http://www.latimes.com/nation/la-na-ff-arizona-dreamers-ninth-circuit-20150716-story.html. Not surprisingly, Judge Pregerson also signed onto the Ninth Circuit opinion suspending a deportation of a transgendered criminal alien by applying international law—the case we cited in chapters 1 and 3. Avendano-Hernandez v. Lynch, No. 13-73744 (9th Cir. Sept. 3, 2015).
32. abc15.com staff, "Mom of Sgt Brandon Mendoza pens emotional letter on immigration to President Barack Obama," ABC15, July 9, 2014, http://www.abc15.com/news/region-southeast-valley/mesa/mom-of-sgt-brandon-mendoza-pens-emotional-letter-on-immigration-to-president-barack-obama.
33. Lauren Vargas, "Family Injured in DUI Crash by Man Deported Six Times Speaks to ABC15," ABC15, July 19, 2015, http://www.abc15.com/news/region-central-southern-az/maricopa/family-injured-in-dui-crash-with-illegal-immigrant-speaks-exclusively-to-abc15.

34. House Judiciary Committee, "Breakdown of the Types of Specific Criminal Convictions Associated with Criminal Aliens Placed in a Non-Custodial Setting in Fiscal Year 2014," http://judiciary.house.gov/_cache/files/718a8157-af82-4d6e-b3e8-a17ee3312fb5/fy14-criminal-releases-total-crimes.pdf.
35. 8 U.S.C. § 1225.
36. Kobach, et al. v. Election Assistance Commission, et al., Nos. 14-3062 and 14-3072., cert denied, (10th Cir. 2014). See Dion Lefler, "Federal Appeals Court Rejects Citizenship Proof Rule for Kansas Voters," *Kansas City Star*, November 7, 2014, http://www.kansascity.com/news/government-politics/article3654328.html.
37. Simone Pathe, "Voting-Rights Advocates Get Win at Supreme Court," *Roll Call*, June 29, 2015, http://atr.rollcall.com/supreme-court-victory-for-voting-rights-advocates/.
38. U.S. Const. art. I, § 4, cl. 1.
39. Alexander Hamilton, *Federalist* No. 59.
40. Ariz. Const., Art. II, §22(A)(4).
41. Or, petition for writ of certiorari. A cert petition, as it is often called, is filed when the losing party wants the Supreme Court to review the lower court's decision. In this case, the Supreme Court denied Arizona's petition for writ of certiorari.
42. Lopez-Valenzuela v. County of Maricopa, 719 F. 3d 1054 (9th Cir. 2013), cert denied.
43. County of Maricopa v. Lopez-Valenzuela, 575 US ____ (cert denied) (Thomas, J., dissenting, 2015) *2.
44. Malia Zimmerman, "'Obvious Flight Risk': Toddler's Brutal Beating Prompts Call to Withhold Bail from Illegal Immigrants," Fox News, October 23, 2015, http://www.foxnews.com/us/2015/10/23/obvious-flight-risk-near-fatal-beating-california-toddler-prompts-call-to/?intcmp=hpbt2.
45. Lora v. Shanahan, No.14-2343, (2nd Cir. 2015). The Court ruled that holding criminal aliens without bail for longer than six months represents indefinite detention. In reality, the government is trying to deport them; however, there are so many criminal aliens and too few judges that it often takes more than six months to go through deportation proceedings. Were these aliens to be released on bail, they would endanger society. Ironically, by affording them their procedural due process against deportation, which takes a long time due to the mass invasion of criminal aliens, our immigration officials are accused of violating their rights.
46. Judges Barrington and Wesley were George W. Bush appointees.
47. Alicia A. Caldwell, "Immigrants Caught at Border Believe Families Can Stay in US," CNSNews.com, October 30, 2015, http://www.cnsnews.com/news/article/immigrants-caught-border-believe-families-can-stay-us.
48. United States v. Meza-Rodriguez, No. 14-3271(7th Cir. 2015) at 13–14.
49. Ibid. The other GOP-appointed judge, Joel Flaum, wrote in his concurrence that he doubts there is a Second Amendment right for an illegal alien. Judge Easterbrook did not sign onto his concurrence. (United States v. Meza-Rodriguez [Flaum, J., concurring]).
50. Friedman v. City of Highland Park, 784 F. 3d 406, 412 (7th Cir. 2015).
51. Jenny L. Flores, et al. v. Jeh Johnson, et al., No. 85-04544-CV (C.D. Cal. July 24, 2015). See Cliff Saunders, "Illegal Surge Continues Despite Surge," AM740 KTRH, August 11, 2015, http://www.ktrh.com/articles/houston-news-121300/illegal-surge-continues-despite-heat-13842998/.
52. Brittaney M. Hughes, "DHS Report: 84% of Illegal Alien Adults Not in Court for Final Case Hearing," CNS News, June 30, 2015, http://cnsnews.com/news/article/brittany-m-hughes/dhs-report-84-illegal-alien-adults-not-court-final-case-hearing.

53. Jose Antonio Franco-Gonzalez, et al., v. Holder, et al., No. 10-02211-CV (C.D. Cal. April 23, 2013) (order granting partial judgment and permanent injunction). See also Associated Press, "Hundreds of deported immigrants with mental disabilities may return to US," Fox News, September 26, 2015, http://www.foxnews.com/us/2015/09/26/hundreds-deported-immigrants-with-mental-disabilities-may-return-to-us/.
54. Section 292 of the Immigration and Nationality Act (8 U.S.C. 1362).
55. Stephen Dinan, "Feds to spend $9 million to provide attorneys to illegal border children," *Washington Times*, September 30, 2014, http://www.washingtontimes.com/news/2014/sep/30/feds-spend-9-million-lawyers-kid-illegals/?page=all.
56. Immigration Act of 1891 Chap. 551 26 Stat. 1084 § 10.
57. Turner v. Williams 194 US 279, 292 (1904).
58. Jeremy Redmon, "Immigrants without Legal Status Sue for Georgia Driver's Licenses," *Atlanta Journal-Constitution*, August 31, 2015, http://www.ajc.com/news/news/state-regional-govt-politics/immigrants-without-legal-status-sue-for-georgia-dr/nnTyZ/.
59. Ian K. Kullgren, "Oregon Driver Cards: Immigrants Sue to Reverse Measure 88 Defeat," *Oregonian* (Portland, OR), November 4, 2015, http://www.oregonlive.com/politics/index.ssf/2015/11/oregon_driver_cards_immigrants.html.
60. "Oregon Votes Down Immigrant Driver's License Law—a Strong Warning to President Obama," Fox News Latino, November 16, 2014, http://latino.foxnews.com/latino/politics/2014/11/16/oregon-votes-down-immigrant-driver-license-law-strong-warning-to-president/.
61. Blake Neff, "Federal Court: Illegal Immigrant and Convicted Felon Can't Be Deported Because He's Transgender," *Daily Caller*, September 3, 2015, http://dailycaller.com/2015/09/03/federal-court-illegal-immigrant-and-convicted-felon-cant-be-deported-because-hes-transgender/.
62. Avendano-Hernandez v. Lynch, No. 13-73744, slip op. at 4 (9th Cir. September 3, 2015).
63. Alfonso Chardy, "Gay Mexican Immigrant Wins Federal Court Case, Can Remain in Miami," *Miami Herald*, December 22, 2015, http://www.miamiherald.com/news/local/community/gay-south-florida/article51041660.html.
64. *Nishimura Ekiu,* at 659. ("As to such persons, the decisions of executive or administrative officers, acting within powers expressly conferred by congress, are due process of law.")
65. Daniel Siegal, "9th Circ. Rules BIA's 'Crime of Violence' Standard Vague," Law 360, October 19, 2015, http://www.law360.com/articles/715769/9th-circ-rules-bia-s-crime-of-violence-standard-vague.
66. Dimaya v. Lynch, No. 11-71307 (9th Cir. October 19, 2015).
67. Howard Fischer, "Federal Judge Agrees to Hear Class-Action Lawsuit on Migrant Conditions," *Arizona Capital Times*, January 12, 2016, http://azcapitoltimes.com/news/2016/01/12/federal-judge-agrees-to-hear-class-action-lawsuit-on-migrant-conditions/#ixzz3x8JcfYZl.
68. Sean Higgins, "Employers Could Get Sued for Following the Law," *Washington Examiner*, January 4, 2016, http://www.washingtonexaminer.com/employers-could-get-sued-for-following-the-law/article/2578952#.Vo7pkIfLF-Y.twitter.
69. Calder v. Bull, 3 US (3 Dall.) 386, 388 (1798)
70. Crane v. Napolitano, 920 F. Supp. 2d 724 (N.D.Tex. 2013).
71. Chris Crane et al. v Jeh Johnson et al., No.14-10049 (5th Cir. April 7, 2015).
72. Daniel Halper, "Obama: 'Consequences' for ICE Officials Who Don't Follow Executive Amnesty," *Weekly Standard*, February 25, 2015, http://www.weeklystandard.com/obama-consequences-for-ice-officials-who-dont-follow-executive-amnesty/article/866479.

73. Eugene Davis was appointed by Reagan; Priscilla Owen was appointed by George W. Bush.
74. Arpaio v. Obama, 797 F. 3d 11 *at 3(D.C. Cir. 2015).
75. Richard Brookhiser, *Gentleman Revolutionary: Gouverneur Morris, the Rake Who Wrote the Constitution*, repr. ed. (Detroit: Free Press, 2004).

CHAPTER 6: OUR FOUNDERS' COMMITMENT TO AMERICAN SOVEREIGNTY

1. Gouverneur Morris, "Debates in the Federal Convention of 1787 by James Madison," August 9, 1787, as posted on the Teaching American History website, http://teachingamericanhistory.org/convention/debates/0813-2/.
2. Ibid. James Madison, James Wilson, and Oliver Ellsworth all disagreed with Morris's amendment to make it harder for immigrants to become qualified to run for Senate. However, their only point of disagreement is that they didn't want to discourage "meritorious" immigrants. Ellsworth: "Mr. ELLSWORTH was opposed to the motion, as discouraging meritorious aliens from emigrating to this country." Madison: "because it will put it out of the power of the National Legislature, even by special acts of naturalization, to confer the full rank of citizens on meritorious strangers; and because it will discourage the most desirable class of people from emigrating to the United States." Wilson: "and the effect which a good system would have in inviting meritorious foreigners among us."
3. James Madison, "Sovereignty" (essay, 1835) in *The Writings of James Madison*, ed. Gaillard Hunt, 9:570–71, on the Online Library of Liberty website, http://oll.libertyfund.org/titles/madison-the-writings-vol-9-1819-1836. It's interesting to note that the one example of a right reserved for the individual in a social compact, even against the majoritarian rule, singled out by Madison in this essay is the right to "conscience." This harks back to the utmost importance the Founders ascribed to religious liberty, as we noted in detail in chapter 3.
4. James Madison, *Federalist* No 42. Madison criticized the status quo of the Articles of Confederation in which some states could grant citizenship to "obnoxious" aliens and ruin the sovereignty of other states. "By the laws of several States, certain descriptions of aliens, who had rendered themselves obnoxious, were laid under interdicts inconsistent not only with the rights of citizenship but with the privilege of residence. What would have been the consequence, if such persons, by residence or otherwise, had acquired the character of citizens under the laws of another State, and then asserted their rights as such, both to residence and citizenship, within the State proscribing them?"
5. 1 Annals of Cong. 1148 (1790).
6. For logistical reasons, questions of citizenship during our founding era were arguably equivalent to questions of immigration in our era. Given modern communications and transportation affording millions of people the ability to come here at any time, we need immigration laws to stem that tide, whereas during the 1700s and early 1800s, before the advent of large passenger ships, there was no fear of mass migration, only the concern of integration into citizenship once the small number of immigrants arrived in the country.
7. Thomas Jefferson, *Notes on the State of Virginia*, Query 9.
8. Ibid., Query XIV.
9. Michael C. LeMay, *From Open Door to Dutch Door: An Analysis of U.S. Immigration policy Since 1820* (Westport, CT: Praeger, 1987) 5.
10. 1 Annals of Cong. 1156.
11. Michelle Fields, "680,000 Green Cards Given to Immigrants of Muslim Countries," Breitbart News, November 25, 2015, http://www.breitbart.com/big-government/2015/11/25/680000-green-cards-given-immigrants-muslim-countries/. These numbers are based on the number of green cards issued to nationals of predominantly Muslim countries from 2009 to 2013.

12. Jefferson, *Notes on the State of Virginia*, Query 9.
13. James Monroe, Seventh Annual Message to Congress, December 2, 1823, as posted on the American Presidency Project website, http://www.presidency.ucsb.edu/ws/?pid=29465.
14. Congress was explicitly barred from regulating immigration before 1808 because of the compromise hashed out at the Constitutional Convention over the slave trade. As part of art. I § 9, cl. 2, Congress had to wait until 1808 to ban the slave trade. But even thereafter, Congress shied away from passing immigration laws because it would inevitably ignite the tinderbox of the growing schism over state representation surrounding population issues and slavery. They relied on states to electively keep out undesirables through state laws. And although the federal government set the conditions for naturalizations, state and local governments wielded significant influence over the process and used it to bar those they disliked from becoming citizens.
15. Naturalization Act of 1790, Sess. II, chap. 3; 1 stat 103 (1790). The Naturalization Act of 1795 added a requirement that the court certify that the alien resided in "good *moral* character."
16. Large passenger ships carrying significant numbers of migrants (as opposed to just cargo) were not widely in use until later in the nineteenth century.
17. The original immigration bill in 1790 required only two years of residency, but that was amended to five years in 1795.
18. Naturalization Act of 1795, Sess. II, chap. 19, 20; 1 stat 414 (1795). An 1824 act of Congress later reduced the interval between declaration of intent and admission from three years to two years.
19. Emerson Edward Proper, *Colonial Immigration Laws* (New York: Columbia University Press, 1900), 20, as reprinted on the *Federalist Papers Project* blog, http://www.thefederalistpapers.org/wp-content/uploads/2013/04/Colonial-Immigration-Laws.pdf.
20. Maldwyn Allen Jones, *American Immigration*, ed. Daniel J. Boorstin (Chicago: University of Chicago Press, 1960) 40–41, 44.
21. Motion by Abraham Baldwin, September 16, 1788, in Anonymous, *Journals of the American Congress from 1774–1788 in Four Volumes* (Washington: Way and Gideon, 1823) 4:867.
22. Gerald L. Neuman, *Strangers to the Constitution: Immigrants, Borders, and Fundamental Laws* (Princeton: Princeton University Press, 1996), 21–22. When the first wave of immigrants arrived in large numbers during the 1830s and 1840s, states with large ports, such as New York and Massachusetts, passed laws establishing a process in cooperation with the federal government for landing officers to collect fees, document the new arrivals, and ensure that the immigrants would not become a public charge. The Supreme Court, in *Mayor of New York v. Miln*, 33 US 120 (1837), upheld the constitutionality of state laws preventing undesirables from entering its territory. Before the '30s there were no waves of immigrants who came en masse, so there was no need to largely regulate it. The rugged individualism involved in making the permanent journey in those days tended to wash out those who would constitute a public charge. The only immigration law passed before the great wave was in 1819, when they began to require documentation of the number of immigrants arriving on each ship.
23. "James Madison Letter to Morris Birkbeck," in 1813, *Letters and Other Writings of James Madison: 1794–1815*, vol. 2 (New York: Worthington, 1884), 576, emphasis added.
24. "To James Madison from Edward Coles, 20 March 1817," Founders Online, National Archives, http://founders.archives.gov/documents/Madison/04-01-02-0017.
25. "Fannie Mae Rolls Out Easy Mortgage, Catering to High-Risk Immigrants," *Investor's Business Daily*, January 7, 2016, http://news.investors.com/ibd-editorials/010716-788747-government-wants-to-lend-more-to-high-risk-immigrants.htm#ixzz3xeXp3xCT.

26. "Madison Debates," August 13, 1787, as posted on the Avalon Project website of Yale Law School, http://avalon.law.yale.edu/18th_century/debates_813.asp.
27. 1 Annals of Cong. 1148 (1790) 1150.
28. Jefferson, *Notes on the State of Virginia*, Query 9.
29. George Washington letter to John Adams, November 15, 1794, in The Writings of George Washington, vol. 12, ed. Worthington Chauncey Ford (New York and London: G. P. Putnam's Sons, 1890).
30. John Sanderson, *Republican Landmarks: The Views and Opinions of American Statesmen on Foreign Immigration* (Philadelphia: J. P. Lippincott, 1856) 315.
31. Maldwyn Allen Jones estimated that 250,000 immigrants arrived between 1783 and 1815, which is an average of 7,575 immigrants per year. Maldwyn Allen Jones, *American Immigration*, ed. Daniel J. Boorstin (Chicago: University of Chicago Press, 1960), 66. That is a fraction of the 30,000–60,000 we admitted even in the most restrictive years of the Great Depression during the shutoff period.
32. "From George Washington to the Hebrew Congregation in Newport, Rhode Island, 18 August 1790," as posted by Founders Online, National Archives website, http://founders.archives.gov/documents/Washington/05-06-02-0135.
33. George Washington, "Farewell Address," September 19, 1796, as reprinted by Gerhard Peters and John T. Woolley, *The American Presidency Project*. http://www.presidency.ucsb.edu/ws/?pid=65539.
34. "From George Washington to the Hebrew Congregation in Newport, Rhode Island," Founders Online.
35. George Washington, letter to Patrick Henry, October 9, 1795, in Ford., ed., *Writings of George Washington*.
36. See "U.S. soccer team booed in their own country as Mexican fans turn LA into an 'away' game," *Daily Mail* (UK), June 27, 2011, http://www.dailymail.co.uk/news/article-2008444/Only-America-U-S-soccer-team-booed-Mexico--California.html#ixzz3xeEGuo6T.
37. Alexander Hamilton, *The Works of Alexander Hamilton*, ed. Henry Cabot Lodge, Federal ed. (New York: G. P. Putnam's Sons, 1904).
38. Alexander Hamilton, *The Papers of Alexander Hamilton: July 1800–April 1802,* vol. 25, ed. Harold C. Syrett (New York: Columbia University Press, 1977) 496.
39. Ibid.
40. John Quincy Adams, letter to Moritz Von Fuerstenwaerther, Department of State, June 4, 1819, printed in *Niles' Weekly Register* 18 (April 29, 1820): 157 https://archive.org/stream/nilesweeklyregis18balt#page/157/mode/1up.
41. Adams to John Wooddrop, February 3, 1786, in *Papers of Thomas Jefferson*, ed. Julian P. Boyd et al. (Princeton: Princeton University Press, 1950) 13:432.
42. Benjamin Franklin, "Information to Those Who Would Remove to America," *The Writings of Benjamin Franklin*, ed. Albert Henry Smyth, 10 vols. (New York: Macmillan, 1905–7.) 8:603–14.
43. Tench Coxe, "An Enquiry into the Best Means of Encouraging Emigration from Abroad, Consistently with the Happiness and Safety of the Original Citizens. Read before the Society for Political Enquiries, at the House of Dr. Franklin, April 20th, 1787," *American Museum* 10 (September 1791):114.
44. As an aside, we can deduce from here that implicit in the grievance expressed in the Declaration against King George's restrictions on desirable immigration was also his nullification of colonial law to restrict undesirable immigrants.

45. See Julia Preston, "White House Campaign Urges Legal Immigrants to Become (Voting) Citizens," *New York Times*, September 17, 2015, http://www.nytimes.com/2015/09/18/us/white-house-campaign-legal-immigrants-citizenship.html?_r=0.
46. Tony Lee, "Feds to Advertise Settlement Allowing Deported Illegals to Return," Breitbart News, August 24, 2015, http://www.breitbart.com/big-government/2014/08/28/feds-agree-buy-ads-on-mexican-media-place-billboards-on-border-to-reach-deported-illegals-allowed-to-return/.
47. Thomas H. Russell, *Life and Work of Theodore Roosevelt* (Chicago, Homewood Press, 1919) 367–68.
48. Jie Zong and Jeanne Batalova, "The Limited English Proficient Population in the United States," Migration Policy Institute, July 8, 2015, http://www.migrationpolicy.org/article/limited-english-proficient-population-united-states.
49. Theodore Roosevelt, "Sixth Annual Message," December 3, 1906, par. 68, as posted on the American Presidency Project website, http://www.presidency.ucsb.edu/ws/index.php?pid=29547.
50. Theodore Roosevelt, "Fifth Annual Message," December 5, 1905, pars. 70–72, as posted on the American Presidency Project website, http://www.presidency.ucsb.edu/ws/index.php?pid=29546.
51. Ibid. par. 71.
52. Theodore Roosevelt, "First Annual Message," December 3, 1901, par. 37, as posted on the American Presidency Project website, http://www.presidency.ucsb.edu/ws/index.php?pid=29542.
53. "Coolidge Appeals for National Unity, Welding All Races," *New York Times*, May, 4, 1925, as posted on the Calvin Coolidge Presidential Foundation website, https://coolidgefoundation.org/resources/speeches-as-president-1923-1928-14/; no longer accessible.
54. Calvin Coolidge, "Third Annual Message," December 8, 1925, as posted on the American Presidency Project website, http://www.presidency.ucsb.edu/ws/index.php?pid=29566.
55. It was actually the progressives of that era who opposed immigration for purely racial reasons. President Woodrow Wilson, a leading progressive intellectual, embodied that mind-set when he said, "Immigrants poured in as before, but . . . now there come multitudes of men of lowest class from the south of Italy and men of the meanest sort out of Hungary and Poland, men out of the ranks where there was neither skill nor energy nor any initiative of quick intelligence; and they came in numbers which increased from year to year, as if the countries of the south of Europe were disburdening themselves of the more sordid and hapless elements of their population."
56. Calvin Coolidge, "First Annual Message," December 6, 1923, as posted on the American Presidency Project website, http://www.presidency.ucsb.edu/ws/index.php?pid=29564; emphasis added.
57. Calvin Coolidge, "Sixth Annual Message," December 4, 1928, as posted on the American Presidency Project website, http://www.presidency.ucsb.edu/ws/index.php?pid=29565.
58. Calvin Coolidge, in a speech to immigrants, October 16, 1924, on the Calvin Coolidge Presidential Foundation website, https://coolidgefoundation.org/quote/quotations-i/.
59. Calvin Coolidge, "Second Annual Message," December 3, 1924, as posted on the American Presidency Project website, http://www.presidency.ucsb.edu/ws/index.php?pid=29569.
60. Immigration and Naturalization Act § 212(f), 8 U.S. Code § 1182.
61. Neil Munro, "No Assimilation Needed in U.S., Obama Tells Millions of Migrants," Breitbart, September 18, 2015, http://www.breitbart.com/big-government/2015/09/18/no-assimilation-needed-u-s-obama-tells-millions-migrants/.

CHAPTER 7: TRANSFORMATION THROUGH IMMIGRATION: REMAKING AMERICA WITHOUT CONSENT

1. Editorial board, "In Praise of Huddled Masses," *Wall Street Journal*, July 3, 1984, http://www.vdare.com/articles/in-praise-of-huddled-masses.
2. Calvin Coolidge, "Calvin Coolidge Says," *Milwaukee Sentinel*, December 15, 1930, https://news.google.com/newspapers?nid=1368&dat=19301215&id=il9QAAAAIBAJ&sjid=8w4EAAAAIBAJ&pg=2166,2547942&hl=en.
3. Pew Research Center, "Where International Migrants Have Gone," Pew Research Center's Religion and Public Life Project, March 8, 2012, http://features.pewforum.org/religious-migration/world-maps/weighted-gone.php.
4. Numbers tabulated using the Department of Homeland Security's *Yearbook of Immigration Statistics: 2013 Lawful Permanent Residents*, table 1, available online at http://www.dhs.gov/publication/yearbook-immigration-statistics-2013-lawful-permanent-residents.
5. Pew Research Center, "Modern Immigration Wave Brings 59 Million to U.S., Driving Population Growth and Change Through 2065" (Washington DC: Pew, September 2015), http://www.pewhispanic.org/files/2015/09/2015-09-28_modern-immigration-wave_REPORT.pdf.
6. Ibid.
7. Analyst in Immigration Policy (name redacted), Congressional Research memorandum to the Senate Committee on the Judiciary, re: "Components and Characteristics of the U.S. Foreign-Born Population—Revised," September 16, 2014, 6, http://c3.nrostatic.com/sites/default/files/CRS%20Memorandum%20on%20Asylees%20Refugees%20and%20Future%20Projections.pdf.
8. Sandra L. Colby and Jennifer M. Ortman, "Projections of the Size and Composition of the U.S. Population: 2014 to 2060," Current Population Reports, P25-1143, U.S. Census Bureau, Washington, DC, March 2014, http://www.census.gov/content/dam/Census/library/publications/2015/demo/p25-1143.pdf.
9. Pew Research Center, "Modern Immigration Wave Brings 59 Million to U.S."
10. Jens Manuel Krogstad and Michael Keegan, "15 states with the highest share of immigrants in their population," Pew Research Center, May 14, 2014, http://www.pewresearch.org/fact-tank/2014/05/14/15-states-with-the-highest-share-of-immigrants-in-their-population/.
11. Ibid.
12. Numbers tabulated using the Department of Homeland Security's *Yearbook of Immigration Statistics: 2013 Lawful Permanent Residents*, table 2.
13. Renee Stepler and Anna Brown, "Statistical Portrait of Hispanics in the United States, 1980–2013," Pew Research Center, May 12, 2015, http://www.pewhispanic.org/2015/05/12/statistical-portrait-of-hispanics-in-the-united-states-2013-key-charts/#hispanic-rising-share. The data point for 2015 is from the United States Census Bureau, Population Projections, "2014 National Population Projections: Summary Tables," tables 10, 11, http://www.census.gov/population/projections/data/national/2014/summarytables.html.
14. Colby and Ortman, "Projections of the Size and Composition of the U.S. Population: 2014 to 2060," 9–10, fig. 8.
15. Mark Hugo Lopez and Jens Manuel Krogstad, "Will California Ever Become a Majority-Latino State? Maybe Not," Pew Research Center Fact Tank, June 4, 2015, http://www.pewresearch.org/fact-tank/2015/06/04/will-california-ever-become-a-majority-latino-state-maybe-not/.
16. Jens Manuel Krogstad, "Reflecting a Racial Shift, 78 Counties Turned Majority-Minority Since 2000," Pew Research Center Fact Tank, April 8, 2015, http://www.pewresearch.org/fact-tank/2015/04/08/reflecting-a-racial-shift-78-counties-turned-majority-minority-since-2000/#table.

17. Karen Zeigler and Steven A. Camarota, "One in Five U.S. Residents Speaks Foreign Language at Home," Center for Immigration Studies, October 2015, http://cis.org/One-in-Five-US-Residents-Speaks-Foreign-Language-at-Home.
18. Camille Ryan, "Language Use in the United States: 2011," U.S. Census Bureau American Community Survey Reports, August 2013, p. 11, table 4, http://www.census.gov/content/dam/Census/library/publications/2013/acs/acs-22.pdf.
19. Ibid., 14, table 5.
20. Piler Menendez, "United States Has More Spanish Speakers Than Spain Does, Report Says," CNN, July 1, 2015, http://www.cnn.com/2015/07/01/us/spanish-speakers-united-states-spain/.
21. Jens Manuel Krogstad, "A View of the Future through Kindergarten Demographics," Pew Research Center, July 8, 2014, http://www.pewresearch.org/fact-tank/2014/07/08/a-view-of-the-future-through-kindergarten-demographics/.
22. Tony Lee, "Gov. Jerry Brown: Nearly 30% of CA Kids Illegal or 'Don't Speak English,'" Breitbart, September 4, 2014, http://www.breitbart.com/california/2014/09/05/gov-jerry-brown-nearly-30-of-ca-kids-illegal-or-don-t-speak-english/.
23. Jonah Bennett, "Almost Half of California Driver's Licenses Went to Illegal Immigrants In 2015," *Daily Caller*, January 10, 2016, http://dailycaller.com/2016/01/10/almost-half-of-california-drivers-licenses-went-to-illegal-immigrants-in-2015/#ixzz3wsPM4iVo.
24. "Kansas School District Copes Increased Ethnic Diversity from Influx of Immigrants, Refugees," Fox News Latino, April 26, 2015, http://latino.foxnews.com/latino/lifestyle/2015/04/26/kansas-school-district-copes-increased-ethnic-diversity-from-influx-immigrants/.
25. John Higgins, "Surprising study may lead to better English-language instruction," The Seattle Times, October 14, 2015, http://www.seattletimes.com/education-lab/one-size-fits-all-for-english-learners-doesnt-fit-south-king-countys-diverse-students/.
26. Andrew Dugan, "In U.S., Six in 10 Dissatisfied with Immigration Levels," Gallup, January 29, 2015, http://www.gallup.com/poll/181313/dissatisfied-immigration-levels.aspx?.
27. In the words of historian Aristide Zolberg, "[T]he greatest irony of all was that a law that expressed the nation's determination to maintain immigration as the marginal feature to which it had been effectively reduced in fact had the opposite effect." Aristide R. Zolberg. *A Nation by Design* (Cambridge: Harvard University Press, 2006), Kindle edition, locs. 4703–4.
28. Colby and Ortman, "Projections of the Size and Composition of the U.S. Population: 2014 to 2060,", 10 (fig. 8). For data from 1980 to 2000, see Frank Hobbs and Nicole Stoops, *Demographic Trends in the 20th Century: Census 2000 Special Reports* (Washington, DC: U.S. Government Printing Office), table 10, https://www.census.gov/prod/2002pubs/censr-4.pdf.
29. United States Census Bureau, "Millennials Outnumber Baby Boomers and Are Far More Diverse," Census Bureau Reports news release, June 25, 2015, http://www.census.gov/newsroom/press-releases/2015/cb15-113.html.
30. Otis L. Graham, *Unguarded Gates: A History of America's Immigration Crisis* (Lanham, MD: Rowman and Littlefield, 2004), 42.
31. For more on the influence of Islamic satellite TV broadcasts in Western countries, see Tomas Precht, *Home Grown Terrorism and Islamist Radicalization in Europe: from Conversion to Terrorism*, research report funded by the Danish Ministry of Justice (December 2007), 59–60, http://www.justitsministeriet.dk/sites/default/files/media/Arbejdsomraader/Forskning/Forskningspuljen/2011/2007/Home_grown_terrorism_and_Islamist_radicalisation_in_Europe_-_an_assessment_of_influencing_factors__2_.pdf.

32. See Ian Smith, "How the Left Shuts Down the Immigration Debate," *Washington Times*, January 20, 2016, http://www.washingtontimes.com/news/2016/jan/19/ian-smith-how-the-left-shuts-down-the-immigration-/. The American Immigration Lawyers Association is staffed with thirteen thousand lawyers and lobbyists.
33. The Congressional Research Service estimates that had Congress passed the Gang of Eight immigration bill in 2013, it would have brought in 10 million additional immigrants—over and beyond the exploding trajectory under existing policy. Analyst in Immigration Policy (name redacted), Congressional Research memorandum to the Senate Committee on the Judiciary, re: "Components and Characteristics of the U.S. Foreign-Born Population—Revised," 6.
34. Elizabeth M. Grieco, "The 'Second Great Wave' of Immigration: Growth of the Foreign-Born Population Since 1970," *Random Samplings*, the official blog of the U.S. Census Bureau, February 26, 2014, http://blogs.census.gov/2014/02/26/the-second-great-wave-of-immigration-growth-of-the-foreign-born-population-since-1970/.
35. James Lee and Katie Foreman, "U.S. Naturalizations: 2013," Annual Flow Report produced by U.S. Department of Homeland Security's Office of Immigration Statistics, May 2014, http://www.dhs.gov/sites/default/files/publications/ois_natz_fr_2013.pdf.
36. Numbers tabulated using the Department of Homeland Security's *Yearbook of Immigration Statistics: 2013 Lawful Permanent Residents*, Table 20.
37. The immigration admission numbers are based on the statistic used earlier in the chapter, comparing the 25.3 million admissions from 1989 to 2013 with the 16.8 million admissions from 1900 to 1924.
38. Maldwyn A. Jones, *American Immigration* (Chicago: University of Chicago Press, 1961), 297.
39. Campbell Gibson and Kay Jung, "Historical Census Statistics on the Foreign-Born Population of the United States: 1850-2000," Working Paper No. 81, table 1, Population Division of the United States Census Bureau, February 2006, http://www.census.gov/population/www/documentation/twps0081/twps0081.html.
40. The native-born population is projected to be 338.6 million in 2060, which is 77% greater than the 1970 population of 191.3. See Gibson and Jung, ibid., for 1970 native born population and Colby and Ortman, ibid., for 2060 projection.
41. See Lee and Foreman, "U.S. Naturalizations: 2013," table 1. There is not a single country from Europe or English-speaking country included in the top twenty countries of origin of recent naturalized citizens.
42. Ronald Reagan: "Farewell Address to the Nation," January 11, 1989. Online by Gerhard Peters and John T. Woolley, The American Presidency Project, http://www.presidency.ucsb.edu/ws/?pid=29650.
43. Ibid.
44. *Notes on the State of Virginia*, in *The Writings of Thomas Jefferson*, ed. H. A. Washington, vol. 7 (New York: Derby & Jackson, 1859), Query 9.
45. Karthick Ramakrishnan and Taeku Lee, *The Policy Priorities and Issue Preferences of Asian Americans and Pacific Islanders* (National Asian American Survey, September 25, 2012), pp. 12 (table 9), 19, http://www.naasurvey.com/resources/Home/NAAS12-sep25-issues.pdf.
46. 2010 Cooperative Congressional Election Study, as cited by Eagle Forum, *How Mass (Legal) Immigration Dooms a Conservative Republican Party: A Comprehensive Review of Surveys in Immigrant Communities Showing Their Support for Big Government*, 2nd ed. (Washington, DC: Eagle Forum, June 2014), 11, table 1, http://www.eagleforum.org/wp-content/uploads/2014/06/2014_ImmigrationBook-6-12-14.pdf.

47. Paul Taylor et al., *When Labels Don't Fit: Hispanics and Their Views of Identity*, pt. 5, Politics, Values and Religion, fig. 4.2, Pew Research Center, Hispanic Trends, April 4, 2012, http://www.pewhispanic.org/2012/04/04/v-politics-values-and-religion/.
48. John Fonte and Althea Nagai, *America's Patriotic Assimilation System Is Broken* (Washington, DC: Hudson Institute, April 2013), figs. 5, 15, http://www.hudson.org/content/researchattachments/attachment/1101/final04-05.pdf.
49. Rebecca Kaplan, "Bobby Jindal: 'Immigration without Assimilation Is Invasion,'" *Face the Nation*, August 30, 2015, http://www.cbsnews.com/news/bobby-jindal-immigration-without-assimilation-is-invasion/.
50. Nancy Rytina, "Estimates of the Legal Permanent Resident Population in 2012," U.S. Department of Homeland Security's Office of Immigration Statistics, July 2013, 4, table 4, http://www.dhs.gov/sites/default/files/publications/ois_lpr_pe_2012.pdf. All but four of the top twenty countries of origin of those immigrants eligible for citizenship are in Africa, Asia, and Latin America.
51. James G. Gimpel, "Immigration's Impact on Republican Political Prospects, 1980 to 2012," table 1, Center for Immigration Studies, April 2014, http://cis.org/immigration-impacts-on-republican-prospects-1980-2012.
52. "The 1965 Immigration Act was not given much contemporary attention in a decade of social upheaval and a war in Vietnam, was not mentioned by Lyndon Johnson in his memoirs, and is routinely allotted one or two sentences in history textbooks." Graham Jr., *Unguarded Gates*, 96.
53. Immigration and Nationality Act of 1965, H.R. 2580, 89th Cong., https://www.govtrack.us/congress/bills/89/hr2580.
54. Ibid. Sixty of the 70 no votes in the House and 14 of the 18 no votes in the Senate came from Democrat members.
55. Hearings on S. 500, Before the Senate, Subcommittee on Immigration and Naturalization, 89th Cong. (February 10, 1965) (statement of Edward Kennedy, senator from Massachusetts).
56. Hearing on H.R. 2580, An Act to Amend the Immigration and Nationality Act, Before the Immigration and Nationality Subcommittee of the House Judiciary Committee, 89th Cong. (March 3, 1965) (statement of Attorney General Nicholas Katzenbach).
57. "We do not anticipate a large increase in those nonquota applications The opportunities here in the United States, the opportunities which attract immigration, are the more sophisticated opportunities, for the educated, for the trained, for the industrial worker, for the technician, for those who can enter into a more sophisticated part in our life than they could if they came in without skills and without any training." Dean Rusk, quoted in Joseph Fallon, "So Much for Promises—Quotes Re 1965 Immigration Act," *Social Contract* 9, no. 3 (Spring 1999), http://www.thesocialcontract.com/artman2/publish/tsc0903/article_952.shtml.
58. Pew Research Center, *Modern Immigration Wave Brings 59 Million to U.S.*, 8.
59. Ibid., 47, fig. 3.11.
60. Ibid.
61. Ibid., 49, table 3.6.
62. Karen Zeigler and Steven A. Camarota, "All Employment Growth Since 2000 Went to Immigrants," Center for Immigration Studies, June 2014, http://cis.org/all-employment-growth-since-2000-went-to-immigrants.
63. Zolberg. *A Nation by Design*, locs. 4715–16.
64. Josh Getlin, "Senate Backs Cap on Immigration; Sets Limit of 630,000; Illegal Aliens Would Not Be Counted in 1990 Census," *Los Angeles Times*, July 14, 1989, http://articles.latimes.com/1989-07-14/news/mn-3675_1_illegal-aliens. This article described the original Senate version in 1989 as "opening the doors to more residents of Western Europe."

65. "The 1990 law, which originated as an attempt to shift the priorities from family- to employment-oriented criteria and to impose an overall cap on legal immigration, resulted instead in the cumulation of the two, holding forth the prospect of a further expansion of the intake." Zolberg, *A Nation by Design*, locs. 5347–48.
66. Hearing on H.R. 2580, statement of Attorney General Nicholas Katzenbach.
67. Malia Zimmerman, "Elusive Crime Wave Data Shows Frightening Toll of Illegal Immigrant Criminals," Fox News, September 16, 2015, http://www.foxnews.com/us/2015/09/16/crime-wave-elusive-data-shows-frightening-toll-illegal-immigrant-criminals.html.
68. Steven A. Camarota, "Welfare Use by Immigrant and Native Households," Center for Immigration Studies, September 2015, http://cis.org/Welfare-Use-Immigrant-Native-Households.
69. Steven A. Camarota, "Welfare Use by Legal and Illegal Immigrant Households," Center for Immigration Studies, September 2015, http://www.cis.org/Welfare-Use-Legal-Illegal-Immigrant-Households.
70. "Subcommittee Chart: More Than 90% of Recent Middle Eastern Refugees on Food Stamps, Almost 70% on Cash Welfare," press release, Office of Senator Jeff Sessions, September 10, 2015, http://www.sessions.senate.gov/public/index.cfm/2015/9/more-than-90-of-recent-middle-eastern-refugees-on-food-stamps-almost-70-on-cash-welfare.
71. Jie Zong and Jeanne Batalova, "Central American Immigrants in the United States," Migration Policy Institute, September 2, 2015, http://www.migrationpolicy.org/article/central-american-immigrants-united-states#Income%20and%20Poverty.
72. Molly Hennessy-Fiske, "Along the Border, Who's an 'Anchor Baby' Is a Guessing Game," *Los Angeles Times*, September 3, 2015, http://www.latimes.com/nation/immigration/la-na-texas-anchor-babies-20150903-story.html.
73. See Sharyl Attkisson, "Polio-Like Illness Claims Fifth Life in U.S.," posted on Sharyl Attkisson's blog, October 4, 2014, https://sharylattkisson.com/polio-like-outbreak-claims-fifth-life-in-u-s/.
74. Katzenbach, Hearing on H.R. 2580.
75. Justice Stephen Field writing the majority opinion in the Chinese Exclusion case, 130 U.S. 608–9 (1889), citing Wharton's *Digest of International Law*, § 206.
76. "Sessions: DHS Letter Confirms Public Charge Immigration Law Not Being Enforced," press release, Senate Budget Committee, February 14, 2013, http://www.budget.senate.gov/republican/public/index.cfm/2013/2/sessions-dhs-letter-confirms-public-charge-immigration-law-not-being-enforced.
77. See "Government Benefits," WelcomeToUSA.Gov, http://www.welcometousa.gov/Government_benefits/default.htm.
78. Sally Kestin, Megan O'Matz and John Maines, with Tracey Eaton in Cuba, "U.S. Welfare Flows to Cuba," *Sun-Sentinel*, October 1, 2015, http://www.sun-sentinel.com/us-cuba-welfare-benefits/sfl-us-cuba-welfare-benefits-part-1-htmlstory.html.
79. Michael Barone, "Immigration Reformers Should Learn from History," *Washington Examiner*, September 22, 2014, http://www.washingtonexaminer.com/immigration-reformers-should-learn-from-history/article/2553621.
80. Karen Zeigler and Steven A. Camarota, "U.S. Immigrant Pop. Hit Record 42.4 Million in 2014," Center for Immigration Studies, September 17, 2015, http://cis.org/us-immigrant-pop-hit-record-42-million-2014#3.
81. Karen Zeigler and Steven A. Camarota, "Immigrant Population Hits Record 42.1 Million in Second Quarter of 2015," Center for Immigration Studies, August 2015, http://cis.org/Immigrant-Population-Hits-Record-Second-Quarter-2015.

82. Jens Manuel Krogstad and Michael Keegan, "From Germany to Mexico: How America's Source of Immigrants Has Changed over a Century," Pew Research Center, October 7, 2015, http://www.pewresearch.org/fact-tank/2014/05/27/a-shift-from-germany-to-mexico-for-americas-immigrants/.
83. Michael C. Lemay, *From Open Door to Dutch Door, An Analysis of U.S. Immigration policy Since 1820*, (Califronia: Praeger, 1987) 7.
84. Michelle Fields, "680,000 Green Cards Given to Immigrants of Muslim Countries," Breitbart, November 25, 2015, http://www.breitbart.com/big-government/2015/11/25/680000-green-cards-given-immigrants-muslim-countries/. These numbers are based on the number of green cards issued to nationals of predominantly Muslim countries from 2009 to 2013.
85. Zeigler and Camarota, "U.S. Immigrant Pop. Hit Record 42.4 Million in 2014."
86. "Poll of U.S. Muslims Reveals Ominous Levels of Support for Islamic Supremacists' Doctrine of Shariah, Jihad," press release, Center for Security Policy, June 23, 2015, https://www.centerforsecuritypolicy.org/2015/06/23/nationwide-poll-of-us-muslims-shows-thousands-support-shariah-jihad/.
87. "The Future of World Religions: Population Growth Projections, 2010–2050," Pew Research Center: Religion and Public Life, April 2, 2015, http://www.pewforum.org/2015/04/02/religious-projections-2010-2050/.
88. See Tammi Rossman-Benjamin, "While Global Anti-Semitism Surges, Don't Forget U.S. Campuses," JNS.org, July 28, 2014, http://www.jns.org/latest-articles/2014/7/28/while-global-anti-semitism-surges-dont-forget-us-campuses#.VOU0Yy6zk7c=.
89. Institute of International Education, "Top 25 Places of Origin of International Students, 2013/14–2014/15," from the *Open Doors Report on International Educational Exchange* (2015), http://www.iie.org/Research-and-Publications/Open-Doors/Data/International-Students/Leading-Places-of-Origin/2013-15. Estimate of breakdown from predominantly Muslim countries was tabulated by adding the number of foreign students from forty-three countries with predominantly Muslim populations. See http://www.iie.org/Research-and-Publications/Open-Doors/Data/International-Students/All-Places-of-Origin/2013-15.
90. Wilfred M. McClay, "American Colleges Are Forgetting to Teach Citizenship," John William Pope Center for Higher Education Policy, January 20, 2016, http://www.popecenter.org/commentaries/article.html?id=3317.
91. Cliff Young and Chris Jackson, "The Rise of Neo-Nativism: Putting Trump into Proper Context," Ipsos Ideas Spotlight, October 9, 2015, http://spotlight.ipsos-na.com/index.php/news/the-rise-of-neo-nativism-putting-trump-into-proper-context/.
92. Jason Gonzales, "Nashville Schools Have Thousands of ELL Students," *Tennessean*, November 14, 2015, http://www.tennessean.com/story/news/education/2015/11/14/nashville-schools-have-thousands-ell-students/75704226/?from=global&sessionKey=&autologin.
93. Conference Report, 66th Cong., 3rd sess., February 22, 1921; S. Rep. No. 1515, at 57.
94. House committee on immigration, 1921, as quoted in Unguarded Gates: A History of America's Immigration Crisis by Otis L. Graham Jr. (Lantham, Md.: Rowman & Littlefield, 2003), 46.
95. 139 Cong. Rec. S11,999 (daily ed. Sept. 20, 1993) (statement of Senator Reid).
96. Pew Research Center, *Modern Immigration Wave Brings 59 Million to U.S.*, 23.

CHAPTER 8: DILUTING AMERICAN CITIZENSHIP AND DISENFRANCHISING AMERICANS

1. Merriam-Webster Online, s.v. "sovereignty," accessed February 16, 2016, "Full Definition of Sovereignty," http://www.merriam-webster.com/dictionary/sovereignty.
2. Hearings on Role of Family-Based Immigration in the U.S. Immigration System, Before the House Subcommittee on Immigration, 110th Cong. (May 8, 2007) (statement of Phil Gingrey, representative from Georgia).
3. Numbers tabulated using the Department of Homeland Security's *Yearbook of Immigration Statistics: 2013 Lawful Permanent Residents*, table 6, available online at http://www.dhs.gov/publication/yearbook-immigration-statistics-2013-lawful-permanent-residents. Ten-year figures are from 2004 to 2013.
4. See Michele Malkin and John Miano, *Sold Out: How High-Tech Billionaires and Bipartisan Beltway Crapweasels Are Screwing America's Best and Brightest Workers* (New York: Threshold Editions, 2015).
5. Department of Homeland Security, *2013 Yearbook of Immigration Statistics*, 26, table 9, http://www.dhs.gov/sites/default/files/publications/ois_yb_2013_0.pdf.
6. See Colin Campbell, "The Twin Cities Have an ISIS Problem," *Business Insider*, September 13, 2015, http://www.businessinsider.com/minneapolis-isis-problem-2015-9.
7. Paul Bedard, "Report: 75% of Population Growth Since 2000 from Immigration, 100 Million More by 2065," *Washington Examiner*, October 26, 2015, http://www.washingtonexaminer.com/report-75-of-population-growth-since-2000-from-immigration-100-million-more-by-2065/article/2574909.
8. William A. Kandel, *U.S. Family-Based Immigration Policy* (Washington, DC: Congressional Research Service, 2014), pp. 29, fig. A-1; 32, table B-1, http://digital.library.unt.edu/ark:/67531/metadc491047/m1/1/high_res_d/R43145_2014Nov19.pdf.
9. Ibid., 15, table 3.
10. Nuclear Family Priority Act, H.R. 604, 114th Cong. (2015).
11. Jessica Vaughn, "All in the Family: Preferences for Relatives Drive U.S. Immigration and Population Growth," Negative Population Growth, Inc., October 2015, 2, http://www.npg.org/wp-content/uploads/2015/10/2015-All-in-the-Family-Forum-Paper.pdf.
12. Jeb Bush speaking at 2016 Republican Candidates "Voters First Forum" in Manchester New Hampshire, August 3, 2015, as broadcast on C-SPAN, http://www.c-span.org/video/?327157-1/2016-republican-candidates-voters-first-forum&live.
13. Immigration Act of 1990, §203(c) (Pub. L. 101-649).
14. Ruth Ellen Wasem, "Diversity Immigrant Visa Lottery Issues," Congressional Research Service, 2011, http://www.fas.org/sgp/crs/misc/R41747.pdf.
15. "Initiated by Representative Brian Donnelly of Massachusetts on behalf of the Irish, it was hailed by New York's Senator Anthony D'Amato as 'affirmative action' on behalf of Europeans more generally." Aristide R. Zolberg, *A Nation by Design* (Cambridge: Harvard University Press, 2006), Kindle ed., locs. 5164–65).
16. Wasem, "Diversity Immigrant Visa Lottery Issues," 6, fig. 2.
17. David North, "Social Security Data Points to Growth in 2nd-Generation Muslim Population," Center for Immigration Studies, January 5, 2016, http://www.cis.org/north/social-security-data-growth-muslim-population.

18. Data computed using FY 2004–2015 numbers from U.S. Department of State, Bureau of Population, Refugees and Migration. "Cumulative Summary of Refugee Admissions," December 31, 2015, http://www.state.gov/j/prm/releases/statistics/251288.htm.
19. United Nations High Commissioner for Refugees, Statistical Yearbook 2014, table 23.
20. Pre-2002 data extracted from the U.S. State Department's Worldwide Refugee Admissions Processing System (WRAPS) as of January 25, 2016. Data from 1993 to 2004 for Somali refugees extracted from Department of Homeland Security, *Yearbook of Immigration Statistics: 2004 Refugees and Asylees*, table 15.
21. U.S. Department of Health and Human Services, *Office of Refugee Resettlement Annual Report to Congress: FY 2013*, 101–2, https://www.acf.hhs.gov/sites/default/files/orr/arc_2013_508.pdf.
22. "Top Ten Refugee Native Languages: Fiscal Years 2008 through 2016," Department of State Bureau of Population, Refugees and Migration, Office of Admissions—Refugee Processing Center, October 31, 2015, http://www.wrapsnet.org/Reports/AdmissionsArrivals/tabid/211/Default.aspx.
23. The Obama administration has increased the caps on refugees from 70,000 annually to 85,000 in FY 2016 and 100,000 in FY 2017 to accommodate the Syrians. Paul Bedard, "Sessions: Obama's Syrian refugee plan to cost $55 billion, demands it be killed," *Washington Examiner*, November 16, 2015 http://www.washingtonexaminer.com/sessions-obamas-syrian-refugee-plan-to-cost-55-billion-demands-it-be-killed/article/2576450.
24. Paul Bedard, "Report: U.S. lets United Nations pick which Syrians come to America," *Washington Examiner*, January 11, 2016, http://www.washingtonexaminer.com/report-u.s.-lets-united-nations-pick-which-syrians-come-to-america/article/2580092.
25. Sylvia Rusin, et al., "Cuban Immigrants in the United States," Migration Policy Institute, April 7, 2015, http://www.migrationpolicy.org/article/cuban-immigrants-united-states.
26. Adrian Glass-Moore, "North Dakota Leads Nation in Refugee Resettlement Per Capita," InForum, October 4, 2015, http://www.inforum.com/news/3853303-north-dakota-leads-nation-refugee-resettlement-capita.
27. Aaron Diamant, "2 Investigates: Local Refugees Deported for Violent Crimes," WSB-TV, November 23, 2015, http://www.wsbtv.com/news/news/local/2-investigates-local-refugees-deported-violent-cri/npSxz/.
28. The United States Refugee Act of 1980, Pub. L. No. 96-212, 94 Stat. 102 (1980).
29. "The Refugee Act of 1980 created The Federal Refugee Resettlement Program to provide for the effective resettlement of refugees and to assist them to achieve economic self-sufficiency as quickly as possible after arrival in the United States." "The Refugee Act," Office of Refugee Resettlement, August 29, 2012, http://www.acf.hhs.gov/programs/orr/resource/the-refugee-act.
30. See Zolberg. *A Nation by Design*, locs. 4854–64.
31. H.R. 2816, 96th Cong., Retrieved from https://www.govtrack.us/congress/bills/96/hr2816.
32. U.S. Department of State, U.S. Department of Homeland Security, and U.S. Department of Health and Human Services, *Proposed Refugee Admissions for Fiscal Year 2011: Report to the Congress*, ii–iii, http://www.state.gov/documents/organization/181380.pdf.
33. Edward Kennedy, "Refugee Act of 1980," *International Migration Review* 15, no. 1/2 (Spring–Summer, 1981): 50, http://www.rcusa.org/uploads/pdfs/International%20Migration%20Review,%20Refugee%20Act%20of%201980%20by%20Edward%20M.%20Kennedy,%20Spring%201981.pdf.
34. Don Barnett, "Creating Isolation, Not Assimilation," *Washington Times*, November 29, 2015, http://www.washingtontimes.com/news/2015/nov/29/don-barnett-reforming-refugee-resettlement-program/print/.

35. Karen Zeigler and Steven A. Camarota, "The High Cost of Resettling Middle Eastern Refugees," Center for Immigration Studies, November 2015, http://cis.org/High-Cost-of-Resettling-Middle-Eastern-Refugees.
36. Jamie Stengle and Betsy Blaney, "Texas leads in refugee resettlements, despite its immigration politics," *Dallas Morning News*, January 4, 2016, http://www.dallasnews.com/news/state/headlines/20150104-in-texas-refugees-find-a-future.ece.
37. Karen Zeigler and Steven A. Camarota "U.S. Immigrant Pop. Hit Record 42.4 Million in 2014," Center for Immigration Studies, September, 2015, http://cis.org/us-immigrant-pop-hit-record-42-million-2014#3.
38. "New Americans in Minnesota: The Political and Economic Power of Immigrants, Latinos, and Asians in the North Star State," American Immigration Council, August 2015, http://www.immigrationpolicy.org/sites/default/files/docs/new_americans_in_minnesota_2015.pdf.
39. Andy Mannix, "Who Are Minnesota's New Americans? Here's What the Data Tell Us," *MinnPost*, October 7, 2015, https://www.minnpost.com/new-americans/2015/10/who-are-minnesota-s-new-americans-heres-what-data-tell-us.
40. Sec. 412 (2)(C) of the Immigration and Naturalization Act. See Jim Geraghty, "Federal Law: Office of Refugee Resettlement Must Consult with States," The Corner (National Review blog), November 17, 2015, http://www.nationalreview.com/corner/427191/federal-law-office-refugee-resettlement-must-consult-states-jim-geraghty.
41. Stephen Dinan, "Obama Changes Rules for Refugees, Further Breaches Trust in Congress," *Washington Times*, February 9, 2014, http://www.washingtontimes.com/news/2014/feb/9/obama-changes-rules-for-refugees/?page=all.
42. Resettlement Accountability National Security Act of 2015, H.R. 3314, 114th Cong. (2015). See "Babin Files Bill to Suspend and Examine U.S. Foreign Refugee Program," press release, U.S. House of Representatives, July 30, 2015, http://babin.house.gov/news/documentsingle.aspx?DocumentID=356.
43. The city of Sandpoint, Idaho, has already taken the initiative by defeating a resolution of support for refugee resettlement in their city. Cameron Rasmusson, "Amid Heated Debate, Sandpoint City Council Withdraws Resolution Supporting Refugees," *Boise Weekly*, January 21, 2016, http://www.boiseweekly.com/boise/amid-heated-debate-sandpoint-city-council-withdraws-resolution-supporting-refugee-resettlement/Content?oid=3698683.
44. See Encarnacion Pyle, "Suicide Risk High among Bhutanese Immigrants in Central Ohio," *Columbus Dispatch*, July 20, 2015, http://www.dispatch.com/content/stories/local/2015/07/20/suicide-risk-among-areas-bhutanese-is-wake-up-call.html.
45. For an estimate of the number of children born to illegal aliens annually, see Jon Feere, Center for Immigration Studies, testimony before House Subcommittee on Immigration, April 29, 2015, http://judiciary.house.gov/_cache/files/9504b34f-9f28-4e49-b31d-7d5a4e86d6c9/feere-testimony.pdf.
46. Jon Feere, "Birthright Citizenship for Children of Foreign Diplomats?" Center for Immigration Studies, July 2011, http://cis.org/birthright-citizenship-diplomats
47. Immigration Stabilization Act of 1993, S. 1351, 103rd Cong. (1993).
48. Birthright Citizenship Act of 2015, S .45 and H.R. 140, 114th Cong. (2015);
49. Jeffrey S. Passel and D'Vera Cohn, "Number of Babies Born in U.S. to Unauthorized Immigrants Declines," Pew Research Center, September 11, 2015, http://www.pewresearch.org/fact-tank/2015/09/11/number-of-babies-born-in-u-s-to-unauthorized-immigrants-declines/.

50. "Most Mexicans See Better Life in U.S.—One-in-Three Would Migrate," Pew Research Center: *Global Attitudes & Trends*, September 23, 2009, http://www.pewglobal.org/2009/09/23/most-mexicans-see-better-life-in-us-one-in-three-would-migrate/.
51. Jon Clifton, "More Than 100 Million Worldwide Dream of a Life in the U.S.," Gallup, March 21, 2013, http://www.gallup.com/poll/161435/100-million-worldwide-dream-life.aspx.
52. See *Times* Editorial Board, "The Problem of Dual Citizenship," *Los Angeles Times*, December 26, 2014, http://www.latimes.com/opinion/editorials/la-ed-dual-citizenship-20141228-story.html.
53. Immigration and Nationality Act § 337(a).
54. Afroyim v. Rusk, 387 US 253 (1967).
55. Paul Goldman and Mark J. Rozell, "Illegal Immigrants Could Elect Hillary," *Politico*, October 3, 2015, http://www.politico.com/magazine/story/2015/10/illegal-immigrants-could-elect-hillary-clinton-213216.
56. Ibid.
57. Ian Smith, "The Immigration Boon to Democrats," *National Review*, July 16, 2015, http://www.nationalreview.com/article/421286/sanctuary-magnet-illegal-aliens.
58. U.S. Const. amend. XIV, § 2: "Representatives shall be apportioned among the several states according to their respective numbers, counting the whole number of persons in each state, excluding Indians not taxed."
59. U.S. Const. art. I, §2, cl. 3: "Representatives and direct Taxes shall be apportioned among the several States which may be included within this Union, according to their respective Numbers, which shall be determined by adding to the whole Number of free Persons, including those bound to Service for a Term of Years, and excluding Indians not taxed, three fifths of all other Persons."
60. Rep. James Blaine (R-ME) clearly expressed these sentiments on the House floor in 1866. He also explained the reason they included "all persons," instead of voters because women and children were not allowed to vote but had a "vital interest in the legislation of the country." Cong. Globe, 39th Cong., 1st Sess. 141 (1866).
61. Timothy Farrar, *Manual of the Constitution of the United States of America* (Boston: Little, Brown, 1867), 403, §450.
62. Ibid.
63. Ibid, emphasis added.
64. Gray v. Sanders 372 U.S. 368, 381 (1963).
65. Reynolds v. Sims, (1964) 377 US 533, 579 (1964).
66. Immigration Act of 1989 Naturalization Amendments of 1989, S. 358 title VI, 101st Cong., vote #217, http://www.senate.gov/legislative/LIS/roll_call_lists/roll_call_vote_cfm.cfm?congress=101&session=1&vote=00117.
67. Gohmert amendment. to H.R. 4745, 113th Cong. (2014), roll call 276, http://clerk.house.gov/evs/2014/roll276.xml.
68. Roxana Kopetman, "IMMIGRATION: Nearly half of state's drivers licenses went to undocumented," *Press-Enterprise*, January 7, 2016, http://www.pe.com/articles/dmv-791142-licenses-state.html.
69. Jesse Richman and David Earnest, "Could Non-Citizens Decide the November Election?" *Monkey Cage* (blog), October 24, 2014, https://www.washingtonpost.com/blogs/monkey-cage/wp/2014/10/24/could-non-citizens-decide-the-november-election/.
70. Elizabeth M. Grieco et al., "The Foreign-Born Population in the United States: 2010," United States Census Bureau, May 2012, https://www.census.gov/prod/2012pubs/acs-19.pdf.

71. (FAIR) State & Local, "One Million Illegal Aliens on the Road in 2016?," ImmigrationReform.com, January 11, 2016, http://immigrationreform.com/2016/01/11/one-million-illegal-aliens-on-the-road-in-2016/?platform=hootsuite.
72. John McLaughlin, "SecureAmericaNow—Public Opinion of the Syrian Refugee Problem," McLaughlin & Associates, November 25, 2015, http://mclaughlinonline.com/2015/11/25/secureamericanow-public-opinion-of-the-syrian-refugee-problem/.
73. *Annals of Congress. The Debates and Proceedings in the Congress of the United States* (February 3, 1790), 1156.
74. "AP: Army of 800 Lawyers to Represent Immigrant Children for Free," Breitbart, September 24, 2014, http://www.breitbart.com/big-government/2014/09/28/help-wanted-free-lawyers-for-immigrant-children/.
75. "The Examination Number VII," in *The Papers of Alexander Hamilton*, vol. 25, *July 1800–April 1802*, ed. Harold C. Syrett. (New York: Columbia University Press, 1977), 491–95.

CHAPTER 9: RECLAIMING THE KEYS TO SOCIETY AND SOVEREIGNTY FROM THE COURTS

1. Mark R. Levin. *Men in Black: How the Supreme Court Is Destroying America* (Washington, DC: Regnery, 2006), 12.
2. See Alan Blinder and Tamar Lewin, "Clerk in Kentucky Chooses Jail over Deal on Same-Sex Marriage," *New York Times*, September 3, 2015, http://www.nytimes.com/2015/09/04/us/kim-davis-same-sex-marriage.html; Darius Rubics, "Christian Pastor In Vermont Sentenced to One Year in Prison after Refusing to Marry Gay Couple," NBC, July 11, 2015, http://nbc.com.co/christian-pastor-in-vermont-sentenced-to-one-year-in-prison-after-refusing-to-marry-gay-couple/.
3. See Genesis 18:20–21; 19:10, 15–16, 24–25.
4. U.S. Const. art. I, §8, cl. 9: "The Congress shall have Power To . . . constitute Tribunals inferior to the supreme Court"; U.S. Const. art. III, §1: "The judicial Power of the United States shall be vested in one supreme Court, and in such inferior Courts as the Congress may from time to time ordain and establish."
5. Max Farrand, *The Framing of the Constitution of the United States* (New Haven: Yale University Press, 1913), Kindle ed., loc. 804.
6. Roger Sherman, "A Citizen of New Haven, II" (Observations on the New Federal Constitution), in *Essays on the Constitution of the United States*, ed. Paul Leicester Ford (Brooklyn: Historical Printing Club, 1892), 130.
7. United States v. Hudson, 11 US 7 Cranch 32, 33 (1812).
8. Sheldon v. Sill, 49 US 8 How. 441 (1850), at 448–49.
9. U.S. Const. art. III, §2.
10. U.S. Const. art. III, §2, cl. 2; emphasis added.
11. Alexander Hamilton, *Federalist* No. 81, emphasis in original.
12. Alexander Hamilton, *Federalist* No. 80, emphasis in original.
13. John Marshall, speech before the Virginia Ratifying Convention, June 20, 1788, *The Papers of John Marshall*, vol. 1, ed. Herbert A. Johnson et al. (Chapel Hill: University of North Carolina Press, 1974) 275–85; emphasis added.
14. He felt the Constitution wasn't clear enough in "limiting and defining the judicial power." Max Farrand, *The Records of the Federal Convention of 1787*, vol. 3 (New Haven: Yale University Press, 1911) 127.

15. "Elliot's Debates: Volume 3: In Convention, Richmond, Saturday, June 21, 1788," as republished by Gordon Lloyd, Ratification of the Constitution," on the Teaching American History website, http://teachingamericanhistory.org/ratification/elliot/vol3/june21/.
16. 2 Annals of Cong. 1760 (August 5, 1790).
17. Edmund Randolph, "Report of the Attorney-General to the House of Representatives," December 31, 1790; AM. State Papers, vol. 1, Misc. No.17 (1790) 24n. 6.
18. Joseph Story, *Commentaries on the Constitution of the United States*, 3 vols. (Boston: Hilliard, Gray, 1833), §1768. He also referred to this constitutional power to except and regulate as "complete." Ibid., §1767.
19. Martin v. Hunter's Lessee, 14 US 1 Wheat. 304, 334 (1816).
20. Yale Professor Akhil Amar is one of the leading scholars who has concocted a tortured reading of Article III to mandate that some federal courts have jurisdiction over any given issue. See Akhil Amar, "A Neo-Federalist View of Article III: Separating the Two Tiers of Federal Jurisdiction," *Boston University Law Review* 65 (1985): 205, 211–12. Also see Robert Clinton, "A Mandatory View of Federal Court Jurisdiction: A Guided Quest for the Original Understanding of Article III," 132 U.PA. L. REV. (1984).
21. See Joel Gehrke, "What Not Even the King of England Could Do," January 13, 2015, *National Review*, http://www.nationalreview.com/article/396261/what-not-even-king-england-could-do-joel-gehrke.
22. Alexander Hamilton, *Federalist* No. 81: "To avoid all inconveniencies, it will be safest to declare generally, that the Supreme Court shall possess appellate jurisdiction both as to law and *fact*, and that this jurisdiction shall be subject to such *exceptions* and regulations as the national legislature may prescribe. This will enable the government to modify it in such a manner as will best answer the ends of public justice and security."
23. Maggie McKinley, "Plenary No Longer: How the Fourteenth Amendment 'Amended' Congressional Jurisdiction-Stripping Power," *Stanford University Law Review* 63 (2011): 1213–43.
24. *Ex parte Virginia*, 100 US 339, 345 (1879), emphasis in original. In Katzenbach v. Morgan, 384 US 641, 651 1966), the court said "Correctly viewed, § 5 is a positive grant of legislative power authorizing Congress to exercise its discretion in determining whether and what legislation is needed to secure the guarantees of the Fourteenth Amendment." Clearly, § 5 of the Fourteenth Amendment alone, even without Art. III sec. 2 powers to strip jurisdiction, would grant Congress the authority to transfer Fourteenth Amendment litigation to state courts.
25. The Judiciary Act of 1789, ch. 20, 1 Stat. 73 (1789).
26. Justice Marshall of all people made it clear that Congress was exercising its "exceptions and regulations" power in 1789 to limit the scope of the court's jurisdiction. Durousseau v. United States, 10 US 6 Cranch 307, 314 (1810): "When the first legislature of the union proceeded to carry the third article of the Constitution into effect, it must be understood as intending to execute the power they possessed of making exceptions to the appellate jurisdiction of the Supreme Court. It has not, indeed, made these exceptions in express terms. It has not declared that the appellate power of the Court shall not extend to certain cases, but it has described affirmatively its jurisdiction, and this affirmative description has been understood to imply a negative on the exercise of such appellate power as is not comprehended within it."
27. The Jurisdiction and Removal Act of 1875, 18 Stat. 470 (1875).
28. The Judiciary Act of 1914, ch. 2, 38 Stat. 790 (1914).
29. Section 25 of the 1789 bill explicitly withheld the power to overturn standard cases heard by state supreme courts. See Felix Frankfurter and James M. Landis, *The Business of the Supreme Court: A Study in the Federal Judiciary* (New Brunswick, NJ: Transaction Publishers, 2007), chap. 1.

30. Section 11 of the Judiciary Act gave the federal circuit courts, together with the state courts, "exclusive cognizance of all crimes and offences cognizable under the authority of the United States, except where this act otherwise provides."
31. James Kent, *Commentaries on American Law*, "Of the Original and Appellate Jurisdiction of the Supreme Court," Lecture 15 (4) http://lonang.com/library/reference/kent-commentaries-american-law/kent-15/.
32. Frank Gaylord Cook, "Oliver Ellsworth" (1745–1807), in *Great American Lawyers*, vol. 1, ed. William Draper Lewis (Philadelphia: John C. Winston, 1907) 335.
33. Wiscart v. Dauchy, 3 US (3 Dall.) 321, 327 (1796).
34. Roger Sherman, "Observations on the Alterations Proposed as Amendments to the New Federal Constitution," originally published in the New Haven *Gazette*, December 4, 1788, reprinted in Ford, *Essays on the Constitution of the United States*, 231.
35. Sherman, "A Citizen of New Haven, II," 237.
36. Mathews v. Diaz, 426 US 67, 83–84 (1976).
37. Northern Pipeline Construction Co. v. Marathon Pipe Line Co., 458 US 50, 64n15 (1982).
38. Ex parte McCardle, 74 US 7 Wall. 506, 514 (1868).
39. Colorado Cent. Consol. Mining Co. v. Turck, 150 US 138, 141 (1893).
40. Some examples include: S. 520, 109th Cong. (2005) (blocking lawsuits against government officials who invoke God); H.R. 1546, 108th Cong. (2003) (stripping lower courts of jurisdiction over abortion) S. 1760, 97th Cong. (1981) (issues pertaining to bussing in school desegregation cases); S. 1742, 97th Cong. (1981) (voluntary prayer in public schools); H.R. 867, 97th Cong. (1981) (abortion); H.R. 2365 and H.R. 2791, 97th Cong. (1981) (gender discrimination in the military); Helms Amdt. to S.210, 96th Cong. (1979) (school prayer); S. 917, 90th Cong. (1968) (state criminal convictions using voluntary confessions); H.R. 11926, 88th Cong. (1964) (state reapportionment plans); S. 2646, 85th Cong. (1957) (subversive activities); H.R. 10,839, 74th Cong. (1935) (stripped lower courts of all judicial review).
41. Marriage Protection Act of 2004, H.R. 3313, 108th Cong. (2003).
42. House Roll Call No. 410, July 22, 2004, 108th Cong. 2d Sess.
43. Pledge Protection Act of 2004, H.R. 2028, 108th Cong. (2004).
44. Prison Litigation Reform Act of 1996, Pub.L. 104–34, 110 Stat. 132. The bill stated that the court "shall not grant or approve any prospective relief unless the court finds that such relief is narrowly drawn, extends no further than necessary to correct the violation of the Federal right, and is the least intrusive means necessary to correct the violation of the Federal right" [18 U.S.C. § 3626(a)(1)(A)].
45. Miller v. French, 530 US 327 (2000).
46. Protect Marriage from the Courts Act of 2015, S. 1080, 114th Cong. (2015).
47. John Fabian Witt, "Stephen Breyer's 'The Court and the World'," *New York Times Sunday Book Review*, September 14, 2015, http://www.nytimes.com/2015/09/20/books/review/stephen-breyers-the-court-and-the-world.html?_r=0.
48. Michael John Garcia, *International Law and Agreements: Their Effect Upon U.S. Law* (Washington, DC: Congressional Research Service, 2015), 19, https://fas.org/sgp/crs/misc/RL32528.pdf.
49. To prevent the misuse of foreign law in federal courts, and for other purposes, H.R. 3052, 114th Cong. (2015).
50. See "Fact Sheet on Judicial Selection Methods in the States," American Bar Association, http://www.americanbar.org/content/dam/aba/migrated/leadership/fact_sheet.authcheckdam.pdf.

51. A. G Sulzberger, "Ouster of Iowa Judges Sends Signal to Bench," *New York Times*, November 3, 2010, http://www.nytimes.com/2010/11/04/us/politics/04judges.html.
52. Mark Levin, *The Liberty Amendments: Restoring the American Republic* (New York: Threshold Editions, 2013), chap. 4.
53. Alexander Hamilton, *Federalist* No. 81.
54. Linda Hirshman, "Why the Next Supreme Court Vacancy Will Favor Liberals, No Matter Who Retires," *Washington Post*, December 31, 2015, https://www.washingtonpost.com/opinions/why-the-next-supreme-court-vacancy-will-favor-liberals-no-matter-who-retires/2015/12/31/12828dce-978b-11e5-8917-653b65c809eb_story.html?postshare=2461451920787214&tid=ss_tw.
55. Oliver Roeder, "Supreme Court Justices Get More Liberal as They Get Older," *FiveThirtyEight blog*, October 5, 2015, http://fivethirtyeight.com/features/supreme-court-justices-get-more-liberal-as-they-get-older/?ex_cid=538twitter:."A typical justice nominated by a Republican president starts out at age 50 as an Antonin Scalia and retires at age 80 as an Anthony Kennedy. A justice nominated by a Democrat, however, is a lifelong Stephen Breyer."
56. Robert H. Bork, "The End of Democracy? Our Judicial Oligarchy," *First Things*, November 1996, http://www.firstthings.com/article/1996/11/003-the-end-of-democracy-our-judicial-oligarchy.
57. Bob Egelko, "At Santa Clara Scalia Says He's a Dissident on a Liberal Court," *San Francisco Chronicle*, October 29, 2015, http://www.sfgate.com/news/article/At-Santa-Clara-Scalia-says-he-s-a-dissident-on-6597321.php.
58. Pat Toomey, *Philadelphia Inquirer*, August 4, 2009.
59. *Calder v. Bull*, 3 US 3 Dall. 386, 395 (1798).
60. Ibid. at 399.
61. Ibid., at 398
62. James Madison, *Federalist* No. 49. ("The several departments being perfectly co-ordinate by the terms of their common commission, none of them, it is evident, can pretend to an exclusive or superior right of settling the boundaries between their respective powers; and how are the encroachments of the stronger to be prevented, or the wrongs of the weaker to be redressed, without an appeal to the people themselves, who, as the grantors of the commissions, can alone declare its true meaning, and enforce its observance.")
63. It can truly be said that James Wilson was one of the most influential of the Founders. Wilson spoke more at the Constitutional Convention than any other delegate except for James Madison. He was one of only six signatories of both the Declaration and the Constitution; he was a member of the five-person Committee of Detail responsible for drafting the Constitution, served on the original Supreme Court, and was one of the most prominent lawyers and legal scholars of his time.
64. Kermit L. Hall and Mark David Hall, eds., *Collected Works of James Wilson*, 2 vols. (Indianapolis: Liberty Fund Press, 2007), 121.
65. Section 1 of the Judiciary Act of 1789 prescribes the rules for quorums on the court.
66. Story, *Commentaries on the Constitution of the United States*, §1752.
67. Judiciary Act of 1789, § 1.
68. Evan H. Caminker, "Thayerian Deference to Congress and Supreme Court Supermajority Rule: Lessons from the Past (Symposium: Congressional Power in the Shadow of the Rehnquist Court: Strategies for the Future)," *Indiana Law Journal* 78, no. 1 (2003): 117–22, http://repository.law.umich.edu/cgi/viewcontent.cgi?article=1067&context=articles.
69. Ibid., 91–93.

70. For current efforts under way to free Arizona from the clutches of the Ninth Circuit, see Maria Baer, "Arizona's GOP Governor Wants out of the Liberal 9th Circuit," *World* magazine, February 1, 2016, http://www.worldmag.com/2016/02/arizona_s_gop_governor_wants_out_of_the_liberal_9th_circuit.
71. Robert Yates (Brutus), Anti-Federalist No. 15, http://www.constitution.org/afp/brutus15.htm.
72. Alexander Hamilton, *Federalist* No. 81. Madison always believed the will of the legislature and the states would easily trump the power of the judiciary. "It is not probable that the Supreme Court would long be indulged in a career of usurpation opposed to the decided opinions & policy of the Legislature. Nor do I think that Congress, even seconded by the Judicial Power, can, without some change in the character of the nation, succeed in *durable* violations of the rights & authorities of the States." James Madison to Spencer Roane, 6 May, 1821), *Madison: Writings*, ed. Jack N. Rakove (New York: Literary Classics of the United States, Inc., 1999), 774.
73. James Madison, *Federalist* No. 48: "As the legislative department alone has access to the pockets of the people, and has in some constitutions full discretion, and in all a prevailing influence, over the pecuniary rewards of those who fill the other departments, a dependence is thus created in the latter, which gives still greater facility to encroachments of the former."
74. Ibid.
75. James Madison, *Federalist* No. 58.
76. Madison, to George Washington,18 October, 1787), in *Madison: Writings*, 140.
77. Gina Holland, "Scalia Criticizes Politics in Nominations," Associated Press, March 4, 2003.
78. Robert H. Bork, *Slouching Towards Gomorrah: Modern Liberalism and American Decline* (New York: Harper Collins, 1996).
79. Thomas Jefferson, *The Works of Thomas Jefferson*, Federal Edition, ed. Paul Leicester Ford, vol. 10 (New York and London, G.P. Putnam's Sons, 1904–5), http://oll.libertyfund.org/titles/806#lf0054-10_div_014.

CHAPTER 10: CONCLUSION: OUR LAST CHANCE TO RESTORE THE REPUBLIC

1. Nick Gass, "Gallup: Share of Democrats Reaches Record Low," Politico, January 11, 2016, http://www.politico.com/story/2016/01/poll-political-party-identify-217562#.li8uxv3:nloe.
2. Caroline May, "Obama Admin. Naturalizing 36,000 Immigrants in One Week," *Breitbart*, September 17, 2015, http://www.breitbart.com/big-government/2015/09/17/obama-admin-naturalizing-36000-immigrants-one-week/.
3. See Alexa Ura and Jolie McCullough, "More foreign migrants make their way to Texas," ValleyCentral.com, October 12, 2015, http://valleycentral.com/news/local/more-foreign-migrants-make-their-way-to-texas. ("As they become hotspots for Asian immigration, Harris and Dallas counties are beginning to mirror California, where major cities have large Hispanic populations and growing Asian populations, [state demographer Lloyd] Potter said.")
4. "New High: 65% Oppose Automatic Citizenship for Children Born Here to Illegal Immigrants," Rasmussen Reports, November 18, 2011, http://www.rasmussenreports.com/public_content/politics/current_events/immigration/new_high_65_oppose_automatic_citizenship_for_children_born_here_to_illegal_immigrants.
5. Travis Weber, "82% Agree: Photographers Have Right to Say No to Gay Weddings," CNS News, August 14, 2015, http://www.cnsnews.com/commentary/travis-weber/82-agree-photographers-have-right-say-no-gay-weddings.
6. James Madison, *Federalist* No. 51.

7. James Madison, "Public Opinion," *National Gazette* (December 19, 1791), *Madison: Writings*, ed. Jack N. Rakove (New York: Literary Classics of the United States, Inc., 1999) 501; Letter from James Madison to Spencer Roane (May 6, 1821), *Madison: Writings*, 774.
8. The Declaration of Independence par. 2 (U.S. 1776)
9. Ibid, par. 32.
10. Ibid, par. 2.

INDEX